D0418735

'Whitaker Wright was one of the great characters of the Victorian age – Methodist minister, businessman, swindler and symbol of excess – whose life inspired some of H. G. Wells's finest books. Henry Macrory has found a glorious subject and tells Wright's extraordinary story in vivid, exciting prose that makes his book a tremendous pleasure to read.'

DOMINIC SANDBROOK, AUTHOR, HISTORIAN AND TV PRESENTER

'One of my reads of the year. Absolutely superb. Henry Macrory's impeccably researched and brilliantly told account of Whitaker Wright's extraordinary life is a page-turner from start to finish.'

GEORGE OSBORNE, EDITOR, *LONDON EVENING STANDARD*

'A fascinating story about an extraordinary man – grippingly told.'

PENNY JUNOR, BIOGRAPHER OF PRINCE CHARLES, PRINCE WILLIAM AND MARGARET THATCHER

'The forgotten story of an extraordinary man, a roguish hustler with a genius for self-reinvention who for a time was the richest man in Britain. The book has been diligently researched and the narrative, with its dramatic last twist, is highly entertaining.'

BLAKE MORRISON, AWARD-WINNING NOVELIST AND AUTHOR OF TWO BESTSELLING MEMOIRS

'This is compelling and revelatory stuff. Henry Macrory reminds us, with commendable power and restraint, that truth really is stranger than fiction. The story of Whitaker Wright has movie written all over it.'

JONATHAN MANTLE, BESTSELLING BIOGRAPHER OF JEFFREY ARCHER AND ANDREW LLOYD WEBBER

'A biography that reads like a thriller – the roaring life of the world's greatest ever fraudster. This MUST become a movie!'

GWYN HEADLEY, ARCHITECTURAL HISTORIAN AND AUTHOR OF THE NATIONAL TRUST BOOK OF FOLLIES

'Rattling good stuff – best biography I've read in a long time. Henry Macrory has the gift of a natural storyteller.'
TIM SATCHELL, BESTSELLING BIOGRAPHER OF STEVE MCQUEEN AND FRED ASTAIRE

'Having been intrigued by the life of Whitaker Wright for many years, I'm delighted to be able to recommend *Ultimate Folly*. Henry Macrory has written a gripping biography which highlights the extreme wealth and ultimate tragedy of a fascinating nineteenth-century swindler.'
SALEMA NAZZAL, AUTHOR OF *THE FOLLY UNDER THE LAKE*

'A tour de force of rip-roaring adventure, treachery and double-dealing. Henry Macrory's compelling tale of this larger-than-life swindler is an absolute joy to read.'
MICHAEL TONER, NOVELIST AND PLAYWRIGHT

'*Ultimate Folly* is a truly fascinating account of an extraordinary man … Would that my grandfather-in-law, Sir James Reid, had never set eyes on Whitaker Wright!'
MICHAELA REID, BIOGRAPHER OF QUEEN VICTORIA'S PERSONAL PHYSICIAN, SIR JAMES REID

'Henry Macrory recounts with consummate panache the gripping story of one of Britain's most remarkable folly builders.'
JONATHAN HOLT, EDITOR OF *FOLLIES* MAGAZINE

'I'm delighted that the full story of my great-great-uncle's fascinating life has been told at last. *Ultimate Folly* brims with adventure and skulduggery and kept me riveted throughout.'
DEREK WRIGHT

THE RISES AND FALLS OF
WHITAKER WRIGHT
THE WORLD'S MOST SHAMELESS SWINDLER

ULTIMATE
FOLLY

HENRY MACRORY

Biteback Publishing

First published in Great Britain in 2018 by
Biteback Publishing Ltd
Westminster Tower
3 Albert Embankment
London SE1 7SP
Copyright © Henry Macrory 2018

ISBN 978-1-78590-378-6

10 9 8 7 6 5 4 3 2 1

A CIP catalogue record for this book is available from the British Library.

Set in Adobe Caslon Pro and Bodoni

Printed and bound in Great Britain by
CPI Group (UK) Ltd, Croydon CR0 4YY

CONTENTS

Acknowledgements   vii

Prologue   ix

Chapter One   Swapping God for Mammon   1

Chapter Two   Roughing It   13

Chapter Three   Tenderfoot   25

Chapter Four   Bridal Chamber   39

Chapter Five   Gold and Guinea Pigs   59

Chapter Six   Illustrious Catch   77

Chapter Seven   Surrey Shangri-La   93

Chapter Eight   Lord of the Manor   109

Chapter Nine   Rogue Spark   123

Chapter Ten   King of the Hill   137

Chapter Eleven   Empty Shell   153

Chapter Twelve   Fin de Siècle   169

Chapter Thirteen Lynch Them!   187

Chapter Fourteen   The Net Closes In   205

Chapter Fifteen   On the Run   215

Chapter Sixteen   Got Him!   227

Chapter Seventeen   A Ball or a Funeral   249

Chapter Eighteen   Homeric Contest   261

Chapter Nineteen   Horror in Room 546   277

Chapter Twenty   Broken-Hearted Widow   289

Chapter Twenty-One   Final Reckoning   299

Bibliography   309

Index   315

ACKNOWLEDGEMENTS

This first full-length biography of Whitaker Wright would not have been possible without the help of many people. First and foremost I am indebted to Derek Wright, WW's great-great-nephew, for his invaluable suggestions and encouragement, and for making available to me his archive of family documents and photographs. I am grateful to Dr Peter Forsaith of the Oxford Centre for Methodism and Church History for supplying me with information about WW's father, and to Ann Laver at Godalming Museum for giving me access to a treasure trove of material about the Wright family, including her own research into their early days in Philadelphia. My thanks to Andrew Plumridge and Mary Bright of the Folly Fellowship for their useful leads about Lea Park, and to Rex Walters for passing on the magical story of how his mother danced the night away in WW's underwater room. I am grateful to Ken Smith of the Friends of Mount Moriah Cemetery for sleuthing on my behalf in Philadelphia, and to Michaela Reid for supplying me with information about her grandfather-in-law, Sir James Reid, whose association with Wright cost him dear. For their time and help I would like to thank Jonathan Mantle, Gabby Bertin, Blake Morrison, Phil Cooper, Tim Satchell, Jonathan Holt, Sarah Womack, Caroline Macrory, David Macrory, and the past and present occupants of WW's Surrey estate, Martin Brown and Gary Steele. For access to documents, letters and other material I am indebted to the staff of the Bodleian Libraries of the University of Oxford, and the Public Record Office of Northern Ireland. My thanks also to Eton College archivist Eleanor Hoare; to Heidelberg University (Germany) archivist Gabriel Meyer; and to the archivist at Heidelberg University, Ohio, Dorothy Berg. I am particularly grateful to the superb team at Biteback Publishing, especially Iain Dale, Olivia Beattie, James Stephens and my brilliant editor, Victoria Godden. I would like to acknowledge the work of Dr Jeremy Mouat of the University of Alberta, whose articles about Wright inspired me to find out more. Special thanks to Gwyn Headley, whose riveting description of the underwater room in the *National Trust Book of Follies* started me off on this journey. Finally, my heartfelt thanks to my wife, Francie, for her unceasing enthusiasm, encouragement and patience.

PROLOGUE

If he was in a state of shock after the judge had passed sentence – the maximum permitted by law – Whitaker Wright was careful not to show it. Dignity was the thing. Dignity coupled with the injured air of a man who has been misunderstood and wronged. Facing the bench, he declared in a firm voice: 'My Lord, all I can say is that I am as innocent of any intention to deceive as anyone in this room.' But the judge was not in a mood to listen. Hostile to Wright from the start, he was already on his feet and on his way out of the court.

The convicted man's solicitor placed a consoling arm on his shoulder and whispered his regret at the outcome of what the newspapers had already dubbed 'the most dramatic trial of modern times'. Wright, determined to stay calm, shrugged. 'Never mind, Sir George. I don't mind a bit.' Then, as a score or more of reporters rushed to file what they assumed was the final instalment of Wright's extraordinary story, he was escorted by two bailiffs to a basement room beneath the court. Here he was to be allowed a few minutes in private with his advisers before a horse-drawn Black Maria took him to Brixton Prison.

His fall from grace could hardly have been more spectacular. Five years earlier, he had reputedly been the richest man in Britain, perhaps in the world. On both sides of the Atlantic he had been portrayed as a god-like figure dextrously pulling the strings in a dazzling puppet show of high finance. He was a friend and adviser to nobility, numbering the Kaiser and the Prince of Wales among his acquaintances. His lifestyle was the stuff of legend. There was a 220ft steam yacht manned by a crew of thirty-three, a six-storey mansion in London's Park Lane and a 9,000-acre country estate where up to 600 labourers at a time attended to his every whim. They built him an observatory, a palm house, a trio of lakes adorned with marble statuary, and moved a hill that was blocking his view. A total of seventy-seven servants – including valets, footmen, secretaries, maids, cooks, grooms – saw to his personal needs. The press drew comparisons with Versailles and the Winter Palace in Saint Petersburg.

His proudest creation – his unique and ultimate folly – was an underwater glass smoking room, fully submerged in one of the lakes like something out of a Jules Verne novel. Here, on summer evenings, as the fish peered in from outside, he entertained his high-born friends and regaled them with tales of his adventures in the Wild West. Not even Versailles and the Winter Palace could boast anything like that.

The magnitude of his achievements was all the more remarkable given his modest background. He had started out without a penny to his name. The course of his career had been as harsh and jagged as a fever chart, but shrewdness, ambition and a seismic energy, almost enough to bend the space around him, kept propelling him to ever greater heights. And then, disaster. Overstretching himself, the too-clever-by-half puppetmaster became entangled in his own strings and the whole show collapsed around him. It was, in the words of *The Spectator*, one of those 'sudden reverses which hurl men from the topmost pinnacle of success to the lowest depth of deserved misfortune'.

Strictly speaking, the court bailiffs who accompanied him into the bowels of the building at the end of the trial should not have left his side until they had handed him over to the police. But Wright said he wanted to be alone with his advisers before the transfer to jail. The bailiffs mulled it over and relented. Even now, crushed and disgraced though he was, Wright's word held sway. He was nothing if not persuasive. As one newspaper had observed: 'He is one of those men at whom a passer-by instinctively looks twice. He has a personality which is commonly called "magnetic".'

Turning a blind eye to the rules, the bailiffs withdrew from the room to allow him some privacy. In the circumstances, it seemed a reasonable concession. He would be out of their sight for only a few minutes, and he would be in the company of respected and responsible men, including his solicitor. It was a decision they would regret. The Whitaker Wright story was not over yet. Always a man who revelled in doing the unexpected, he had one last, dreadful surprise to spring.

CHAPTER ONE

SWAPPING GOD
FOR MAMMON

As a boy he was plain James Wright. Not until he was an adult did he replace his first name with his middle name and metamorphose into Whitaker Wright. This altogether more imposing moniker, which he liked to shorten to 'WW', had a solid, reliable ring to it. It was, he believed, perfectly suited to a man of his vaunted dependability and stature.

That he was bright and capable was evident from early on, but nothing in his conventional, chapel-going background pointed to the breathtaking heights he would reach. His father, also James, was the son of a brick-maker. Born in 1815, the elder James had been brought up in the Cheshire silk-making town of Macclesfield. At a young age he was sent to work in a factory, an experience he was fortunate to survive unscathed, for the town's silk mills were among the most notorious in Britain. Crowded, damp, insanitary and deafeningly noisy, they were nurseries of disease and deformity. Children as young as five and six made up a significant proportion of the workforce. By the time they were eight, they were expected to work six fourteen-hour days a week for 1s 6d (7.5p), rising to 2s 6d (12.5p) when they were nine. Their misery was exacerbated by the harsh discipline. In 1833, eleven-year-old Sarah Stubbs died in a Macclesfield mill after she was repeatedly beaten with leather thongs for not tying broken silk threads at the required rate. In the town as a whole, the annual death rate from illness and disease was more than twice the national average.

Nothing in Wright's background pointed to the breathtaking heights he would reach. His father, James, was a Methodist minister. His mother, Matilda, was a domestic servant.

At the age of thirteen, the elder James began to find solace from factory life in the Methodist Church. In due course, his faith also gave him a means of escape from his gruelling existence. Every Sunday, the one day in the week when he could break free from the mill's slavery, he rose before 4 a.m. to attend scripture meetings in his local Methodist chapel and to lend a hand with services. He devoted the rest of the day to bible

study and Sunday school. According to church records, he 'began to con-
template the salvation of his fellow sinners, and earnestly apply himself to
a preparation for a life of usefulness'. His mother, Mary, was his guiding
light, a pious woman who 'planted in his mind the precepts of life, wa-
tered them with her tears, and nourished them by her example'.

At the age of twenty-four, he became a full-time Methodist New
Connexion preacher in Worcestershire. (The New Connexion was a
dissenting Methodist movement formed in 1797 with the aim of giving
the laity a greater say in church affairs.) Six years later, in 1845, he moved
north and became a minister on the Stafford circuit. The same year he
married a 31-year-old domestic servant, Matilda Whitaker, the daughter
of a Macclesfield tailor. The couple was allocated a modest house in
Foregate Street, Stafford, close to the River Sow, and here, on 9 February 1846, their first child, James Whitaker Wright, was born.

The proud father can have seen little of his son as he grew up, for the
work of a Methodist minister was long and arduous. He was required to
preach a minimum of eight sermons a week in different places, often in
the open air and in all weathers. When not preaching, he was expected
to hold prayer meetings, distribute religious tracts and to make house-
to-house calls to steer people away from sin. His many other duties
included comforting the sick and afflicted and officiating at baptisms,
weddings and funerals. All this for a salary of £100 a year, raised from
the collections he made at meetings. To set an example to his flock, he
was obliged to behave in a blameless manner at all times. The slightest
infringement was liable to punishment. In 1837, one of his fellow Methodist ministers in Staffordshire, James Clay, was suspended 'for going to
see the railway on a Sunday with his wife'.

Leadership and an ability to communicate were high on the list of attributes the Methodist Church looked for in its clergy. The elder James

possessed both, and they were qualities he would pass on in abundance to his eldest son. Little is known about WW's boyhood, although he would say in later life that he was brought up in 'the depths of poverty' and that he reached adulthood with nothing but his native wit to help him on in the world. Always given to exaggeration, he seems to have overstated the privations of his youth. Census records show that a domestic servant, Lydia Hall, worked for the family at the time of his birth and continued to live with them for several years. This suggests at least a degree of comfort, as does the fact that he was spared the horrors of factory life and received a good education.

The house in which he was born stood in the shadow of Stafford Jail, a grim eighteenth-century building which was regularly the scene of executions in the mid-1840s. It is possible that its forbidding presence made an impression on the infant James, providing him with an early lesson that straying from the path of righteousness generally had a cost, but his memories of Stafford were so slight that in interviews years later he said he believed that he was Cheshire-born like his parents. Certainly, his upbringing was strict. Compulsory church attendance and bible study, reinforced by corporal punishment, were the tools his father employed to keep him on the straight and narrow. Methodist documents reveal that his father was a 'vigilant' man who was 'careful to both practise and enforce discipline'. He was perhaps thinking of his eldest son when he wrote in a religious pamphlet:

Let us imitate the example of the little boy, whose father, having just cause to chastise him, took hold of the child's tiny hand firmly in his own, and inflicted a slight blow with a cane. The judicious father would not have spared for his crying, but as he raised his hand to inflict a second stroke, the dear little fellow gently pressed his lips to his father's hand, and kissed it, saying, 'I have been naughty long enough.' The evil spirit was gone, and that kiss instantly stayed the uplifted blow.

Two more biblical names were added to the family when a second son, John Joseph – 'JJ' as he became known – was born in Great Yarmouth in Norfolk in 1847 (Methodist ministers led an itinerant life and the Wrights were constantly on the move). Later, three other children – Matilda, Robert and Frederick – swelled the brood, all of them being born in different parts of England as their father moved from living to living. By 1851, the Wrights were based in Alnwick, Northumberland, and from there they moved south to Derby in 1853.

Young James now began to reap the benefits of being a minister's son. He and JJ were sent to Shireland Hall School in the Birmingham suburb of Smethwick, a boarding establishment funded by charitable donations which catered for the sons of clergymen of all denominations, especially dissenting ministers who might not be able to afford a proper education for their children. The school demanded high standards of its 'young gentlemen' and promised that in return they 'could not fail to become useful members of society'. Under the guidance of the principal, a Baptist minister named Thomas Morgan, the Wright boys thrived. They had inquiring minds and a bent for science, with James in particular displaying an aptitude for chemistry. They were rigorously instructed in Latin and Greek, and in later life James, a gifted linguist, was fond of dropping Latin quotations into his conversations. The school also believed in practical training and supplied the pupils with a printing press to 'combine the advantages of [a] useful and profitable profession with study'. This apparatus appears to have captured the imagination of at least one of the Wright boys' contemporaries, a Congregational minister's son by the name of George Newnes. As Baron Newnes, he was to own several influential journals, including the *Strand Magazine*, the *Westminster Gazette* and *Country Life*. In years to come his publications would devote many column inches to the exploits of one Whitaker Wright, many of them far from flattering.

But, for now, he was still James Wright. He too was apparently intrigued by the Shireland Hall printing press, for when he left school at the age of fifteen he found work as a printer's apprentice, or 'devil', in the Yorkshire town of Ripon, where the family had recently settled. His career in printing, which involved tasks such as mixing tubs of ink and fetching type, was brief. It was an age when eldest sons were generally expected to take up their father's professions, and the dutiful James was no exception. As soon as he was old enough, and probably under considerable pressure from his parents, he followed his father into the Methodist Church. At the age of eighteen, he undertook an intensive course of religious training, at the end of which he was required to deliver a sermon to church elders on a topic of their choice, a daunting challenge for a lad so young. He must have demonstrated that he was a gifted speaker, for he carried out the task to their satisfaction and was admitted into the church as a preacher. His talent for making converts from a public platform would serve him well for the rest of his life. Years later, a journalist who heard him address a shareholders' meeting wrote: 'He played upon his hearers like a virtuoso upon a delicately toned instrument, alternately smiling, suggesting, arguing and thundering, threatening, never pleading, and what had first been unanimous bodies of shareholders against him became violent pro-Wrights.'

In 1866, when still only twenty, he became a fully fledged minister. He was based first in North Shields, Northumberland, and is known to have preached regularly at Sand Yard Chapel in Milburn Place. He may have found some of his duties unchallenging, as when he addressed the 'annual tea meeting' at Salem Chapel on 'the growing prosperity of the church' and was joined on the platform by a Miss Shipsides, who sang 'a touching and simple melody' called 'Little Daisy Darling'. Sometimes there were weightier tasks to be carried out. During his first summer as a minister he officiated at the marriage in South Shields of one J. B. Wright (probably a relative) to Mary Ann Birieson.

In 1867, he was assigned to the Stockport circuit in Cheshire, but the posting came to an abrupt end the following year when he resigned from the ministry citing 'ill health'. The New Methodist Connexion Conference in June 1868 accepted 'with much regret the resignation of the Revd J. W. Wright' and complimented him on his 'youthful fervour'. The nature of his 'illness' was not recorded, but judging from his subsequent active life he made a quick and full recovery. 'Ill health' was almost certainly a euphemism for disinclination. He was a young man of wide interests and it is possible that Charles Darwin's evolutionary theories, first published nine years earlier, caused him to question the very foundation of his faith. More likely, he could not countenance a life of financial hardship. Whatever the reason, his decision to leave the church must have come as a grave disappointment to his father. As it turned out, an even greater shock awaited the head of the household.

Swapping God for Mammon, WW joined forces with JJ, who had also worked as a printer's 'devil' after he left school, and in May 1868 they founded a printing and stationery business in the West Yorkshire town of Halifax, where their father had recently been assigned. Trading as 'Wright Brothers', they set up shop at 77 Northgate, opposite the Temperance Hall, selling and binding books as well as supplying stationery and fulfilling printing orders. In a respectful nod to their father, the books they stocked were mainly bibles, prayer books, hymn books and collections of church music. In his spare time, WW was an enthusiastic member of the Low Moor Cricket Club near Halifax and played most weekends during the summer months.

The business did not survive for long. The brothers quickly ran into financial difficulties, and disaster struck a year later when they went bankrupt. They only just avoided going to prison. Filing for bankruptcy was viewed harshly by nineteenth-century society, and around 10,000 bankrupts were jailed every year. (Charles Dickens's father notoriously spent three months in a debtors' prison because he owed £40 to a baker, a harrowing experience which inspired his son to write *Little Dorrit*.) Following a public examination at Halifax Bankruptcy Court, where it emerged that their liabilities outweighed their assets by more than two to one, the brothers were ordered to pay their creditors eight shillings (40p) for every pound of debt, the money to be handed over in three stages over the course of six months. Under the terms of the order, their father was required to act as a guarantor. It was probably his involvement in the arrangement that saved them from jail.

It was another cruel blow to this proud minister of the gospel. All his career he had warned his flock that debt – 'the improvident habit of borrowing and not repaying' – was an evil to be avoided at all costs if they were to find salvation. Seeing his name appear alongside those of his two eldest sons in the official reports of bankruptcy proceedings in the *London Gazette* would have left him burning with shame, and it may be no coincidence that weeks later he contracted a severe cold which gnawed away at his once-strong constitution and left him too weak to leave his bed. He wrote to a friend of his 'dark and painful' suffering and his 'great distress' at not being able to attend to his pastoral duties. Unable to shake off his illness, he struggled through an unusually warm winter and died in April 1870 at the age of fifty-four. The 'mournful event' earned him a fulsome obituary, very different in tone from his eldest son's obituaries more than three decades later, in the *New Methodist Connexion Magazine*:

> The Christian character of this estimable brother was of a superior order. High moral worth and sterling integrity distinguished him as a servant of the most high God. He was a good man. He lived as well as preached the Gospel ... by his instrumentality many were saved and brought into the Church.

Shortly after their father's death, the two elder Wright boys turned their backs on England and moved to Canada, then a highly popular destination for British migrants. They may have believed that the New World offered a more exciting and prosperous future than England ever could (their nomadic childhood had made them adaptable to change and probably helped to imbue in them a pioneering spirit) but the real motivation for their departure almost certainly stemmed from their unsuccessful venture in Halifax. Then as now, the stigma of bankruptcy was difficult to shake off, and for either to regain a foothold in business in Britain would have been next to impossible in the foreseeable future. Banks would have refused to advance them credit, and suppliers would have demanded cash on the nail. Probably they felt they had brought disgrace upon the family. Better to put the whole humiliating affair behind them and to start afresh in a new country. As far as it is possible to know, neither ever spoke of their failed partnership again.

The two brothers arrived in Canada towards the end of 1870 and moved into rented rooms in the Niagara district of Toronto, a predominantly working-class neighbourhood which housed numerous immigrants. A street directory the following year listed JJ as an engineer and his 25-year-old elder brother as a commercial traveller. Close in age and temperament, they got on well. They had inquiring minds, great energy and shared interests. Living as they did near the shores of Lake Ontario, they developed a lifelong passion for boats. JJ acquired an old steam engine from a printing shop, and on a day off work he and his brother manhandled it down to the bay where they attached it to an even older boat. They then motored noisily around the bay in what they claimed was the city's first steam yacht. There would come a time when both owned steam yachts vastly larger and more luxurious than that early makeshift contraption.

Back in England, their mother had been left in a financially parlous position by her husband's death. To make ends meet, she worked for a time in a grocer's shop in Birmingham. A year or so later she too emigrated to Canada, along with her other three children, and set up home with JJ in Toronto's Moss Park district. WW, meanwhile, branched out on his own. Little is known about his life during this period other than that he worked for the Victoria Chemical Works, based near the harbour. His job as a commercial traveller probably entailed hawking agricultural products across Ontario and, if his young self was anything like his older self, he would have been a gifted salesman with considerable powers of persuasion and an ability to lay on the charm. His manager, James Smith, probably valued him highly, although his wages are unlikely to have topped $20 a week (the equivalent of £4). There was no indication yet that he was set to become one of the world's richest men.

Wright appears to have marked time in Toronto for two or three years. Coincidentally, he was living in the city when one of Britain's most distinguished diplomats, Lord Dufferin and Ava, arrived from London in 1872 to take up his post of Governor-General of Canada. It is unlikely that their paths crossed, but a quarter of a century on, by which time Wright was one of the most powerful men in the City of London, the two would form an intimate and highly significant business relationship. The partnership would end up wrecking the final years of the peer's life.

In 1873 or thereabouts, Wright decided to leave Toronto and try his luck in the United States. Oil was the magnet that drew him to the Land of the Free, and to Pennsylvania in particular. A pretty Philadelphian girl became a reason for him to stay there. Pennsylvania's oil boom had been triggered a decade and a half earlier by a former railroad conductor, Edwin Drake. In 1859, he began drilling in a remote creek near Titusville, 300 miles north-west of Philadelphia. He knew oil was down there somewhere. The native Delaware Indians had told tales of a black liquid bubbling to the surface. They thought it was the blood of the Evil One oozing out of the earth. Drake knew better. For five months he toiled away beneath blazing skies to no avail. Local farmers dubbed him 'Crazy Drake'. Then, just as his funds were running dry, his drill bit struck black gold at a depth of 69ft. It was the start of America's first oil rush. Within months, scores of wells and refineries had shot up across the region. The population of Titusville surged from 250 to 10,000. Railroads expanded into western Pennsylvania to ship petroleum to the rest of the country. Within ten years, the state's wells were producing a third of the world's oil.

To an adventurer like Wright, on the hunt for lucrative challenges, the lure of Pennsylvanian oil would have been irresistible. Arriving in Philadelphia, he acquired an office in Chestnut Street in the heart of the so-called Quaker City's financial centre and set up shop as a broker. If you were daring, confident and persuasive – and Wright was all three – there was good money to be made. 'I do not believe in luck,' he would say in a newspaper interview years later. 'It is all a matter of good judgement, a clear head and knowing how to take advantage of opportunities.'

The state's output of crude had soared from 220,000 barrels a year in 1860 to 4 million in 1869 and 10 million in 1873. One Titusville well was reported to be generating $15,000 profit for every $1 invested. The precise nature of Wright's commercial activities during this period is lost to time, but probably he was trading in the oil and pipeline certificates which helped to finance the booming industry. With a temperamental love of gambling, he thrilled to the vagaries of the market, embarking on a series of profitable deals, not just in oil, but also in grain, wool and cotton, which enabled him to acquire a house in the city's fashionable Oxford Street, a mile or so west of the Delaware River.

Even in those early entrepreneurial days he had a habit of sailing close to the wind. In 1877, he and four other men were accused of making false claims in the prospectus of a business they had set up, the Philadelphia Woollen Manufacturing Company, and a grand jury charged them with conspiracy to defraud stockholders. Wright's role in the affair was minor, and the case against him seems not to have been pursued, but his brush with the law must have brought back uncomfortable memories of his bankruptcy in Halifax. He does not appear to have learned from the episode. It was precisely this kind of cavalier attitude towards the information he gave investors that would lead to his sensational downfall a little over two decades later.

CHAPTER TWO

ROUGHING IT

Wright evidently sent back glowing reports about Philadelphia to his family, for in due course he was joined there by his mother, his sister and JJ. The latter pitched up in the city in 1876 to attend the Centennial International Exhibition, a six-month extravaganza held in Philadelphia's Fairmount Park to celebrate the 100th anniversary of America's independence. He was among the ten million visitors who flocked to the 450-acre site on the banks of the Schuylkill River, and it can be taken as read that his inquisitive elder brother paid the fifty-cent entrance fee and went along too.

The USA's first official World's Fair was everything that two bright and ambitious young men could have hoped for. It showcased all the latest New World innovations, including Alexander Graham Bell's telephone, which produced the incredulous response from Dom Pedro II of Brazil: 'My God, it talks.' Other marvels on show were a Pullman Palace railroad car, an elevated monorail and a mechanical calculator. For fifty cents visitors could have a personal letter written on a new machine called a 'type-writer'. Also making early public appearances were Heinz ketchup, sugar popcorn, soda water and bananas. In the evenings, new-fangled electric lamps shone out from a lakeside statue of the right arm and torch of what would become the Statue of Liberty. Fireworks displays staged by an English firm, Brock's, lit up the Pennsylvanian sky.

Anna Weightman, described as 'a petite handsome brunette', was just sixteen when she married Wright in Philadelphia.

JJ's chief reason for attending the fair was to see the array of modern electrical gadgets on show. While in Toronto, he had become interested in the science of electricity, and so he made a beeline for Booth 188, where one Thomas Edison was creating a stir with various ingenious devices. These included an electric pen and a telegraph which could transmit four messages simultaneously over a single wire. JJ stayed on in the city for several years, enrolling for lectures on electricity at Philadelphia's Central High School and finding work with a local electrical engineering firm. Before returning to Canada in 1881, he helped to install Philadelphia's first electric-arc street lamps and pioneered the concept of placing electrical wires underground. Back home he developed Canada's first electric motor, which was used to grind coffee in a Toronto store, and opened the city's first commercial power station. Later he installed electric light in the East Wing of the White House and led the development of Canada's first electric street railways. Like his elder brother, he was a driven man for whom a desire to compensate for that early failure in Halifax may have been a significant motivating force.

Not that everyone approved of his innovative work. Denouncing him in a church sermon in the 1880s, a Canadian minister described his electric motor as 'an instrument of evil since it releases girls from honest toil to wander about the streets and fall prey to the wiles of Satan'. In years to come, WW would also be excoriated by men of the cloth, but for very different reasons. It was perhaps just as well that their God-fearing father died when he did. To have seen both his elder sons condemned from church pulpits would have been an excruciating torture.

WW himself, while no doubt fascinated by Edison's inventions, was probably more interested in the 'products of the soil and mine' showcased in Fairmount Park's vast main hall. Among the exhibits was one of the original wooden derricks used by 'Crazy Drake' at Titusville, but it would have been the displays of rock and minerals – gold, silver, coal, marble, quartz – that held him in thrall. He probably foresaw – correctly – that the Pennsylvania oil boom would not last for ever (the initial rush had already subsided) and it may have been the Centennial Exhibition that sparked in him what would become an all-consuming interest in mining.

Somewhere along the line – exactly where and when is unknown – he became skilled at assessing the quality and content of ores and metals. A few months after his arrival in Toronto in 1870, the city's first College of Technology had opened up not far from his lodgings. Its wide-ranging curriculum included a course of evening classes in mining geology and assaying. Both were areas in which he became an expert. No records exist to show if Wright enrolled on one of these courses, but two decades on, when he was wheeling and dealing on the financial markets in London, the letters MA began to appear after his name in company prospectuses. This was a curious adornment for someone whose formal education had ended when he left school at fifteen, but given his penchant for swagger and exaggeration he may have decided that his attendance at evening classes in Toronto justified this hard-to-disprove embellishment. There are, of course, other possibilities. Many years later, members of his family were under the impression that he had studied geology or a related subject at Heidelberg University. (In a letter to a cousin in the 1970s, one of Wright's granddaughters said she had been told this by her mother.) Like the MA after his name, the Heidelberg course seems to have been a flight of fancy, of which there were many over the course of Wright's life. Neither Heidelberg University in Germany nor its namesake college in Ohio has any record of a student named J. W. Wright. Whatever the truth about his academic qualifications, he determined in around 1878 that his future lay in the mining industry. A quarter of a century later, he told an American newspaper reporter:

My father died, leaving nothing except an annuity of £100 for my mother. I was cast entirely on my own resources, without a penny in capital. But he had given me a good education, and as I had been much interested in inorganic chemistry and assaying I came to this country to try my fortunes as an assayer.

It was a time of high hopes in the land of opportunity. 'Go west, young man,' the *New-York Tribune* editor, Horace Greeley, had famously advised a few years earlier. The Civil War was not long over, and men were pouring across the Mississippi to try their hand at ranching, farming and mining. Scenting low-hanging fruit, Wright joined them, armed with blankets, tobacco, water canteens and not much else as he followed the winding trail to the Rockies. The iron horse had yet to reach many of the frontier towns, and travelling across the dusty, unmarked terrain by wagon and stagecoach was gruelling and uncomfortable. No photographs exist of Wright in early life (and precious few in later life), but his son, whom he closely resembled, was portrayed in a 1904 sketch at the age of twenty as a well-built, square-chinned young man with dark good looks. This probably accurately describes Wright himself in his Wild West days. At nearly 6ft tall, with tar-black hair, a winning smile and an English accent, he had the commanding presence and know-how to strike a good deal. His strongest and most marked characteristic was an unshakeable belief in himself. Given his intelligence and resourcefulness, he would have cut a powerful and impressive figure as he crossed the continent, eager for adventure and intent on becoming rich. In the words of a New York journal, the *Albany Review*, he was 'a big, burly, masterful man; everything in his personality breathed pluck, energy, ambition'.

Wright did not confine his work to carrying out assays for others. He would recall in later life that to scrape a living he worked as 'a mule driver, a baggage man to a western outfit, and a mining labourer … There were tough times before I made good.' Demonstrating an inner resolve that was never to desert him, he started prospecting for gold and silver himself, particularly in the mountainous regions of Idaho and Montana, divining the metal content of a rock by sight, heft, intuition and crude chemistry. Laden with picks, drills, gads, crowbars, shovels, cans of blasting powder and coils of fuse, he hacked at the earth in the search for silver and panned for gold in the riverbeds, marking his claims with piles of rocks, or by pounding wooden stakes into the ground and posting a written notice. If he found nothing, he 'pulled up stakes' and moved on to mark a new claim. Samuel Clemens – better known by his pen name of Mark Twain – had prospected in the Wild West a few years earlier. He described the thrill of hunting for silver in the Rockies in his book *Roughing It*:

> Presently I found a bright fragment and my heart bounded! I hid behind a boulder and polished it and scrutinised it with a nervous eagerness and a delight that was more pronounced than absolute certainty itself could have afforded … of all the experiences of my life, this secret search among the hidden treasures of silver-land was the nearest to unmarred ecstasy. It was a delirious revel.

Life for the prospectors was hard. Their leather boots fell apart and their clothes were torn to shreds as they trekked through the sagebrush and clambered among the rocks. The primitive shacks they built for themselves out of scraps of wood and canvas, with a corner left open to serve as a chimney, were infested with lice and rodents. Life was dangerous, too. Cool nerves were needed, and Wright seldom went anywhere without a gun, holstering it by day and keeping it close to his side by night. Rattlers, bears and bandits were the least of his worries, however. The greatest threat was from Native American Indians, who tended to resent any intrusion within 100 miles of their reservations. As the *San Francisco Call* newspaper noted: 'They have a way of disposing of the hardy prospector which does not make farther investigation in that particularly locality very attractive to others.' In years to come, Wright liked to tell the story (perhaps embellished) of how his life was once saved by a young Native American Indian bride who was camping near his shanty on the banks of Snake River in Idaho. Noticing that the woman and her husband were watching him smoking, Wright gave them a plug of tobacco, which they gratefully accepted. Shortly afterwards, a party of braves rode up intent on exterminating every white man in the area. Their leader made for Wright's hut, but the young woman ran after him, caught the bridle of his horse and spoke to him for several minutes. To Wright's surprise and great relief, the war party left him in peace and rode on. They proceeded down the river and, according to Wright, massacred three men who had been working with him. Though he never found out what the woman had said, he was in no doubt that her intervention had saved his life.

Despite the discomforts of prospecting – the long days working under a hot sun, the drenching rain that came out of nowhere, the smudge fires to keep off the midges, the hours spent standing in cold mountain waters – Wright thrived and prospered. In due course he began trading on a small scale, buying up the mining claims of fellow prospectors and re-selling them at a profit. In his quest for riches, he appeared to be a man possessed, as if trying like his brother to make amends for the shame and unhappiness that the hot breath of bankruptcy had brought on his father, not to mention the distress he had caused his parents by resigning from the church. Perhaps, too, he wanted to prove to the rest of his family that he was not the failure that the disaster back in Halifax had seemed to suggest. Many years later, he told a newspaper reporter:

There was never any difficulty about my making money. I had to struggle at first, of course, as does any young man without capital, but after I made my first 10,000 dollars the rest was easy. In fact, it is my experience that any man with a fair insight into human nature, a clear head, and absolute integrity ought to make a comfortable competence at least, if he can once accumulate 10,000 dollars. How did I get that start? Why, I went west, and as I made a little money I saved it, and bought a few shares in a mine that looked as if it would be profitable. It was only a few dollars at first, but all the time I was adding to my investment. I bought a mining claim for 500 dollars, and sold half my interest in it for enough to pay me back my original investment and provide working capital. The mine proved profitable, and a little later I sold out my remaining half interest for a good profit. Then I did the same thing with other properties, and kept on doing it until I was dealing in amounts that made the profit worthwhile.

To use his own words, Wright was on his way to 'making a pile' by the time he was in his early thirties. Ever the optimist, he was confident that he had the business acumen to build on this promising start and make a substantial fortune. He had also struck gold on the domestic front. In between his travels he had fallen in love with Anna Edith Weightman, a Philadelphian girl barely half his age. Where and how they met is not recorded, but an encounter at one of the top-drawer social events which Wright increasingly liked to attend can almost certainly be ruled out. Anna had only recently turned sixteen when she met Wright. She was from a relatively poor family (most of the Weightman men had led a hand-to-mouth existence for many generations as blacksmiths and ironworkers) and the likeliest scenario is that she worked for him as a domestic servant, either in his Oxford Street home or at his Chestnut Street office.

Anna's brief life had been troubled. Her father, Isaac Weightman, had fought for the Union during the Civil War, initially with the Illinois 4th

Cavalry (Anna was born in Illinois) and later as a corporal in the Pennsylvania 29th Volunteers. He survived the Battle of Gettysburg in 1863 but was killed the following year at the Battle of Pine Knob in Georgia, aged twenty-nine. He was buried in only his trousers near some railroad tracks close to the battlefield, his grave marked by a piece of cracker box inscribed with a lead pencil. Anna was just three years old at the time of his death.

Anna's mother, Sarah, remarried in Philadelphia in 1866, but the union was not happy and ended in divorce. Anna and her brother and sister all left home at a young age, probably driven away by the stepfather they detested. When the wealthy, well-connected and good-looking Wright began romancing her, she must have felt that she had landed on her feet. Wright, too, was evidently bowled over. Judging from an early photograph of Anna, she was a highly attractive young woman. Contemporaries described her as a 'petite, handsome brunette' with a lively intelligence and great charm. Wright's nephew, Walter, who met her in later life, thought she was 'beautiful'.

The couple were married by a Methodist pastor, the Revd R. J. Carson, at the Union Methodist Episcopal Church in Philadelphia in May 1878. Anna was still five weeks shy of her seventeenth birthday at the time. Wright, who was thirty-two, may not have been entirely straight with his bride about how old he was. Certainly, he was less than truthful with the marriage registrar, giving his age as thirty when signing the certificate. In 1880, when the census takers called, he again knocked two years off his age. For her part, Anna was clearly in awe of her high-flying and frequently absent husband, although she must have often wondered what she had let herself in for. From the start their marriage was a roller-coaster ride, with extreme highs and extreme lows, but her devotion and loyalty to Wright remained constant. His adoration and respect for her – despite a roving eye which threatened their partnership in later years – was equally steadfast.

Ever with an eye to self-advancement, Wright took the opportunity at the time of his marriage to acquire American citizenship (or so he made out – doubts were raised later as to whether he actually filled in his naturalisation papers). His new status entrenched him firmly in Philadelphian society and no doubt lubricated the passage of some of his business deals. The couple set up home in Wright's Oxford Street house, and within a week or two of their wedding Anna was expecting their first child.

Parenthood came at a heavy cost, and three tough and traumatic years lay ahead. On 6 February the following year, three days before Wright's thirty-third birthday, Anna gave birth to a son, Ernest. In material terms, the little boy had a good start in life. His well-off father took his parental duties seriously and was unfailingly generous with his money. Wright's neighbours recalled later that he always 'bought the best goods in the market for household consumption and paid promptly'. For a dollar a day each he employed two live-in Irish servants, Mary O'Connell and Maggie Summerville, to do the laundry and other domestic chores. But even in the city's well-to-do households, and especially among the vulnerable new-born, one in six of whom did not survive to their first birthday, death had a habit of striking suddenly, and Ernest succumbed to a viral infection at the age of five weeks.

Putting this blow behind them, the Wrights tried for another child, and in April 1880 Anna gave birth to a daughter, Mabel. The little girl thrived, and the couple's happiness seemed to be complete when a son, Jay, was born in March 1882. Wright's financial situation continued to improve, and that year the family moved from their well-appointed but comparatively small Oxford Street home to a substantial brick and stone house on the corner of Locust Street and 36th Street on the east side of the Delaware River. The property, which cost $12,000, had four storeys and a basement, along with a sizeable garden in which the children could play. It was purchased in Anna's name, presumably to protect the couple from any costly business claims against Wright in person. It was acquired with the help of a $10,000 mortgage, suggesting that Wright's income at this time was more substantial than his cash reserves.

But the reaper was not finished with the young family. Philadelphia in the 1880s boasted that it was the 'workshop of the world', but a cost of rapid industrialisation was dangerously polluted air and water. The couple's happiness was shattered at the end of that year when both children died within six days of each other in the run-up to Christmas. Mabel's cause of death was registered on her death certificate as acute enteritis, Jay's as dysentery. The Schuylkill River, from which all the city's water supplies originated at the time, was also the recipient of much of its sewage, and both were probably victims of the same contaminated food or water. Even by the harsh standards of the 1880s, when more than one in three children in Philadelphia died before the age of ten, the deaths of all three of the couple's offspring in fewer than three years was an unusually cruel tragedy. 'Mr Wright is a man of tender home affections and the blow that has fallen upon his fold will no doubt have a crushing effect upon his nature,' noted the *Las Vegas Daily Optic*.

Wright's mother, Matilda, who had been living with JJ half a mile away in Samson Street, also died during this period as the result of a stroke. She and her three grandchildren were buried in the same plot at Mount Moriah Cemetery in south-west Philadelphia, a popular rural burial ground for the city's Victorian elite. The black granite tomb Wright erected there in their memory was vast and ostentatious, and stands to this day. Even in tragedy he liked to leave his mark on the landscape.

CHAPTER THREE

TENDERFOOT

Towards the end of the 1870s, Wright decided that the time had come to parade his financial tail-feathers on the stock exchanges of Philadelphia and New York. With this in mind, he hatched plans to buy mining properties he could promote as money-spinning assets and float them on the market, hopefully making vast profits for himself in the process. In his dealings in oil he had impressed members of Philadelphia's affluent Quaker community with his business acumen, his hair-trigger alertness and his genius for organisation. His special gift was as a salesman. Those with whom he did business found him affable, suave and generous, and enjoyed his keen sense of humour. His conversational prowess gave him an aura of brilliance, all the more so when, as he sometimes did, he slipped into French or German. He was a welcome contrast from the usual wooden-faced financiers. With the witchery of the powerful preacher he had once been, he drew venture capital from these eastern capitalists – the prosperity of the late 1870s had left them with money to burn – and headed west again. 'The people want to be skinned, and I am going to skin them,' he reportedly told a Philadelphia friend at around this time.

Edward Drinker Cope was Wright's business associate in Colorado and New Mexico. The brilliant palaeontologist would bitterly regret their partnership.

His first target was the silver-mining town of Leadville, Colorado, 1,700 miles west of Philadelphia in the heart of the Rocky Mountains. Here, 10,000ft above sea level on the crest of the continent, a bonanza had been sparked in 1877 when miners realised that the black sand they had been tossing aside while looking for gold on the upper reaches of the South Platte River was actually silver. Men flocked to the area in their thousands and hacked away at the rocky soil in the hope of striking lucky. Within two years, they had driven some 5,000 shafts at random into the surrounding hills, of which around 100 were yielding enormous riches. Often, they worked alone for weeks on end, their only possessions being a blanket, tools and basic provisions. Come the winter they poured into town looking for eastern capitalists – 'tenderfoots' as they called them – to buy their claims.

Wright arrived in Leadville in bitterly cold weather at around the end of 1879, as determined and as resourceful a 'tenderfoot' as any who had ever set foot in the city. ('City' was rather a grand word for what was essentially an enormous ramshackle camp tucked away among the snow-capped peaks.) The mines there were producing ore worth $1.5 million every month, and he wanted his share of the booty. It was a long haul getting there. The railroad journey from Philadelphia to Denver, via Indianapolis and Kansas City, would have taken him several days. From Denver he would have had to endure a bone-jarring stagecoach ride to Leadville along primitive roads littered with abandoned wagons and dead horses. Knowing the importance of making a good impression, he came expensively dressed and carried his possessions in a black metallic trunk with his initials – J. W. W. – emblazoned in gold on the side.

Even before he reached the city he would have seen the head-frames that pierced the sky above the hillside mines and heard the dull crack of explosions as miners blasted at the rock with sticks of dynamite. He would have passed the wagon teams that endlessly hauled rich ore down the dusty roads to Leadville's booming smelters, and all the while he would have cast a predatory eye over the tens of thousands of acres of mountainous land that had yet to be exploited. Leadville, where 'the rasp of the saw and the tattoo of the hammer were heard from daylight to dusk seven days in the week', and where the only talk in the saloons and around the camp fires was about the acquisition of sudden wealth, was Wright's kind of place. 'The most lively town in the world, if rather ungodly,' wrote a Welsh visitor, the Revd William Davies Evans. A correspondent for the *Illustrated London News* observed that 'life here tends to prodigality among all classes'. Oscar Wilde, who visited Leadville in the early 1880s, declared:

I'm a little bit scared … and have noted with alarm that the average
bicep size here is thicker than my waist … They afterwards took me to
a saloon where I saw the only rational method of art criticism I have
ever come across. Over the piano was printed a notice: 'Please do not
shoot the pianist: he is doing his best.'

Armed with $300,000 of his own and his clients' money, Wright began
scouting around for suitable mining properties. He needed to have
his wits about him. Conmen abounded, and swindles were frequent,
as when 'Chicken Bill' Lovell duped Horace Tabor into paying a large
sum for his barren pit by dumping a wheelbarrow-load of silver-rich
ore into it – 'salting the claim' as the practice (not yet illegal) was called.
Tabor had the last laugh when his men dug deeper and discovered a
rich seam of ore. On another notorious occasion, the managers of the
Little Pittsburg mine surreptitiously sold off their shares after the ore
ran out. Scores of investors subsequently discovered that their stock was
not worth a 'hoorah in hell'. As the *Detroit Free Press* observed in 1881:
'A mine is a hole in the ground. The discoverer of it is a natural liar.' The
Salt Lake Tribune was equally scathing about the industry's get-rich-
quick shysters: 'Colorado today presents an example of a mining territory nearly ruined by the villainous frauds of a class of men in whom
there is neither honour nor integrity.'

Like Oscar Wilde, Wright was an outgoing man with a quick wit and
a ready charm. According to one acquaintance, he was a 'capital racon-
teur'. He made friends freely and found himself at ease in Leadville's
saloons and gambling dens. He enjoyed the rough-and-tumble life of
the Wild West and claimed in years to come that he had witnessed
'fierce revolver fights in the dancing halls'. The town's hotels offered
basic comforts (though they were 'more popular with bedbugs and body

lice than they were with travellers', according to a visiting judge), but in his quest to obtain inside information Wright was quite prepared to bunk at the mines, dispensing drinks, swapping stories and playing cards with the men who did the blasting, mucking and tramming. For much of that first winter he lived high up in the mountains in a shanty built of tongue-and-grooved boards, backed up with logs and lined on the inside with cotton sheeting. Most nights the thermometer dropped so low that he slept fully clothed. If we are to believe his description of wintry nights on Leadville's slopes, which he gave to a newspaper reporter years later, the pitcher of water by his bed was usually iced up by morning, and on more than one occasion a tin of water on his stove froze solid even though the fire was still smouldering. He was happy to put up with the discomfort, however, for all through that winter he picked up useful information and made valuable contacts. A London friend, Roland Belfort, wrote of him many years later:

He saw nascent mining magnates, apparently models of conservatism and integrity, scrambling to buy at bargain prices worthless holes in the ground. He observed that no claim could be so unpromising, no assay so preposterous, no prospectus so fraudulent, that it would not attract subscriptions from the pockets of people bitten by speculation. He observed the eagerness with which people infected with the rabies of gambling would buy anything and everything. The higher the prices of shares, and the more hopeless the enterprise, the more brilliant the success of the flotation. How could he escape becoming cynical in such an atmosphere?

Teaming up with a seasoned mining engineer, William Shedd, Wright took a wagon to Leadville's eastern outskirts and alighted at Fryer Hill, hailed by some prospectors as the richest silver depository in the world. A careful examination of the rocky slopes convinced him that the area had plenty of untapped potential, and during December and January he paid $195,000 for three claims – the Denver City, the Shamus O'Brien and the Quadrilateral – and incorporated them into the Denver City Consolidated Silver Mining Company. The game was on.

During this period, Wright became acquainted with a flamboyant San Franciscan mining promoter, George D. Roberts, who combined guile and energy with a readiness to engage in sharp practice, skilfully loading the dice so that he always won the game. He was, according to one description, 'an unpretentious little man with a big round head, a quick eye and a pleasant smile that belied the hard edge of his soul'. Wright's meeting with Roberts in the mountains of Colorado was probably the most significant of his career and helped to set the pattern for his own business operations over the next two decades. From Roberts he learned much about the psychology of the investing public, of the manipulation of mining shares, and of the value of different mining properties.

Sometimes referred to as 'His Satanic Majesty', Roberts had organised shady mining ventures in California and Nevada and had gained notoriety for his role in the great diamond hoax of 1872, in which barren land in Colorado had been 'salted' with South African diamonds to fleece gullible investors. His method of mining promotion never varied and, where his own pocket was concerned, seldom failed, the object being to make his money not through dividends but on wild fluctuations of share prices. He would take an option on a profitable mine and create a corporation with a much higher capitalisation than the option price and the known value of the ore reserves. He then exercised the option and floated the company on the stock market. To attract investors, he lured eminent individuals onto the board of directors to provide respectability – the Wild West equivalent of celebrity endorsements. Preferably these hired luminaries would have little or no knowledge of the mining industry, and so be unlikely to interfere in the running of the business. Bringing in his own team of cronies to operate the mine, Roberts maximised output while minimising expenditure on development. For a time, he paid the largest dividends possible and fired a barrage of self-glorifying news at the press to whip up excitement. This pushed up stock prices and gave him and his fellow insiders the chance to sell out near the top once they had paid the bulk of the dividends into their own pockets. Where possible, he raised and lowered the stock prices numerous times by skilful manipulation of the news, so making a profit in both directions. He aimed to complete each swindle within twelve months. After that, with the easily accessible ore exhausted, he unshackled himself from the corpse and it was downhill all the way for the remaining investors.

Wright's mines on Fryer Hill were only 600ft from properties owned by Roberts. He could not have avoided becoming friendly with Roberts's managers and admiring the shrewd Californian's stock market successes. The two met in either 1879 or 1880 and appear to have established an instant rapport. In due course they would form a ruthless partnership, but in the meantime, Wright adopted almost to the letter Roberts's tried-and-tested formula for fleecing investors. The only significant difference was that he operated on a longer time frame, aiming to form companies that would produce dividends for at least five years, as opposed to Roberts's one year, so reducing his exposure to charges of fraud.

To find the all-important distinguished figurehead for his mines in Leadville, Wright did not have to look far. The man he enticed on board was Edward Drinker Cope, a leading American palaeontologist and prominent Quaker, who was in Leadville on the hunt for fossils and mining prospects. As a professor of zoology and a prolific writer of scientific papers, Cope was highly regarded in the upper echelons of East Coast society. As with many clever men, he was also naive, and fell immediately under Wright's spell. The Englishman not only sweet-talked him into becoming the treasurer of Denver City Consolidated, but cajoled him into buying a large holding in the company.

Cope's involvement set the seal on a successful $5 million flotation on the Philadelphia and New York stock exchanges in March 1880. It would turn out all too soon that $5 million was far in excess of the company's actual worth, but investors were encouraged by Shedd's predictions of spectacular profits and they snapped up the $10 shares. Wright, as president of the company, pocketed a substantial number of Founder's shares, barrelling him to a large paper fortune.

To begin with, in accordance with the George D. Roberts blueprint for doing business, Denver City Consolidated seemed to offer endless riches. To keep stock prices buoyant, Wright missed no opportunity to trumpet the company's potential, and sent numerous carefully worded telegrams about ore production to the press. R. G. Dill, editor of the *Leadville Herald Democrat*, became a useful ally, writing of the 'perseverance and energy' of Wright's venture and predicting that it was on course to strike the 'richest and most extensive' ore veins in the region. In a flurry of publicity-generating activity, Wright had the Denver City's existing 320ft shaft re-timbered and named it after himself – 'The Wright Shaft'. He built a surface plant and hoisting apparatus, used a drill to 'ascertain that the shaft contains wonderful richness', and hired thirty-six men to dig out the ore. The *Herald Democrat* enthused: 'The Denver Consolidated is continually pushing and is doing well. It has magnificent buildings and machinery. The shipments of ore from development work alone more than pay all expenses of working the mine.'

Encouraged by the vigorous take-up of shares, Wright acquired interests in the prosperous Lee Basin mines and Iowa Gulch mines on Leadville's Yankee Hill, and became a director of the Sovereign Silver Mining Company nearby. On the slopes of Breece Hill, he bought six more claims and floated them in early 1881 as the Chippewa Consolidated Mining Company with a capitalisation of $2.5 million. 'There is considerable development on all the claims,' he boasted in Chippewa's rose-coloured prospectus. As before, there was a healthy demand for shares and Wright's wallet grew fatter. If the whole process seemed breathtakingly simple, it was because it was. As Mark Twain explained in *Roughing It*:

> Surely nothing like it was ever seen before since the world began. You could go up on the mountain side, scratch around and find a ledge (there was no lack of them), put up a 'notice' with a grandiloquent name in it, start a shaft, get your stock printed, and with nothing whatever to prove that your mine was worth a straw, you could put your stock on the market … [T]o make money, and make it fast, was as easy as it was to eat your dinner.

Despite a readiness to play fast and loose with other people's money, Wright was careful to cultivate a reputation for straight dealing with the operators on the ground, so winning himself admiration and respect in the industry. Denver speculator William Burchinell, who sold him an interest in a Leadville mine, had nothing but praise for the Englishman's methods. In a newspaper interview nearly a quarter of a century later, he recalled:

> He invested $300,000 in mines near Leadville and made a great deal of money. I should say that Wright's most striking characteristic was his personal magnetism. We were all impressed with it at the time. Of

course, when he came to Colorado he was a man of small repute. He did not have much money, but he was a man, even then, who could command money. In appearance he was handsome. He was tall and athletic, with black hair and flashing dark eyes. He was well groomed, though his personality was so impressive that one forgot his clothes. He was not dandified. An excellent conversationalist, he made friends readily. I knew him only in a business way, yet I remember distinctly how convincing his manner was and how winning. He was in Leadville a great deal of the time and he had a large acquaintance there. His transactions in Colorado were marked by their honesty. He paid promptly and square. All the men who had business dealings with him will say the same thing. He was regarded as an up-to-date business man. He was not considered a 'sharper' though he was shrewd in driving his bargains. As far as Colorado is concerned, his transactions would reflect credit on any man.

By his own account, Wright made costly mistakes while in Leadville. He would admit in later life that he and his partners paid $1 million for a mine that turned out to be practically worthless, sinking shafts to 300ft but failing to find enough good-quality ore to cover their costs. Adjoining their property was a fifteen-acre site whose owners were in the same dire position. They offered to sell their site to Wright for a song, but the Englishman suspected their shafts were as barren as his own. 'Gentlemen,' he told them, 'I wouldn't give you fifteen cents for your fifteen acres.' They went elsewhere to raise cash to work the property, and 3ft further down they struck a rich ore vein, which, according to Wright, went on to earn them $3 million. No other details of the episode exist, but it is probably the origin of the statement in the *Dictionary of National Biography* in 1912 that 'at Leadville he made and lost two fortunes'. Given Wright's tendency to exaggerate, the incident may not have been as dramatic as he later made it sound, and it is unlikely that much if any of the cash was his own. Nonetheless, the event served to illustrate how fortunes were made and lost in the Wild West with spectacular speed.

As it turned out, silver production in Leadville peaked in 1880 – the year Wright floated Denver City Consolidated – and a long, slow decline set in the following year. Press reports about Wright's companies ceased to be favourable. The *Denver Republican* newspaper noted a feeling among investors that elaborate equipment installed in his mines was the 'height of extravagance'. (It became a feature of Wright's career that any expenditure on his mines was generally undertaken to impress speculators rather than to facilitate mining.) Wright probably realised by the end of 1880 that Denver City lacked enough high-grade ore to cover its debts and that it would never make a profit, but he did a good job of keeping this quiet. To raise more cash, he hived off the Lee Basin as a separate corporation and sold shares in it, a move that even the normally supportive *Herald Democrat* branded 'ridiculous'. Meanwhile, he strung along investors with assurances that an expensive ore-concentration plant would quickly deliver the long-awaited returns. 'Dividends will soon be in order,' he declared in January 1882.

He could only maintain the charade for so long, however, and there inevitably came a point when the stockholders began to get the jitters. Shares that had originally sold at $10 apiece dropped to below $1.50 that year, and by 1883 they were being traded at a desultory ten to twenty cents. Neither the Denver City Consolidated nor the Lee Basin ever paid a dividend. The *Herald Democrat* noted in 1886: 'While promising much at various stages in the development of the properties, the net returns continued small and unsatisfactory.'

Wright himself lost no sleep over the ultimate failure of his Leadville ventures, for by the time they hit the skids he was long gone. In what would become part of a familiar pattern, he offloaded his shares at a good profit, spun the wheel again and moved on, leaving the remaining investors to lick their wounds. The *Leadville Chronicle* commented bitterly of this all-too-common way of conducting business in the mining industry:

> Too many men have gone East and told lies about their prospects. Too many mine managers have promised dividends, well knowing that the promises could not be fulfilled. Too many men are walking around Leadville proclaiming the enormous value of prospects which might be dear at $1, and all this wholesale lying has produced its natural fruit.

A quick-change artist of considerable panache, Wright next showed up in the bustling boom town of Frisco in Beaver County, Utah, 500 miles to the west of Leadville. Here he and Edward Drinker Cope inspected the rocky terrain at the base of the San Francisco mountains and launched the North Horn Silver Mining Company in 1881. The usual breathless prose accompanied their $10 million flotation – 'the immensity of the ore body continues to be the wonder of the company', declared the *Southern Utah Times* – and there was a brisk take-up of the $25 shares. As at Leadville, the prospects initially looked good, and for a while the mine shipped 150 tons of ore a day. But the good times and the generous dividends that went with them did not last. In 1884, the *Southern Utah Times* reported that 'the abandoned silver smelter and their equipments have nearly all been taken apart and moved out of camp'. Early the following year, a catastrophic cave-in, the result of inadequate timbering of the maze of tunnels, closed the Horn's main shaft and shut off the richest part of the mine. Wright, of course, was nowhere to be seen. He had moved on long before the rot set in, having sold his shares in the company for a good profit and leaving others to sort out the mess. Not that his exit from the scene appears to have damaged his standing in the industry. His flair for self-promotion, and his ability to paint failures as victories, meant that his reputation remained largely intact, so much so that in 1881 he was elected president of the prestigious Philadelphia Mining Stock Exchange.

In due course, Edward Drinker Cope would become one of many business associates who rued the day they met him, but by and large Wright escaped censure from the investing public. American shareholders tended to be philosophical about their losses and did not bay for blood. Wright knew that he could rely on the balm that a fatalistic attitude and the passage of time dispensed on most victims of his failed enterprises. In an interview with the *Washington Evening Star* two decades later, he explained what he believed to be the essential difference between English and American speculators:

When Americans speculate and lose, they never squeal. In this country you have a secret admiration for the manipulator who does you, and who 'gets away with it' as you say. You make a lot of noise in crying out against him, but that is all. Americans, even when they are out of pocket – even when they are quite broke, I might almost say – have a sort of sly respect for the manipulator who has 'had' them. They look upon the arrangement as a sort of dog-eat-dog affair. 'I got mine, and got it good,' the speculating American says when his 'good thing' is hashed, and then he pockets his loss and makes up his mind that the next fellow who gets him has got to be a good deal smarter than the one who has already done him. It is different in old England. They scream over there, and for personal vengeance.

With this philosophy in mind, Wright cast around for bigger and better properties to exploit in the land of opportunity. He did not have to look far. The scope for 'doing' investors appeared to be limitless.

CHAPTER FOUR

BRIDAL CHAMBER

Wright's next port of call was Lake Valley in New Mexico, 200 miles south-west of Albuquerque, in the shadow of Lizard Mountain. Silver ore had been found there in 1878 when a cowboy prospector named George Lufkin dismounted his horse to tighten the saddle and spotted a strange-looking rock. The rock was so heavy that he had it professionally tested. To his astonishment, it assayed several thousand ounces of silver to the ton. He and others immediately began to file a number of claims along an outcrop where the surface was braided with silver. It was the start of another bonanza. 'The ground here is simply bristling with high-grade silver ore,' a visiting Cornishman, William Trembath, wrote to his family at Penzance in the early 1880s. Not all the news was good. The *American Naturalist* journal observed that 'large numbers of prospectors, miners, mechanics and a fair percentage of professional scoundrels have flocked into the country'. One of these 'scoundrels' was Whitaker Wright.

Far to the north, word of Lake Valley's treasures reached him and his role model, George Roberts. Wright's ambition, as he revealed years later in a newspaper interview, was to retire young with 'a snug little nest egg of fifty million dollars or so'. Lake Valley seemed to offer a route to that dream, and in the spring of 1881, he and Roberts joined forces in the hope of making a quick killing. As before, Philadelphia's wealthy Quaker community was Wright's principal target for investment. Once again, the game was on.

The two men despatched a Leadville mining engineer, George Daly, to Lake Valley to assess the finds. Described in his obituary six months later as 'a very wide-awake and enterprising man', Daly judged the area ideal for stock promotion. There and then he bought eight claims. He telegraphed Wright that there was big money to be made and urged him to head south and see the area for himself. Travelling by railroad and buggy, Wright arrived in the secluded valley in April and liked what he saw. During a tour of the site, he personally located two new mining opportunities, which he named Fairview and Little Chief. Canny operator that he was, he collected fossils from the limestone deposits and sent them to Edward Drinker Cope in Philadelphia. His aim was to match the age of the limestone with that of immensely lucrative silver mines in northern Mexico. If they could be shown to be of similar age, the investing public would be inclined to assume the presence of pockets of fabulously rich silver ore which could be mined for years.

Confident that he was on to a winner, Wright bought eight more claims, bringing his and Daly's total outlay to around $300,000. Back in Philadelphia, he and Roberts formed four mining companies – the Sierra Apache, the Sierra Bella, the Sierra Madre (later to become the Sierra Grande) and the Sierra Plata – to work between four and six claims each over an area of 350 acres. Each was capitalised at $5 million, divided into 200,000 shares with a par value of $25. The quartet of companies was placed under the overall control of the Sierra Grande Silver Mining Company, based in Philadelphia and headed up by Wright. Roberts took responsibility for selling stock on the New York market, while Wright assumed control of the Philadelphia market.

Wright quickly got cracking with publicity. That summer he started or acquired a supposedly independent Philadelphian publication called *Mining Journal*, which promoted his own interests so shamelessly that some readers took to calling it *Wright's Organ*. The *Journal* missed no opportunity to sing the praises of the Lake Valley mines, even though there was scant proof as yet that they harboured great riches. As at Leadville and Fresco, Edward Drinker Cope proved useful. Intrigued by the fossils Wright had sent him, he travelled to Lake Valley. He estimated there was 'seventy million in silver ore' in the mines and pronounced them a top-notch acquisition. At Wright's suggestion, he invested most of his spare cash in the venture. He also agreed to become president of Sierra Apache and an officer of its three sister companies. He would soon curse his gullibility.

In the meantime, George Daly's miners were busy digging shafts. Daly, a student of the Wright school of hyperbole, told the local press that 'even the weeds growing over the mine give large assays of silver', but this was sheer bravado, and for two frustrating months his men drew a blank. To add to their problems, a band of Chiricahua Apaches were on the rampage in the area, torching ranches and shooting up mining camps. On 19 August, the pugnacious Daly formed a posse and went after the marauders, only to be killed when he and his men were ambushed by Apache warriors 10 miles west of Lake Valley. He appears to have seen his death coming, for in a note written the previous day he requested that 'my friend, Whitaker Wright' be the sole executor of his $500,000 estate.

The timing of his murder was supremely ironic. At almost the exact moment that his body was brought back to camp, his miners there hit the jackpot. Thirty feet down they found a solid mass of silver 4ft thick. It turned out to be part of an ore body composed of silver chlorides and silver bromides nearly 200ft long. It was christened the Bridal Chamber because of the glistening appearance of the ore in candlelight. Worth $10 a pound, some of the silver was so pure that it required no smelting.

Wright hotfooted it to Lake Valley, ostensibly to sort out Daly's affairs, but in truth to feast his eyes on the Bridal Chamber. The great repository did not disappoint. With some justification, he hailed it as the richest silver mine ever discovered and encouraged the curious to come and see it for themselves. Anson Safford, the former Governor of Arizona, was so impressed that he offered $50,000 for all the ore he could personally remove in ten hours. Another visitor, a miner named S. S. Robinson, wrote to a colleague in the industry: 'I have before seen nothing like it by which I could judge of its merits. Leadville never showed anything richer or more easily got at ... there is millions in it for speculation.' At the end of his letter, he added a warning note: the silver, he predicted, would not prove extensive. His caution was echoed by a correspondent of the *Tombstone Republican* newspaper:

> I have been to Lake Valley and was all through the mines ... there is one rich sort of cave, called the Bridal Chamber, in which there is about a million dollars in sight. You can take your knife and wherever you stick it in, it feels like pushing it into a bar of lead. But outside of this rich bunch, I don't think it is as good as represented.

In 1882, Wright and Roberts invited a 35-strong group of dignitaries, scientists and speculators to travel with them to Lake Valley in order to view its splendours. Wright's days of roughing it in primitive shanties were long behind him, and to impress his guests he hired the finest Pullman Hotel car that the Atchison, Topeka and Santa Fe Railway could provide to take them south to New Mexico. At the end of the line, they alighted at Nutt Station, in the foothills of the Good Sight Mountains, where carriages ferried them the 16 miles to Lake Valley. They were accompanied across the sterile plains by a military escort supplied by a Civil War veteran, General Phil Sheridan, whom Wright had befriended back east. This was partly to protect the visitors from Apaches and outlaws, but no less importantly to impress on them that their hosts were men of wealth, influence and stature.

The highlight of the visit was a tour of the Bridal Chamber. Wright led the expedition into the cavern himself, telling the visitors to hold up their candles against the rock to gaze at the abundant veins of silver. They were duly impressed. When the tour was over, Wright went into the mining offices and telegraphed long, laudatory despatches to the East Coast newspapers. He told the *New York Tribune*:

> The body of ore in the Bridal Chamber is so rich and porous that at many points a candle-flame will melt it into silver globules. The property is looking better today than I have ever seen it. Stock will rise to a high point once investors realise the immense richness of the mine.

A key member of the party was Benjamin Silliman Jr, a renowned Yale chemistry professor whom Wright had asked to come along to assess the Lake Valley mines for potential investors. 'Can I tempt you with a little call on La Plata?' he had written to him. Though highly regarded in the oil industry, Silliman's reputation in mining had taken a drubbing in the 1870s when he grossly overestimated the extent of ore reserves in Utah, causing hundreds of investors to suffer heavy losses. Wright did not give a jot about Silliman's dubious record. On the contrary, he hoped the professor's report on Lake Valley would display a similar penchant for unfounded optimism. Silliman did not disappoint, and he duly obliged Wright with a glowing assessment which concluded that 'nothing since the discovery of California and Australia is comparable'.

Delighted to have Silliman's unqualified seal of approval, Wright began pumping out press releases promising huge returns in the months and years ahead. The Sierra Grande prospectus made the dramatic claim that there were '144 million in silver ore in sight'. The expression 'ore in sight' was a legally safe term used by promoters to convey the impression of proven ore reserves, when in fact it was merely an opinion. The press gave powerful backing to the venture. The *New Mexico News* quoted 'experts' (probably Silliman and Wright) as saying that Lake Valley had 'the richest ore and largest bodies ever discovered in the world of knowledge'. The editor of the *Mining World* of Las Vegas, having been wined and dined by Wright at Lake Valley, called the mines the 'richest on earth'. The *Las Vegas Optic* declared: 'Certain are we that New Mexico can today show to the world in the Lake Valley mines a marvel of wealth which neither California nor Nevada ever approached.'

For a time, the barrage of good news had investors scurrying for their cheque books. In vain did the *Engineering and Mining Journal* of New York advise the public 'not to touch the Lake Valley stock'. It warned that Silliman's record in the examination of mines 'is such as to make it necessary to receive his estimates with extreme caution'. The San Francisco-based *Daily Exchange* said Silliman's assessment of the Lake Valley mines was 'superficial and the conclusions mere guessing'. In a report dripping with sarcasm, it added:

We learn that the new litter of untamed kittens ... being suckled down in New Mexico for the Philadelphia market have about got their eyes open ... each is provided with a long and imposing list of officers whose names we presume are used as files to dull the claws of the kittens as they grow to maturity.

But the public took no notice of the killjoys. Over the previous three years, America had enjoyed a period of unparalleled prosperity, powered largely by the expansion of the railroad industry. People were flush with cash and they were up for a gamble. Such was the enthusiasm for buying shares that many mining companies kept 'sucker lists' of gullible investors. In this buoyant climate, Wright and Roberts had no trouble selling twenty million dollars' worth of Lake Valley stock. Everyone, it seemed, wanted a slice of the action, and for a time the town boomed. Saloons opened up around the clock, miners paid for their drinks with stolen lumps of ore, gunfights took place almost every night and the Bridal Chamber kept delivering. On one occasion it yielded a single 640lb chunk of silver worth $7,000. Ever with an eye for publicity, Wright had the find displayed at Denver's National Industrial and Mining Exposition, where it created a sensation.

At first, in accordance with the George D. Roberts master plan for making a fast buck, the Sierra Grande Mining Company rewarded its investors with handsome returns. For the first five months it paid out $100,000 a month in dividends as more than a million dollars in silver was brought to the surface. The company's share price soared. Among those who acquired stock was the poet and essayist Walt Whitman, whose writing had made him a national institution. A well-wisher gave him 200 Sierra Grande shares at the end of February 1883. Each had a par value of $25 and came with the assurance of a 25-cent dividend per share every month, or 12 per cent interest. It was the only stock Whitman ever owned, and the writer was delighted to receive his first dividend of $50 a week later. In the Whitman household, toasts were raised to the great Whitaker Wright.

But the good times did not last for long. The canary in the mine that warned of trouble ahead was Wright's decision in April 1883 to bar access to any further visitors. He claimed that 'out-of-towners' were helping themselves to valuable specimens and interrupting operations. His reasons for the edict did not ring true to the local *Rio Grande Republican* newspaper. It slammed his explanation as 'bosh' and suggested there was a 'deeper motive at work'. The paper was right to be suspicious. The 'deeper motive' was almost certainly that Wright did not want investors to learn that Lake Valley output had slowed to a trickle. By the summer of that year, the 'seventy million in ore' predicted by Cope, and the '144 million' emblazoned in the prospectus, were some way shy of just two million.

Realising the way things were going, a Lake Valley mining engineer, Henry Sawyer, wrote to Benjamin Silliman saying that he felt sorry for 'the poor Philadelphia Quakers who are being humbugged … waste, thievery could not be worse if it was plotted openly … of all badly managed ventures this Grande is the worst … having warned these Philadelphia people I am astonished – they do nothing but suck their thumbs.' Wright could not conceal the truth for ever, and investors knew things were going wrong when the company's flashily printed business cards were replaced by rubber-stamped strips of cheap cardboard. The Bridal Chamber was played out by the summer of 1883, profits and share prices fell dramatically, and monthly dividends were changed to quarterly dividends. 'What has become of the Lake Valley mines?' asked the *New York Daily Stock Report* when the payments began to dry up. 'They are never heard of any more.' With a hint of 'we-told-you-so' smugness, the *Engineering and Mining Journal* noted that 'there is now utter stagnation' in Lake Valley stock. It did not help that some of the company's machinery was not up to the task of fully exploiting what was left of the deposits. Sierra Grande's $20,000 smelter 'would have done credit to a museum of antiquities', scoffed the same journal. San Francisco's *Daily Exchange* noted bitterly:

> Valueless properties are thrown upon the market, and, by incessant newspaper puffs, and fraudulent reports, are sold to confiding speculators. We have an example of this in the Sierra mines of New Mexico, the stock of which was floated in Philadelphia and which has since proven to be utterly worthless.

The presence on the board of George Roberts added to the problems. His notoriety began to spook investors, and in response he sold his shares to Wright and removed himself from the scene. Much good it did. Shares prices continued to plummet, and investors came increasingly to the view that they had been sold a pup. Although silver continued to be extracted from the Lake Valley mines for several more years, all five companies in which Wright was the leading light ended up losing money. So did those shareholders who did not get out in time, which was nearly all of them – the two notable exceptions, predictably, being Wright and Roberts. Walt Whitman's experience was typical. His stock paid a few dividends, and then became worthless. He wrote to a friend: 'My loss … is worse than I expected. I knew all the spring and early summer there would be *something*, for I was feeling too well & prosperous & sassy.' On his death in 1892, one of his executors scrawled on his Lake Valley stock certificate: 'It has no value.'

Whitman took the loss in his stride, but Edward Drinker Cope, saddled with a large stake in the Lake Valley mines, was furious about the disastrous turn of events. During the course of that ruinous summer he helped to oust Wright from the board amid claims that the investors had been misled about the mines' prospects. 'It must be apparent very soon what a swindler Whit. Wright is, and how weak or mistaken are those who believe him honest,' he wrote to his wife, Annie, in September. 'I take to myself the credit for having broken their game. Several of them, including WW, dare not show their faces in this part of the country. I will not go to the poor house yet.'

Flying in the face of the evidence, Yale chemistry professor Benjamin Silliman Jr gave Wright's New Mexico mines his unqualified seal of approval.

By then, however, it was too late. Cope did not go to the poor house, but three years later he was forced to give up his worthless stock and move out of his four-storey home in Philadelphia to a smaller property next door. His heavy investment in Wright's Leadville and Lake Valley companies was not the only cause of his financial downfall, but it was a major contributory factor, costing him most of the half-million dollars he had inherited from his father. So severe were his losses that he was eventually obliged to sell a large part of his fossil collection to make ends meet. The American Museum of Natural History bought it for a song, and today the 10,000 items are the core of its palaeontological collection. Writing about the Lake Valley episode a quarter of a century later, an American mining expert, Henry B. Clifford, criticised the 'manipulations of value' and 'misquoted experts' reports' which he said characterised Wright's methods. He concluded:

The Lake Valley mines of New Mexico were being floated by the late Whitaker Wright ... If there were years of dishonour from 1880–1884, we may class that period as crown of them all. The people were told that ore bodies were unlimited, that the values increased with depth and that millions would positively result from mines, that, even to this day, are non-commercial ... The promoter of today is a butcher when compared to the handlers of the fine stiletto that those men plunged into the vitals of the public.

Wright himself, of course, did not see it that way. Blaming the problems in New Mexico on the deceit of others (a ploy he would use again in subsequent ventures), he returned to Philadelphia a richer man than before. He did not make as much money from the escapade as George Roberts, who was estimated to have walked away with a million dollars, but he would claim later that Lake Valley had set him on the path to becoming a dollar millionaire. According to the *San Francisco Chronicle*, he was also involved with Roberts in the so-called State Line Swindle in Nevada in 1880, when the latter incorporated a near-worthless mine in Death Valley for $20 million. Shares rose from $1 to $25 after their cronies, including Silliman, called it 'the greatest gold mine on the continent'. Only after the promoters had cleaned up did cold reality set in. The ore averaged less than $10 a ton – not $100 as touted – and the share price quickly fell back to $1.

Wright's reputation took a battering during these shenanigans, but not fatally so. A New York credit agency, R. G. Dun & Company, which kept tabs on the finances and ethics of American businessmen, noted in 1884: 'He is a smart fellow and understands this bus[iness], but seems to have lost the hold of some Capitalists here.' The *Philadelphia Evening Bulletin* would later recall that while in the city 'he was mixed up with many "get-rich-quick" concerns and speculations of a doubtful sort'; *The Times* of Philadelphia claimed that 'none of the reputable brokers would have anything to do with him'. But these were mainly retrospective opinions, voiced long after he had left Philadelphia, and they may not have reflected the general view of Wright at the time. A 3rd Street broker quoted in the *Philadelphia Inquirer* was more generous: 'We transacted considerable business with Wright, and always found him perfectly straight in his transactions.'

Damaged reputation or not, Wright was like one of those round-bottomed toys that always flips upright no matter how many times you knock it over, and he was soon back in business. As ever, it helped that most investors understood and accepted the risks associated with mining stock, tending to concur with the old Yankee saying that 'a man who steals a nickel is a thief, but the man who steals a million is a genius'. They enjoyed a flutter on the markets and Wright was the kind of man who appealed to their gaming spirit. Despite his poor record in Leadville and Lake Valley, his ability to charm money out of people's pockets remained as potent as ever. As an English journalist, Arnold White, wrote of him two decades later: 'He cast a binding spell over every individual, high or low, with whom he came into contact. With such signal abilities success was at his command in almost any walk of life he chose to tread.'

The entrance to the Bridal Chamber in Lake Valley. Wright hailed it as the richest silver mine ever discovered.

Wright's command of language was perhaps his greatest asset. In the words of a Philadelphia broker, William Huey, he was a 'persuasive talker' who enjoyed the challenge of winning round an audience to his way of thinking. Rhetoric was his Excalibur. He had a natural gravitas that would have invested the recital of the Baltimore and Philadelphia Railroad timetable with significance. At meetings of directors and potential investors, he often used homespun philosophy and parables from his preaching days to press home a point. One of his favourite and most effective allegories concerned a farmer from Buckinghamshire whom he claimed his father had known. Every Saturday the farmer would take a sack of grain to the mill to be ground, balancing the sack over the back of his horse by putting a large stone in one end and the grain in the other. One day the farmer's son, being a 'shrewd, enterprising and inventive' boy, realised there was no need for the stone. All that was necessary was to put half the grain at one end of the sack and half at the other end. His father would have none of it. 'Boy,' he growled, 'you have a dangerous bent of mind. Take down that sack at once and put a rock at one end immediately. That is how your grandfather carried grain to the mill in his day, and that is how it's done in mine.' Wright would pause for effect before alighting his gaze on those of his listeners he had marked out as staid, and who were likely to be cautious about opening their wallets. He urged them: 'Gentlemen, let us not be here in Philadelphia like that old farmer from Buckinghamshire.'

During the rest of the 1880s, Wright had his foot in the stirrup of numerous business ventures. Soon after his return from Lake Valley, he launched the Colorado-based Security, Land, Mining and Improvement Company to develop and sell gold, silver, lead, coal and iron mines to the west of Denver. The company had a capital of $1 million and by the middle of the decade it was paying quarterly dividends of 2.5 per cent. He also joined the board of the Penn Conduit Company, which had recently won a lucrative contract to modernise Philadelphia's sewage system. It is not unreasonable to assume that his involvement in the drive to stamp out typhoid, dysentery and other water-borne diseases in the city was sparked by the deaths of his two younger children. During his tenure the company was caught up in a scandal involving the bribery of public officials, but there is no evidence that Wright himself was implicated.

On sundry occasions over the next few years he was described variously in city directories as an 'individual broker', a 'broker of real estate', a 'capitalist', and once, mysteriously, as a 'meteorologist' (this was probably a mishearing or an erroneous transcription of 'metallurgist'.) Demonstrating his nose for a good deal, he bought more than 18,000 acres of land near Pecos in New Mexico and re-sold them two years later to his friend George Roberts for a large profit. Between 1885 and 1887, he was based in offices in Philadelphia's Merchants' Exchange Building and declared his interests as cotton, grain and petroleum. He liked to think of himself, not unreasonably, as the 'Mr Big' of Philadelphia, an assessment endorsed by the local press, which often described him as the city's 'most prominent mining broker'. Despite his chequered past, he exuded a high degree of respectability, and was a member of both the American Institute of Mining Engineers and the Consolidated Stock Exchange of New York. He numbered among his close friends such eminent figures as A. J. Cassatt, vice-president of the Pennsylvania Rail-road, and the future Pennsylvanian steel magnate Charles M. Schwab. He travelled frequently to New York, where he brokered valuable grain deals and entertained leading industrialists.

The brash Englishman who had begun his career in a North Shields pulpit as the Revd James Wright had good reason to feel proud of his achievements, if not of his ethics. In the intervening years he had evolved into the prospector James W. Wright, then into the mining promoter J. Whitaker Wright, and now into his final persona of busi-ness magnate Whitaker Wright. By 1886, he had accumulated enough cash to be able to afford a seaside holiday home near Long Branch, New Jersey, an exclusive resort popular with theatrical celebrities and Presidents of the United States. Here, during the summer months, he enjoyed long lunches with business associates, taking them sailing in his yacht – another new acquisition – while the ladies perambulated along the beach.

In a measure of his increasing wealth, he and Anna left Locust Street that year and moved to the prosperous suburb of Haverford, 9 miles north-west of Philadelphia. The couple's new home, Eldridge House, which Wright bought outright for $40,000, was a magnificent colonial-style property with extensive grounds. Close to the wooded campus of Haverford College and the renowned Merion Cricket Club, it was situated in what a city guidebook of the time called 'picturesque countryside of extensive cultivated estates and wide stretches of meadow and forest … resembling Surrey in England'. The couple were listed in the street directory as 'prominent residents' and numbered George Philler, president of the First National Bank of Philadelphia, among their close neighbours.

It was at Eldridge House that Wright first began to indulge his taste for the lavish and ostentatious – and, in the eyes of some, the vulgar – when he supervised the installation of a $5,000 marbled bathroom. 'The bathroom was his hobby,' said a neighbour, who added disparagingly that Wright was 'a high liver and was less refined in his tastes than some men of his class'. Both he and Anna were dedicated social climbers, and to their considerable pleasure their names began to appear regularly in the society pages of newspapers and periodicals. When Anna took herself off to the fancy Brighton Hotel in Atlantic City for some sea air, her visit was recorded in the prestigious *Times* of Philadelphia under a column entitled 'Movements of fashionable folk and people of prominence in Philadelphia'. No up-and-coming socialite could have asked for greater recognition.

One likely reason for the move to Haverford was that the couple had started a family again and wanted to bring up their children in a healthier environment than that offered by the city centre. A boy, John Whitaker, was born to them in 1884, and was followed by two girls, Gladys, born in 1886, and Edith, in 1888. Far removed from the befouled and smoky city, they thrived in Haverford's rural environment and all three would survive into adulthood. Little is known about the family's domestic life at this time, although residents later recalled that Wright 'made few friends and took no interest in the affairs of the neighbourhood', spending days and sometimes weeks away from home on business. In due course he became a dollar millionaire, but exactly when is not known. He had certainly achieved millionaire status by 1887, and by some accounts he did so at least a decade earlier. He would recall in years to come that the news reached him after he had spent an afternoon sailing on Lake Michigan. He had set off 'a moderately rich man'. When he came ashore in the evening, a telegram told him he was worth a seven-figure sum.

Ever on the lookout for new opportunities, Wright crossed the continent to California at the beginning of that year and embarked on yet another mining venture. Temporarily basing himself in the coastal city of San Rafael, he acquired the Crown Point gold mine in Nevada County, one of more than fifty mines clustered together in the gold-rich Grass Valley district. Perhaps concerned that his name had become too toxic even for American investors, he set his sights on the British share-buying public. He appointed a local mining engineer, Charles Hoffman, to oversee Crown Point's operations and floated the concern on the London stock market in April 1887 with a capitalisation of £160,000 in £1 shares. The prospectus brimmed with his usual trademark superlatives. It boasted that Crown Point possessed 'the strongest vein of gold ever opened in the district', with one shoot of rock alone containing 'hundreds of thousands of dollars'. A profit of £25,000 a year was forecast, producing an expected dividend of 15 per cent. If all went well, claimed the blurb, this return might easily be trebled. Intriguingly, a 'Senator L. S. Robinson' was quoted in the prospectus as saying of Charles Hoffman: 'He is a man whose judgement about a mine I would prefer to that of any other person I know, and I know all the mining and civil engineers on the coast … as a metallurgist he stands among the best, and in the manipulation of ore has no superior.'

This may well have been an accurate description of Mr Hoffman, and no doubt the ringing endorsement impressed investors in far-off London, but whose words they actually were is a mystery, since neither then nor since has there ever been an American senator called L. S. Robinson. Like the MA that would soon begin to appear after Wright's name, the obliging senator appears to have been the figment of a fertile imagination. Not that Wright's British shareholders ever thought to question L. S. Robinson's authenticity. They had no reason to doubt that he was the real deal and the fiction went undetected. The Crown Point venture was highly profitable for Wright if not for others, and by 1888 he was reportedly earning $30,000 a month from his Californian activities, enabling him, in the words of *The Times* of Philadelphia, to enjoy life 'both sybaritically and sensibly'. His halcyon days were numbered, however. Just as he was starting to contemplate retiring altogether from business and leading a life of leisure, he came badly unstuck.

He purchased at least one other Grass Valley gold mine – the Riley mine in Boston Ravine – but according to the *San Francisco Chronicle* its acquisition was mired in 'litigation and trouble'. This in itself did not seriously damage him. His real difficulties stemmed from the collapse of the Gunnison Mining Company in Colorado. Several years earlier, Wright had bought stock in this company at $6–$8 a share, eventually acquiring a controlling interest. In what was by now his standard business model, he generated cash by splitting the original company into three separate concerns – the Gunnison Mine Company, the Gunnison Coal Company and the Gunnison Land Company. Each was capitalised at between $2 million and $5 million, the total being more than three times the capitalisation of the original company. His methods did not go down well with the other stockholders. They suspected that he was up to no good and Benjamin Johnson, a banker who represented a number of minority shareholders, denounced him as a 'schemer'. In due course the share price plummeted to ninety cents and all three companies went belly up. This time Wright did not get out in time. 'I had expected to retire from business,' he recalled subsequently. 'I thought I had enough money so that I would never feel the want of anything, but hard times came on and the value of my securities shrank considerably.'

That was putting it mildly. The Gunnison debacle not only cost him much of his fortune but nearly saw him jailed. Three of the company's Philadelphian investors, Ellis Stokes, Emanuel Lehman and a Mr Maybaum, tried to have him arrested for the alleged misappropriation of $40,000. Simultaneously, another Philadelphian, Charles Graham, began pursuing him through the courts for the return of $32,000. They were not the only ones chasing him for money. The New York Bank Note Company was separately after him for $1,116, and a Chicago brokerage firm claimed he owed them $2,000 in respect of grain transactions. There were probably other indignant creditors, too, but attempts by warrant officers to serve summonses on Wright failed. The 'Mr Big' of Philadelphia was not to be found at his Haverford mansion or at his Long Branch holiday home when they rapped on the door. As he had done as a young man in Halifax, and as he would do again in the future when he was in a tight spot, he had upped sticks and made himself scarce. In modern parlance, he had done a runner.

His vanishing act was carried out quickly and efficiently. As far as is known, he never set foot in Philadelphia again. With his mines in Colorado and Lake Valley played out, with most of his ventures having descended into a limbo of things dead and forgotten, with his reputation tarnished, and with creditors breathing down his neck, he decided that the time had come to reinvent himself in the land of his birth.

CHAPTER FIVE

GOLD AND GUINEA PIGS

A lthough Wright was no longer a millionaire when he arrived back on English soil in 1889, either in pounds or dollars, he was far from broke. Initially the family moved into a four-storey terrace house – 3 Bolton Gardens – in the leafy and rapidly developing London suburb of Kensington. Coincidentally, their neighbour at No. 2 was a barrister, Rupert Potter, whose artistic daughter Beatrix had begun formulating ideas about an adventurous rabbit who in time would help her to become a landowner almost on a par with Wright himself at the height of his career.

Now advancing into middle age, Wright had lost the athletic good looks of his youth and had put on several stone in weight. His small, near-sighted eyes peered out from behind gold pince-nez spectacles attached to a black ribbon, and a large moustache compensated in part for his fast-receding hairline. Ever aware of the importance of making a good impression on potential clients and business partners, he always dressed immaculately. London in the final years of the nineteenth century was the capital of one of the largest empires in history and at the height of its influence, and he considered it essential to maintain the highest standards if he was to make his mark. While at work or when attending social events, he generally wore a frock coat cut after the American style, along with a silk top hat, patent-leather shoes and a dark-red neck-tie. Family holidays were spent at the sumptuous Norfolk Hotel in fashionable Brighton where he mixed with the privileged and the wealthy from the Home Counties and touched the lower hem of the aristocracy. His comportment was always impeccable. 'He has the manners of an Admirable Crichton,' noted one City journalist. 'He is a veritable Machiavelli for suavity.' That said, according to friends, he was not above uttering 'powerful American profanities' in the privacy of his office.

Nearly twenty years in Canada and the States had not deprived him of his rugged Northern burr (some said they could detect an American twang as well) and he made no attempt to conceal this. He believed that his accent, like the alliterative qualities of his name, inspired confidence in those with whom he did business. While not without social pretensions, he displayed no signs of the snobbery and pomposity so prevalent in the upper echelons of Victorian society. He had not forgotten his humble background and it was one of his great strengths that he was able to mix easily with people of all classes. Walking into a Kensington corner shop one day, he fell into conversation with the man behind the counter and sought his advice on where to educate his son, whom he wanted to go to Eton College when he reached thirteen. Flattered to be consulted by a man who exuded such intelligence and prosperity, the shopkeeper proffered the name of a local preparatory school. All his life Wright liked to act on impulse, and he took up the recommendation without further inquiry. The boy became a pupil at the school the following term and in due course, much to his father's pride, he won a place at Eton.

Where his work was concerned, Wright exuded the same energy, ambition and guile that had characterised his career in America. He had tasted the life of a millionaire, and he wanted to savour it again. Setting up shop in a modest office in Copthall Avenue in the City of London, not far from the Stock Exchange, he re-launched himself as 'a financier with mining interests'. With his intimate knowledge of all aspects of the industry, he cut a compelling figure. In his own words, he had 'been though the mill, knew all the shady tricks of the mining sharks and Wall Street hustlers, had seen ruinous panic and fabulous profits'. The impression that he had an insider's grasp of mining lured many into trusting his word and putting their faith in his abilities. Spraying his sentences with superlatives and linguistic magnifiers, he impressed potential collaborators and investors with tales of his spectacular American triumphs, safe in the knowledge that only the most persistent of sleuths would find out that there had been spectacular failures as well. In an article in *The Nineteenth Century and After* journal, his friend Roland Belfort wrote of him:

> From the moment that Whitaker Wright invaded London he impressed us all as a 'coming man.' Everything in his person breathed pluck, power, primeval energy, unscrupulous daring. His manner imperious, his eye keen, his words few but pointed, tinged with Americanisms ... Fresh from the savage life of the Wild West mining regions and the comparatively uncouth methods of Wall Street, he enjoyed the more leisurely, cultured, suave social atmosphere of London.

Of his first two years back in England there is almost no record, but to begin with he seems to have met with limited success as he began the task of rebuilding his fortune. In those early days he was relatively

unknown outside City circles, and on the rare occasions when his name
appeared in the financial press he was usually described wrongly as
either an Australian or an American – 'a gentleman from the land of
the cornstalks'. An English journalist, Arnold White, who in due course
would become Wright's sworn enemy, wrote of this period in his life:

> He did not set the Thames on fire by any manner of means. He had
> not much cash and but little credit, and got into very low water indeed.
> His printers could not get paid and they seized on his office furniture
> … If not absolutely impecunious, he was glad to receive very small
> favours from his acquaintances.

As in the past, the mines Wright promoted were on the American continent, which necessitated frequent trips across the Atlantic. According
to a passenger manifest, he returned to the States in a first-class cabin on
the SS *Servia* in December 1889, describing himself on his immigration
papers as a stockbroker when he arrived in New York on Christmas Eve.
He had five pieces of luggage with him, suggesting a long stay. Why
he needed to be in America over the Christmas period is not known,
but the visit was presumably connected to one of his new endeavours.
The first of these was the Chloride Mining and Reduction Company,
created to exploit idle mines in Inyo County in the Death Valley region
of California. He helped to launch the venture in 1890, but it made little
impact and was not his hoped-for route back to great wealth. Next, he
set his sights on Mexico. The mining industry there was expanding, the
economy was growing and the Mexican president, Porfirio Díaz, was
keen to attract foreign investors. The opportunities appeared limitless.
F. W. Edelsten, editor of the *Los Angeles Mining and Metallurgical Journal*,
noted during the 1890s: 'The mining possibilities of Mexico are on a

scale well-nigh inconceivable … many states are enormously wealthy and are as yet virgin territory.'

Words like these were a powerful lure to Wright, and he wasted no time acquiring three silver mines – the San Cristóbal, the San Juan de Los Lagos and the Victoria – a mile outside the city of Zacatecas in North-Central Mexico. He floated these on the London Stock Exchange as the Abaris Mining Corporation, with a capitalisation of £200,000. Abaris was a legendary sage in Greek mythology who was said to have been endowed with the gift of prophecy, and there was no shortage of startling prophecy in Wright's 1891 prospectus. Radiating the usual roseate hue, it forecast that ten tons of high-grade ore would be shipped out every day for processing in San Francisco, generating a daily profit of £540, or around £200,000 a year. (Some £20 million in today's money.) For good measure, it added: 'The San Cristóbal vein appears to have the same geological formation as that of its famous neighbour, El Bote, which has been in bonanza over thirty years, and has given its lucky owners a million dollars yearly in dividends.'

There is no evidence that Wright ever visited Zacatecas, but it can be taken for granted that he did, not only because he was an inveterate traveller and liked to see his properties for himself, but because the traditional Mexican handing-over ceremony would have appealed to his fondness for the theatrical. After the singing of hymns, the previous owner would take the new owner by the arm and lead him into the mine, picking up a handful of ore and placing it in the purchaser's hands to signify the change of ownership. A judge would then complete the proceedings by reading out a declaration of titles and calling on 'anyone present who knows of any true or just impediment to speak now or hold his peace forever'. It sounded straightforward enough, but Wright's business dealings were seldom simple. According to the *San Francisco*

Chronicle, he narrowly escaped indictment at the time of the flotation 'as he had issued debentures, having no title to the property in question'.

Wright spent the summer of 1891 overseeing the venture from San Francisco, making enough money to be able to send for Anna and the children and install them for most of August in the Sea Beach Hotel in Santa Cruz, one of California's most luxurious establishments. At one point he travelled to Amsterdam to try to persuade a Dutch syndicate to invest in his Mexican venture, but failed to win their backing. During the following three summers he again based himself on America's west coast. Abaris remained at the centre of his operation, but he set up at least one other Mexican mining company, Oro Bar, and, according to the *San Francisco Call* newspaper, he tried 'to float some gigantic mining scheme in South America'.

As before, he represented himself as a man of great wealth and stature in a bid to gain the confidence of speculators. He spent weekends at San Jose's Hotel Vendôme, a first-class establishment frequented by San Francisco and Bay Area society, with a ballroom, swimming pools, tennis courts and stables. There he regularly entertained potential investors, flashing his cheque book and insisting on meeting all their costs. Anna arrived with the children for part of each summer, and the couple were reportedly 'well received in the highest social circles'. Life was good, but for Wright it was nothing like good enough.

It was probably while staying at the Vendôme that he developed what would become an absorbing interest in astronomy, for the hotel was within easy reach of the newly built Lick Observatory on nearby Mount Hamilton, the first permanently occupied mountaintop observatory in the world. Visitors were encouraged to make overnight calls and to view the heavens through a 36-inch telescope, an experience that a man of Wright's curiosity would have found hard to resist. Speculation was rife at the time that the so-called canals on Mars proved the existence of intelligent life on the Red Planet. Wright was intrigued by the notion of extraterrestrial civilisations, and in years to come his speeches to shareholders sometimes referred jocularly to 'our Martian neighbours' and their so-called canals. His brother, JJ, with whom he shared many interests, had already built a private observatory in a turret-shaped room at his Toronto house, and Wright hankered after one too. He would not have long to wait. The only difference was that his would be on a spectacularly grander scale than his brother's.

Despite Wright's persuasive skills and lavish spending, Abaris failed to stand the test of time, and the 'snug little nest egg of fifty million or so' continued to elude him. The *Financial Times* later reported that 'the enterprise gained little market or public attention, and procured for him neither much profit nor celebrity'. The company was eventually wound up at the turn of the century, but by then, as was his wont, Wright had long since departed the scene. Back in London, his interest had been piqued by exciting developments on the far side of the world.

In 1892, the discovery of gold in a remote part of Western Australia called Fly Flat had sparked a rush centred on Coolgardie, 350 miles east of Perth. Undeterred by the absence of a railroad, a ragged cavalcade of prospectors armed with picks and shovels descended on the arid, dust-blown site. Some went on horses and camels, some bicycled, others simply walked, carrying their provisions – flour, oatmeal, tinned meat, sugar, tea and tobacco – on their backs for days on end or pushing them in wheelbarrows. They dangled corks from their slouch hats to keep the flies from their faces and held on to their gallon water bags as if they were their wallets. Many suffered agonising deaths in the bush, usually from dehydration or from typhoid fever. Some went mad, throwing off their clothes and chasing mirages. The first sound they heard on arrival at the goldfields was the curious rattle of gravel falling on tin dishes; the first sight the clouds of fine red dust. 'A bird or a beast finds it difficult to live in the waterless sand and gravel,' wrote a visiting London journalist, Raymond Radclyffe. Many completed the journey only to die soon afterwards from disease. Gold diggers became grave diggers, burying the dead in coffins hammered from old packing cases. But the lucky ones found hundreds of ounces of gold gleaming on the soil.

Everything in his person breathed pluck, power, primeval energy, unscrupulous daring…'
Wright in the early 1890s. © GETTY IMAGES

In June the following year, there was another rich find 25 miles away near Kalgoorlie. Three Irish prospectors were passing Mount Charlotte when one of their horses cast a shoe. During the halt in their journey, they spotted alluvial gold at the base of the mountain. A stampede of biblical proportions began within hours of the discovery being made public. Camp fires spread like stars in a clearing sky. Around 400 men were prospecting in the area within three days, cutting spidery paths across the scrub. Within a week their number had swelled to more than a thousand. A hurricane of further finds quickly established Australia as the quarry of the world. Western Australia's Agent-General, Sir Malcolm Fraser, declared that 'every day will show that these finds are one of the most wonderful realities of the century'. Twelve thousand miles away, Whitaker Wright prepared to pounce.

When word of the Australian finds reached London, investors were electrified and the City promoters got cracking. The Stock Exchange was ripening for a boom. Financial panic in America and Australia had cut the outlets for investment in the New World. So many Englishmen were on the hunt for profitable places to sink their cash that by 1894, London banks, awash with money, had dropped interest rates on deposits fourfold to half a per cent. This was not the first time there had been a City craze for mining shares. Earlier booms had revolved round Cornish tin, Indian gold and American silver. Now it was the turn of Australian gold. Pumped up by the chance of a quick profit, British investors began pouring their cash into the new goldfields in Western Australia. The market for shares was insatiable. Every Australian mail steamer arriving on British shores disgorged sun-tanned prospectors eager to hawk a promising vein in Coolgardie or Kalgoorlie. For a time, the excitement in London matched that of the Oscar Wilde libel case, soon to enthral England and the literary world. For Wright, the stars he liked to study were aligning.

He was not the first British promoter to drum in the boom – that honour went to a mining engineer called Albert Calvert – but he was not far behind. His interest in Western Australia, he said later, was sparked in the winter of 1893, when a contact told him about a mine near Coolgardie. Two young prospectors had visited the area the previous year and camped at the site of a native waterhole, probing for gold while their horses grazed. Their initial finds were not encouraging. They discovered a tin plate nailed to a post, along with the skeletons of two earlier prospectors, who had been speared by aborigines. Undaunted, they carried on searching, and over the following weeks they extracted more than 500 ounces of gold from the rocky terrain. They reported their discovery and were awarded a 5-acre lease. Opinions about the value of the site differed, but on reading detailed reports Wright believed the mine had promise. He recalled: 'It was sneezed at by a so-called expert, but I determined to do a little investigating on my own account and sent several responsible men into the country to prospect. They decided it was likely to prove a better gold field than was supposed.'

Wright had read the stars accurately. Confident that enormous wealth lay within his grasp, he gave up on Abaris and launched the West Australian Exploring and Finance Corporation in London in September 1894 with a share capital of £200,000. He laid the groundwork for the flotation with care and precision. The company's stated aim was to exploit the 'marvellous developments' in the new goldfields by acquiring as many viable mining leases as possible and developing them into going concerns. These would then be either re-sold at a profit or be formed into new companies. Needing an able man on the spot, he hired a canny and technically brilliant American mining engineer, Charles Kaufman, whom he knew from his Wild West days. (Kaufman had managed the notorious State Line mine in Nevada for George Roberts.) On the then enormous salary of £10,000 a year, Kaufman arrived in 'Westralia' and acquired numerous mining properties on Wright's behalf. Some, like the Golden Crown, the Cambria and the Salisbury, turned out to be little more than surface splashes of gold. Others, like Mainland, Golden Crown, Paddington and Wealth of Nations, were healthy concerns and in due course were floated as separate enterprises.

The new company's prospectus, in which the letters MA first made their mysterious appearance after Wright's name,* brimmed with the superlatives that flowed so easily from his pen. He claimed there would be lucrative results even if only one in twenty of the acquired properties was successful. 'Very few persons', he added, 'have any conception of the enormous mineral wealth which until lately has been dormant in that colony.' Describing his breakthrough some years later, he recalled:

> Discoveries were rapidly made, and in a few months there was wild excitement. Prospecting parties went in every direction and made what appeared to be rich finds day after day. I saw my chance of making another fortune and plunged into the gamble. Becoming satisfied that the colony would develop into a satisfactory gold mining camp, as the ores were of high grade, I instructed my agents to buy up all the richest discoveries that could be had for a reasonable price. In this way I acquired the very best 'shows' on the gold fields, some of which may well be described as golden treasure houses, whose gold glittered on the surface of the ground like a jeweller's window. In some cases huge boulders of pure gold were found.

Wright's watershed moment had finally arrived. The breakthrough was rapid and dazzling, and for a time there appeared to be no stopping him. Glowing reports about the West Australian Exploring and Finance Corporation's prospects began to appear in the press. The praise of newspapers like the *Financial Times* drowned out the critics who complained that Wright had a bad record on both sides of the Atlantic

---

* The letters MA may have been a deliberate corruption of ME, which stood for Mining Engineer. This did not necessarily denote someone who had graduated from mining school, but rather someone who claimed experience in mining. As a letter in the *Mining Journal* in 1871 pointed out: 'It is claimed by every person who can wheel a barrow or drive a span of mules over the road that he is an ME.'

and who called the venture a 'blind pool' without clear investment goals. Although it was one of nearly fifty 'Westralian' mining companies launched in London in the autumn of 1894, a combination of Wright's organisational brilliance and Kaufman's expertise on the ground made it a frontrunner. Wright started to be identified in the public mind as a man who had been there and done it himself. He had rolled up his sleeves, taken risks and got his hands dirty. He was a man who knew his way around the industry and who could be trusted to guide investors through the maze of mining enterprises which were shooting up by the score. Without someone of Wright's savvy, how were they to distinguish between the Mimosa Gold Mines, the Burbank Southern Gold Fields, the Golden Secret and the Last Shot? Wright was the man who seemed to know which of these alluring prospects had potential and which did not. One newspaper commented that his new company 'bids fair to be one of the biggest successes of all ... [T]here is every probability that the required capital will be subscribed about ten times over.' It was an accurate forecast. All 150,000 shares on offer were snapped up as soon as they became available (Wright reserved 50,000 Founder's shares for himself) and hundreds of would-be investors were left disappointed.

At a meeting in London three days after Christmas 1894, West Australian's shareholders received glad tidings. They were told that Kaufman 'is perfectly elated' by the prospects in Australia, and that the 'consensus is that his acquisitions include some of the best mines in that country'. Exactly who constituted 'the consensus' was not stated, but no one could argue with the £47,000 profits to date. To set the seal on a successful meeting, the board announced an interim dividend for the first half-year of not less than 20 per cent (which in Wright's case meant a windfall of £10,000, or around £1 million in today's money). The shareholders left the meeting in a festive mood. Those who had set eyes on Wright for the first time liked his smooth, persuasive manner. Word spread that he was a man to be watched. Few – if any – realised that he was treading exactly the same path he had followed in Colorado, New Mexico and California. 'He believed in two things,' recalled Roland Belfort. 'His star, and the imbecility of the public.'

Just as he had lured Edward Drinker Cope into his American businesses, he furnished West Australian with a patina of respectability by sweet-talking titled individuals to sit on the board of directors. He was not alone in using this technique. Most promoters with their eye on the ball considered it essential to have 'big names' on their boards. Some were so desperate that they manufactured fake celebrities if real ones were not available. In America, a man named Guggenheim, quite unrelated to the legendary industrialists, had hired himself out to mining promotions, knowing that the public would assume the backing of his more illustrious namesakes. Unscrupulous Texas oil promoters had found an old janitor named Robert E. Lee and named him the figurehead of their new enterprise. The General Lee Development Company took in almost $2 million on the strength of the widespread belief that the revered Civil War general was its chairman.

In Britain, the practice had been pioneered by the crooked British promoter Ernest Terah Hooley, the one man Wright regarded as a true rival. Hooley paid the Earl De La Warr £25,000 to be a director of the Dunlop Pneumatic Tyre Company and had a string of other titled men on his books, including Lord Albemarle, Lord Randolph Churchill and the Earl of Winchilsea. The literary periodical *Temple Bar* coined the term 'guinea pigs' to describe such functionaries – 'the pleasant name for those gentlemen of more rank than means who have a guinea and a copious lunch when they attend board meetings'. Their titles made them invaluable publicity tools, guaranteeing that a company would be mentioned in the society columns of the newspapers as well as on the financial pages. Some saw the presence of such men on the boards of speculative companies as indicative of Britain's economic and social decline, or even its moral degeneracy. By the end of the nineteenth century, the practice was so tarnished that cartoonists lampooned it by picturing peers in sandwich boards advertising companies outside the House of Lords with a sign proclaiming: 'Peers for Hire'. *Punch* ran a cartoon of aristocrats and sportsmen in a drawing room in full evening dress with advertisements emblazoned across their white shirt fronts. Gilbert and Sullivan used the practice as a comic device in a duet between a duke and a duchess in their 1889 operetta *The Gondoliers*:

> I sit, by selection,
> Upon the direction,
> Of several companies bubble.
> As soon as they're floated
> I'm freely bank-noted –
> I'm pretty well paid for my trouble…
> In short, if you'd kindle
> The spark of a swindle,
> Lure simpletons into your clutches –
> Or hoodwink a debtor,
> You cannot do better
> Than trot out a Duke or a Duchess!

Such ridicule did not bother Wright. All that mattered to him was that the share-buying public were suckers for coronets and gold lace, and he spared no effort in the search for suitable 'guinea pigs'. One of those he invited to join West Australian's board was Lieutenant-General the

Honourable Somerset Gough-Calthorpe, the 7th Baron Calthorpe, a veteran of the Crimean War (he had served as ADC to Lord Raglan) and a friend of Queen Victoria. A second draftee was another Crimean War veteran, Lord Edward Pelham-Clinton, a former Liberal MP and now Master of the Queen's Household. In time, both men would grace the boards of several Whitaker Wright companies.

Wright selected these distinguished ornaments of the late Victorian scene not merely for their high-ranking names and impressive pedigrees. Of almost equal importance to him was their almost total ignorance of financial affairs. Neither was a purist of precision and small print, nor an authority on balance sheets and company accounts. Both were happy to sign off any decision made by Wright, as managing director, without question or interference. In the WW firmament, only one star shone brightly, and that was how he intended it to remain. The elderly Gough-Calthorpe, in particular, being extremely deaf, played no discernible role in West Australian's affairs. He was at his most comfortable attending soirées at Buckingham Palace or speaking at regimental dinners, where he liked to reminisce about the battles of Alma and Inkerman and raise toasts to the 'survivors of the Charge', 'The memory of the dead' and 'Florence Nightingale'. In a City boardroom he was utterly out of his depth. In return for his director's fee of £2,000 a year, he was content to be as pliant and as unchallenging as Wright required him to be, treating the managing director's every word as a divine instruction from the burning bush. Pelham-Clinton was equally yielding. When it came to business matters, he was a 'hopeless imbecile', according to a waspish article in *Pearson's Magazine*. If, on rare occasions, a director raised questions at board meetings, Wright would become 'fretful', according to those present. Howard Spensley, an Australian lawyer who later joined the board of one of Wright's companies, was one of the few

73

to query his edicts. His interrogations angered Wright, who claimed they showed a lack of trust. A City friend said Wright was determined 'to brook no criticism, no opposition', and added that the other directors were afraid of him.

For most of Wright's 'guinea pigs', things did not end well. Several years later, when he found himself in the dock accused of making untrue statements in the prospectus of one of Wright's companies, Gough-Calthorpe underwent one of the most humiliating cross-examinations ever faced by the director of a public company.

Mr Hughes KC: Were you a director of the West Australian Exploration Company, General?

Gough-Calthorpe: I do not know. [Laughter in court.]

Mr Hughes: Do you mean that seriously? You were a director of this great company, and you did not know it?

Gough-Calthorpe: I was so often abroad that I might not have known of my directorship. Anyhow, I will say I was a director. [Laughter in court.]

Mr Hughes: Now, you were a director and the chairman of the Caledonian Copper Company?

Gough-Calthorpe: I was not chairman. Certainly not.

Mr Hughes: Oh yes, you were. Where are the mines of the Caledonian Copper Company? Do you know that?

Gough-Calthorpe (after long pause): In New Caledonia. [Merriment in court.]

Mr Hughes: May I take it that when Mr Whitaker Wright asked you to become a director of a company you did so without any questions?

Gough-Calthorpe: Usually. Mr Whitaker Wright and the other directors knew more about finance than I did. I knew nothing.

Mr Hughes (incredulously): You knew nothing about finance?

Gough-Calthorpe: Nothing whatever.

Mr Hughes: And yet you became a director of this great financial corporation?

Gough-Calthorpe: I was a fool for doing so.

Gough-Calthorpe's answers shone a hard light on how little Wright's board members knew about the workings of his organisation. But the retired general's public ordeal was trivial when compared to that of the most distinguished director of all.

CHAPTER SIX

ILLUSTRIOUS CATCH

Throughout 1895 and 1896, the prevailing headwinds remained firmly in Wright's favour. Market conditions were buoyant, confidence was high, and investors were free with their money. Only a handful of Cassandras said the boom in Australian gold was too good to be true. Perth's *Inquirer and Commercial News* was one of them. As early as April 1895 it cautioned that the prospectuses of 'Westralian' mining properties flooding the London market were 'full of mis-statements and perversions'. Without singling out any company by name, the paper went on:

Western Australia is being made the innocent victim in London of a set of company mongers and market riggers, who, if their machinations are not exposed in time, will wreak incalculable mischief. With people preying on the public at every turn, and offering alleged mines at monstrous prices before anything whatever has been done to test their value, it is clear that unless examples are made of a few of the worst harpies a severe blow will be inflicted on the industry. The gang of thieves and the coterie of scoundrels who are taking advantage of the good fortune of Western Australia to ply their nefarious trade must be broken up and scattered.

In the mother country, doom-laden warnings such as this were few and far between. It should have been crystal clear that sooner or later something would give, but no one was thinking much beyond tomorrow. Far from sounding the alarm, British newspapers encouraged the spree in Australian mining shares and applauded Wright's every move. (It emerged later that he had a large number of influential journalists in his pocket.) *The Spectator* and *The Economist* cautioned periodically that the bonanza would end badly, but for nearly two years the magazines were rare voices of prudence. In retrospect, their occasional salvoes were like the first shower of stones warning that an avalanche may descend at any moment.

In the spring of 1895, Wright served up a second heady brew by launching the London and Globe Finance Corporation, again with a share capital of £200,000, and again with the object of acquiring mining properties. (In years to come, shareholders would recall wryly that it was registered on All Fools' Day.) Like West Australian, Globe was not a mining company as such, but a vehicle for purchasing mines and, where possible, launching them on the market as subsidiary companies. The name was designed by Wright to exude strength and reliability, and it immediately became a byword for success among the share-buying public.

As he approached his fiftieth birthday, the former preacher was at the top of his game, a shark cruising effortlessly through the well-stocked waters of the City. He paid himself a managing director's salary of £2,000 for each company, a substantial income by any standards but dwarfed by his other proceeds from the two ventures. As with West Australian, he reserved 50,000 free Founder's shares in Globe for himself at £1 apiece, and saw their value rise rapidly and dramatically. By the end of 1895, his holdings in the two companies were worth around £240,000 – the best part of £25 million in today's money – and rising.

He endowed Globe with one of the most glittering array of 'guinea pigs' yet seen. Early appointments to the board were his two trusty stalwarts, Pelham-Clinton and Gough-Calthorpe. They were followed by two more high-ranking grandees, Sir William Robinson and Lord Loch. The elderly and cultured Sir William (unlike Wright's MA, the CMG, KCMG and GCMG after his name were genuine enough) was an experienced and highly regarded colonial administrator, and a polished public speaker. He was also a gifted musician, and his appointment as Governor of South Australia in 1883 had been marked by the public performance of his own composition: 'Unfurl the Flag'. Sir William had returned to England in 1895 following his early retirement from the colonial service. A grand dinner was held to fete his homecoming, and Wright won the old boy's favour by inveigling himself onto the banqueting committee. In need of cash, Robinson was easily seduced by Wright into becoming chairman of both Globe and West Australian. He was not noted for his financial acumen and he had little or no business experience. This was just how Wright liked it. Sir William would do exactly as the managing director told him.

The other new recruit, Lord Loch, was a former Governor of Victoria, and had previously been High Commissioner for South Africa. Wright was so keen to lure him on board – for his Australian connections as well as for his peerage – that he reputedly gave Pelham-Clinton a £5,000 bonus for persuading him to become a director. Before joining the colonial service, Loch had enjoyed an adventurous military career, taking part in the Anglo-Sikh War of 1845–46 and the Crimean War a decade later. The most talked-about aspect of his life was the rumour that for more than thirty years he had been married to the wrong woman. Society gossip had it that he had erroneously proposed to his intended bride's twin sister and, afterwards, out of pride or honour, we know not which, refused to admit that he had made a mistake. Like Robinson, he had recently retired as a colonial administrator and needed an injection of funds to maintain the lifestyle to which he had become accustomed. Wright was happy to oblige. It went without saying that Loch knew little about finance.

One man who resisted Wright's blandishments was a brilliant American mining engineer, John Hays Hammond, who had managed mines in California and Mexico before briefly basing himself in London in the 1890s. Wright went to see him and asked him to become Globe's consultant engineer in Australia. 'We've a fine board of directors as you'll see by this list,' Wright told him. Hays Hammond recalled in his memoirs:

> I took the paper and noted suspiciously the inclusion of many titled directors. Since I was familiar with Wright's questionable mining reputation, I suspected that these noble lords were being prepared for fleecing. Wright held out the inducement of a yacht for my accommodation if I would go in with him; even so, I refused.

Hays Hammond's rebuff was a minor irritation only. All that really mattered to Wright was that the boom in Australian mining shares showed no sign of abating. In one month alone – April 1896 – eighty-one West Australian mining companies were floated in London, harvesting more money from the investing public than had been collected in gold during

the previous two years. By the end of the year, the number had risen
to nearly 800. During this rip-roaring period, Wright led the way. He
seemed to be everywhere, dabbling in mines across the southern hemi-
sphere, buying them up cheaply and floating them in London dearly.
He ruthlessly controlled the news that flowed from his company headquarters, concealing any information that might be damaging not only
from the press and public but also from his fellow directors. He knew
all too well the tendency of mineral veins to disobey the promises of
promoters, and he stayed quiet when the rich deposits found near the
surface of many of his mines petered out after just a few feet. Pumping
out good news only, he kept the ball rolling with continued infusions of
fresh capital. With a whirl of publicity, he floated numerous subsidiary
companies to work various gold-mining leases, including Mainland
Consols and Paddington Consols. 'Speculators have periods of madness when they will plunge to the depths,' he told a friend. 'That's the
moment to lure them on.'

The use of the word 'consol' was a typically cunning Wright ploy.
Consols – short for 'consolidated annuities' – were a British government security generally seen as exceptionally safe investments. Wright
shamelessly hijacked the word in a successful bid to snare 'suckers'.

Needing directors for his subsidiary companies, he cast around
for more worthies. Plenty were ready and willing to climb on board.
Among them were the Irish peer, Lord Donoughmore; the former
Solicitor-General of Australia, the Hon. Howard Spensley; Francis
Greville, the Earl of Warwick; and a minor English aristocrat, Lieutenant Colonel Edmund Cradock-Hartopp, who was related by marriage
to Pelham-Clinton.

Wright's reputation was further enhanced when he acquired two
exceptionally lucrative Kalgoorlie mines: the Lake View, which he

re-floated in London in 1896 with a capital of £250,000; and the Ivanhoe, which he re-floated the following year with a capital of £1 million in five-shilling (25p) shares, even though it had been originally capitalised at only £50,000. Though not superstitious, Wright was drawn to Lake View partly because of its name. For years the word 'lake' had seemed to bring him good luck. The Leadville mines in Lake County, Colorado, and the Lake Valley mines in New Mexico had both fattened his wallet. The same would go for Kalgoorlie's Lake View (although it would also be the breaking of him). He recalled in a subsequent newspaper interview:

> The fact that my other Australian mining properties, though so rich at the surface, did not go deep, gave me much food for thought, and one night when my wife was ill and the physician had advised me not to retire, I sat in my dressing-room in front of a fire, and thought all through the night, ruminating on the conditions of these mines. Finally I thought of a little property called the Lake View mine, owned by a few practical miners who, with their modest development and paltry appliances, were still taking out £300 a month. I thought to myself that it might be wiser to buy this property than to keep on acquiring undeveloped mines.

His hunch was right. Both Lake View and Ivanhoe proved outstandingly successful purchases and began delivering large profits. Within months, Lake View Consols had risen from £1 to £10, and later reached £28. Local miners called the mine the Duck Pond: it was full of golden eggs, and month after month the company gathered them up and produced a ton of gold. In truth, its acquisition was principally the work of Charles Kaufman, but Wright was happy to take the credit. Never a slave to restraint, he boasted to the shareholders that it was 'the richest gold mine in the world', with known reserves worth £6 million. Plundering all that he could from Lake View and Ivanhoe – 'the mother milking the babies', as one City cynic put it – he told Kaufman to keep buying mining properties. Derek Walker-Smith, in his 1934 study of the career of Lord Reading (who as Rufus Isaacs KC would do battle with Wright in the courtroom), wrote of him:

> No one gave so huge and vivid an impression of rugged force and financial genius; no one was so lavish in the ostentation which advertised his great position ... The prestige of WW, as he came to be known in the City, was enormous. He was looked upon as a sort of Midas, who had only to touch a scheme to turn it into gold. His shares were taken up with alacrity, and his invitations to subscribe responded to with enthusiasm. His actions were watched and his example followed; his advice was sought and his nod attended to.

To his grateful followers, who increasingly accepted new shares in lieu of dividends, he was a larger-than-life figure with almost supernatural powers. In the press, he was dubbed the 'Modern Monte Cristo' after the rags-to-riches hero of Alexandre Dumas's celebrated novel. It was reported that if he left a London dinner party early, the entire room would stand respectfully as if he were royalty. The words '*Veni, Vidi, Vici*' seemed to be emblazoned on the braces above his ever-expanding waistline. All he needed to do, he told himself, was to keep on producing prospectuses filled with golden dreams, and to print share certificates for sale to the members of each new company.

Colonel Isaac Peyton, an American businessman who had dealings with Globe during the mid-1890s, would recall that Wright 'enjoyed the implicit confidence of the leading financial men in London … he was associated with a class of people who brought him into close contact with the highest financial circles of the British Empire … a promoter pure and simple, but he operated on a gigantic scale.' The powerful impression Wright made on people was reinforced in numerous newspaper articles. Describing him as an 'extraordinary personality', the *Auckland Star* observed:

> He is one of those men at whom a passer-by instinctively looks twice. He has a personality which is commonly called 'magnetic'. With inches little short of seventy-two, with avoirdupois approaching eighteen stone, he is a massive man, an impressive man. Yet there is nothing assertive in his appearance. Clean shaven save for a moustache, he abhors that glitter of diamond ring and gleam of golden watch-chain whereby the self-made man is apt to advertise his worldly success. Whitaker Wright dresses quietly in black, and is unadorned by a speck of jewellery.

In early 1897, Wright made another killing when he combined his two main companies, West Australian and Globe, into one entity – the revamped London and Globe Finance Corporation – with a share capital of £2 million. Based in plush new offices at 43 Lothbury, next to the headquarters of the London & Westminster Bank, the company's aim was, as before, to buy up and launch mines as subsidiary businesses. Amid a frenzy of interest, nearly 9,000 people bought shares in the restructured company. For Wright, it was a pinnacle moment. As compensation for his original shares being taken over, he allotted himself 388,000 £1 shares in the new London and Globe. By the end of the year, these had more than doubled in value to forty-five shillings (£2.25), netting him a paper profit of around £50 million in today's money and putting him well on the way to becoming the richest man in Britain. 'Under the skilful direction of Mr Whitaker Wright,' wrote the *Pall Mall Gazette*, 'the Globe is now recognised as being one of the greatest and most successful of City issuing houses.' As usual, there was only a handful of dissenting voices. The *Investors' Review* was one of them. It said the new Globe was of a 'dangerous and flimsy character' and should not be 'regarded as anything but a mockery of a company without serious purpose'.

Needing a chairman for Globe (Sir William Robinson had died in May 1897), Wright aimed high. According to Roland Belfort, 'he endeavoured to create an international sensation by securing as chairman a scion by marriage of royalty'. Writing later about the planned coup, Belfort did not reveal the name of the royal personage in question, but it was almost certainly 61-year-old John Campbell, the Marquess of Lorne, who was married to Queen Victoria's sixth child, her fourth daughter, Princess Louise. At Globe's headquarters, Wright worked late into the night with a team of clerks and secretaries putting the final touches to the prospectus – to be printed the following morning – which would reveal the company's gilt-edged acquisition. Belfort recalled:

Great excitement prevailed. Wright, flushed with success, the master of millions, became imperious, dominating, and already visualised the royal chairman sitting on the board. What he did not know was that the nominee for this flattering appointment had considered it respectful to consult Queen Victoria and was met with an emphatic 'no'. It was on the stroke of midnight that a trusty friend of the proposed royal chairman notified this categorical denial to WW.

The latter expressed his disgust in American expletives, powerful and picturesque, and ordered the name to be struck out.

Never one to be thwarted, Wright consulted his friend, Daisy Greville, the Countess of Warwick, about procuring the next best thing to an empress's son-in-law. She came up trumps. He had come to know this glamorous society beauty (who was the inspiration for the popular music hall song *Daisy Daisy)* because her husband, the Earl of Warwick (previously styled Lord Brooke), was on the board of a Globe subsidiary, Victorian Gold Estates. Daisy was a lavish spender (her coming-out ball in 1879 at the family seat in Essex was a celebration of such grandeur that Mr Carlo, 'the eminent Knightsbridge coiffeur', was brought from London to crimp and powder the footmen's hair), and when she had asked Wright for advice on how to alleviate her debts, he was more than happy to help. The fact that Daisy was in the throes of a passionate affair with the Prince of Wales at the time made her, in his eyes, a particularly useful contact. Taking up his recommendation to acquire Lake View stock, she was delighted when the share price soared. In time she made a profit of £160,000 from her Lake View and other Wright-inspired transactions.

As a reward for turning around her financial fortunes, Wright was regularly invited to Daisy's London soirées. She was an accomplished hostess, and few could resist her bidding. Men of power and influence were drawn to her not only because of her looks (according to one newspaper, 'the countess is so well preserved that her colouring, her clear eyes, her figure, her grace and youthful buoyancy, make of her a veritable proposition in peaches'), but because she was also highly indiscreet and could be relied upon to impart tip-top gossip. One of her titbits – a rumour that a blue-blood had cheated during a game of baccarat attended by the Prince of Wales – had earned her the sobriquet of 'Babbling Brooke'. Wright profited greatly from her friendship, persuading many of the wealthy men he met in her Belgravia drawing room to invest in his companies.

Just as importantly, Daisy was instrumental in finding him a top-notch 'guinea pig' to chair the reconstituted London and Globe, helping him to reel in a catch who, if anything, was even more illustrious than the Marquess of Lorne. Frederick Temple Hamilton-Temple-Blackwood, 1st Marquess of Dufferin and Ava, was one of the most respected men of his generation. In a glittering diplomatic career, he had been Viceroy of India, Governor-General of Canada, and ambassador to Russia, Turkey, France and Italy. He had also served in Gladstone's government as Chancellor of the Duchy of Lancaster. During the course of an extraordinary life, he had played patience with the Duke of Wellington (who recounted to him how one of his aides-de-camp had asked him if he had ever seen Elizabeth I), shot with Prince Albert, dined with Bismarck, conversed with Sitting Bull ('only one eye and nose of brilliant hue'), and had nearly been rejected by Queen Victoria as one of her Lords-in-Waiting on the grounds that he was 'much too good-looking and captivating'. An all-round sportsman, he had sailed in the Sea of Marmara, played lawn tennis in Istanbul, curled on the Canadian lakes and skated on the frozen waters of the Bois de Boulogne. He 'loathed being idle' and in 1895, as he approached his seventieth birthday, he took it upon himself to learn Persian. He wrote in his diary on 30 December: 'During this year I have learned by heart 786 columns of a Persian dictionary, comprising about 24,000 words. Of these, I have learned 8,000 perfectly, 12,000 pretty well, and 4,000 imperfectly. In three months' time I hope to have completely mastered the whole.' His 1903 biographer, Charles Black, wrote that he was 'one of the ablest, most versatile, most successful, and most fascinating of our public men in the latter half of the reign of Queen Victoria'. His nephew Harold

Nicolson recounted in a memoir about Dufferin how he once asked his nanny: "'Miss Plimsoll, is Uncle Dufferin a great man?' She raised her eyes and fixed them on the picture above the mantelpiece … then she turned and faced me … enraptured. 'He is,' she answered slowly, 'the greatest man in the world.'"

Dufferin's one great weakness was a recklessness with money, and he was forever battling to keep his income within hailing distance of his outgoings. He had lived beyond his means for most of his life and had been forced to mortgage his estates in Ireland to thaw out the iron frost of insolvency. In one five-year period alone, between 1873 and 1878, he entertained no fewer than 35,838 people at dinners and balls in his Irish home. 'I hear terrible things about your expenditure,' the Duke of Argyll once wrote to him. 'People say that you will be entirely ruinated.' After his retirement from the diplomatic service in 1896, Dufferin was keen to avoid further pecuniary embarrassment, and when Daisy introduced him to Wright the following year, both men saw it as the perfect match. Far from disdaining the company of the brash magnate, Dufferin was fascinated by him, in the same way that he had been captivated by the spectacularly wealthy Indian princes and American plutocrats he had met during his far-flung travels.

Wright, for his part, saw Dufferin as the ultimate 'guinea pig' and courted him assiduously. Over tea at the Savoy, he showed him maps of his Australian gold finds and thrilled him with tales of the fabulous riches waiting to be brought to the surface. Lord Loch, keen to offload some of his duties, added his own siren voice to the courtship, as did Pelham-Clinton. (Both men were reputedly paid large cash bonuses for helping to win him over.) Gough-Calthorpe also weighed in with words of encouragement, writing to Dufferin: 'Our friend [Whitaker Wright] is always so sanguine. One ought to catch the confidence he wishes to inspire.'

Dufferin had already turned down several invitations to join the boards of other companies, but he found Wright's blandishments irresistible. Seduced by the heady scent of riches – a substantial lump sum reputed to be £10,000, a salary of £4,000 a year and an array of perks – he overcame any lurking doubts he had about Wright's business methods and agreed to become chairman of Globe. He went further. Although he had once warned one of his daughters never to speculate ('first because it is ruinous; and secondly because it is wrong'), this normally astute man showed his confidence in the company by ignoring his own advice and buying 5,000 Globe shares at thirty shillings (£1.50) each. Feeling fully exonerated when, within weeks, they were worth 50 per cent more than he had paid for them, he bought yet more stock. In due course he increased his holdings in Wright's companies to more than £70,000 and encouraged his son-in-law, the Liberal MP Sir Ronald Munro Ferguson, to become a fellow investor. On the back of his newfound wealth, Dufferin enlarged his estate in Ireland, acquired a luxury yacht, *Brunhilde*, and wrote to Ferguson: 'We must build adjoining palaces in Park Lane.'

Before accepting the chairmanship of Globe, Dufferin had inquired about the duties of such a role and was comforted to learn that the financial interests of the company would remain in the hands of the managing director. All that was required of him was to be a figurehead. He knew practically nothing of mining and science and claimed jocularly that as a boy he had 'succeeded in blowing up an assembly of ladies and gentlemen to whom I was giving a chemical lecture'. A letter he received from Wright ahead of his first shareholders' meeting made it plain who was calling the shots: 'My dear Lord Dufferin, I enclose the substance of what should be said at the meeting which, when put into your elegant diction, will, I am sure, be very satisfactory to the shareholders.' Dufferin had no qualms about becoming the wax palette on which Wright inscribed his epistles. He added a little aristocratic flavouring to the boss's words, as he did with all his subsequent chairman's speeches, but relied entirely on Wright to provide the framework. A concerned friend of Dufferin, Fanny Burns, wrote to him: '*Do* be careful of Mr Wright. ("Wrong" would be more appropriate.) Remember he is a Yankee! Too sharp and clever for most people.' But Dufferin was feeling too flush with cash to heed her warning. Besides, Wright wasn't a fly-by-night Yankee. He was British, trustworthy and honest...

The Marquess of Dufferin and Ava was one of the most respected men of his generation. Becoming involved with Wright turned out to be the worst mistake of his life.

The shareholders welcomed Dufferin's appointment. His biographer, Charles Black, stated that large numbers of them invested in Globe 'secure in the easy conviction that all must go well in a concern with which so distinguished and honoured a name as that of Lord Dufferin was connected'. *Pearson's Magazine* noted in 1904:

The capture of Lord Dufferin was the greatest coup Mr Whitaker

Wright ever made – it was far and away the best name that ever appeared on a company's 'front sheet' and served to sanctify the company it adorned, as well as the directors who adorned it. It would have been as reasonable to doubt the stability of the Bank of England as that of the London and Globe.

The *Saturday Review* was almost alone in sounding a warning. Lord Dufferin, it said, 'is a charming and intellectual personality, but in matters of detailed finance he is singularly incapable'. For his part, Dufferin seized every opportunity to say all the right things about his new colleagues. Wright preened himself as the new chairman told the audience at his first Globe shareholders' meeting that he had accepted the position because the directors were 'men of the highest calibre' and because of the 'financial ability and unblemished integrity of Whitaker Wright'. In Wright's eyes, these words alone (which, of course, he had written himself) made the peer worth every penny of his salary. Later during the same meeting Dufferin drew appreciative laughter when he said: 'I confess that when I first joined the board I was imperfectly acquainted with the mysteries of the Stock Exchange, the subterranean machinations of the "bulls" and "bears", and the effect on the value of mining and other shares produced by the financial press.' The admission did him no harm. Even the cynics were won over by his self-effacing tone. *The Economist* commented:

Like the skilled diplomatist that he is, he has displayed conspicuous ability in making rough places plain, and in glossing over apparently difficult points in such a way as to impress the average shareholder with the conviction that things are really much better than they look and that everything is for the best in the best of all possible enterprises.

Dufferin could hardly believe his luck when, that winter, he and his wife, Hariot, embarked on an all-expenses-paid Mediterranean cruise on a fully manned steam yacht provided by Wright as a reward for his becoming chairman. Practically all the good fairies seemed to have gathered at his feet at once. When his old friend Sir Mountstuart Grant Duff sent him a friendly warning about the risks of being associated with someone like Wright, he wrote back blithely: 'All is well. I never do anything without consulting my solicitor.' To his friend Lord Spencer he explained that 'I have taken every precaution and Lord Loch has been my principal guide'. But his friends were right to urge caution. Becoming involved with Wright would turn out to be the most disastrous mistake of his life.

CHAPTER SEVEN

SURREY SHANGRI-LA

Never before and never since has a private residence matched the sheer outlandishness of the home Wright began creating for himself in Surrey in 1896. It was not just the vast house, with its thirty-two bedrooms, observatory, velodrome, private theatre, and its enormous grounds, with their lakes, fountains, marble statuary and lavish stables, that scaled the heights of ostentation and indulgence. What earned Lea Park its place in folklore, and constituted Wright's lasting memorial, was the extraordinary secret that lay (and lies to this day) beneath the surface of one of the lakes.

Since his return to England, Wright had yearned to own a country pile. Successful financiers of the late Victorian era – those who had made their money from what Lady Bracknell called the 'purple of commerce'– considered a large mansion with extensive grounds essential for parading their newfound wealth and prestige. That same year, Wright's rival company promoter, Ernest Terah Hooley, later to serve two prison terms for fraud, had bought the 2,000-acre Anmer estate in Norfolk for £25,000. The flamboyant financier Horatio Bottomley, who would also end up in prison, kept a string of racehorses on his estate at Upper Dicker near Eastbourne, employed eight full-time gardeners and boasted an island summerhouse equipped with a telephone. John North, who had made his fortune from nitrates, rubber, waterworks and freight railways, and who was soon to die from the effects of consuming a plateful of oysters, owned a 600-acre estate near Eltham in Kent.

Wright resolved to outdo the lot of them. He wanted the biggest and the best, bells and whistles, the whole works. He had originally planned to return to his Midlands roots and buy Mount Vernon, a rambling house with extensive grounds in the Nottinghamshire village of Ordsall. The property was on sale for £13,000, with an art collection thrown in for an extra £1,000. He and Anna spent the weekend there as the guests of the owner, a solicitor named George Marshall. In a characteristic negotiating ploy, Wright told Marshall that if he would let him retain the purchasing price he would 'double it in six months' by investing it in Globe shares. Before Marshall had time to consider the offer, Anna said she would prefer to live in the south of England, and Wright withdrew the bid. Renewing his search for a suitable property, he found the perfect place at Witley, an hour's train ride from London's Waterloo Station. It was at least twenty times more expensive than Mount Vernon, but with cash pouring into his coffers at an unprecedented rate there was effectively no upper limit to his spending power.

The parish of Witley, 4 miles south of Godalming in the southwestern corner of Surrey, encompasses some of the finest countryside in England. The area was once occupied by Saxons, and the name is believed to derive from Witta's 'leah' or clearing. By the time of the Domesday Book, the Manor of Witley was held by Gilbert de Aquila, whose Norman grandfather had been killed at the Battle of Hastings.

Its several thousand acres were then valued at £16. Later it belonged to Edward I and was briefly the centre of England when he held court there for five days in 1305 and went hunting in Witley Park. Several other monarchs, including Richard II, Henry VI and Elizabeth I, held the manor before it passed to barrister Philip Carteret Webb in 1763. In 1825, the pamphleteer and radical MP William Cobbett rode through Witley's fields and remarked on the profusion of game to be found there. The novelist George Eliot had a summer home in the parish in the 1870s, and Tennyson liked to walk on the local hills. Sir Arthur Conan Doyle acquired a house on the southern outskirts of the park in the 1890s and wrote *The Hound of the Baskervilles* there.

Witley's ceremonial manorial rights remained with the Webb family until 1896, when the fifth-generational Richard Webb decided to sell up and move on. The new Lord of the Manor was every bit as colourful as any of his illustrious predecessors, and brasher by far. True to form, Whitaker Wright took Witley by storm. Here, in the words of Lord Dufferin's biographer, Harold Nicolson, he 'revived the luxuries and the enterprise of the Roman emperors'. With money no object, he bought two large tracts of land to the west of the village, paying £150,000 for the Lea Park estate, which included the nineteenth-century manor house, and a further £100,000 for the adjacent South Park Farm estate. This gave him a total of 9,000 acres, or a little over 14 square miles. As well as bestowing on him the Lordship of the Manor, the acquisitions gave him ownership of two local beauty spots, Hindhead Common and the Devil's Punch Bowl, areas once notorious for highwaymen and lawlessness. In a nostalgic throwback to his adventures in the Wild West, he also found himself the possessor of two disused iron mines, situated in the parkland to the west of the main house. To the south, he could walk the 3 miles to Haslemere Station without leaving his land.

Striding around his new estate, with its 90 miles of roads, lanes and paths, its 900 acres of sporting woodland, its five lodges and its ten farms (they included Brook Corner, The Willows, Winkford Farm, Lower House and Parsonage Farm), he set his swirling imagination to work. With an acreage more than twice that of Hooley, Bottomley and North combined, there was no lack of scope. Ambitious vision followed ambitious vision. If he had been a pharaoh in ancient Egypt, he would have built himself a pyramid. In Babylonian times, he would have created hanging gardens. Wanting something to match these wonders, he turned his thoughts to a tributary of the River Wey, which meandered north to south through the grounds. It was allowed only a short run of fluvial life, but he immediately began to develop grand ideas for it. In his mind's eye he saw a series of great lakes, complete with islands, gulfs and hidden channels. And something more besides...

His compulsion to own the most magnificent estate in Britain probably went beyond mere social climbing and the ostentatious display of wealth and power. That early failure in Halifax, and the ever-nagging feeling that he had let down his father, undoubtedly sparked a burning need to prove to both himself and to others that he was a man of outstanding ability and success. Most of the more exotic ideas for his Surrey Shangri-La were his own, and it is possible that he was inspired in part by his visit to Philadelphia's Centennial Exhibition twenty years earlier. The great glass dome of the Memorial Hall, the fountains and statuary, the graceful arches and exotic plant life of the Horticultural Hall, the 153 acres of flowerbeds and lawns, the undulating Pennsylvanian grounds enclosed by 3 miles of fencing – all these he replicated to some degree at Witley.

To turn whim into gold-plated reality, he gathered together a team of talented professionals. A London architect, Paxton Hood Watson, was contracted to turn the existing manor house into a pleasure palace, and royal warrant-holders George Jackson and Sons, who had carried out work at Buckingham Palace and Sandringham, were entrusted with the ornamental plasterwork. Edwin Lutyens, who had been brought up in the neighbouring village of Thursley, and who was at the onset of a glittering architectural career, was asked to design some lakeside buildings. The horticulturalist Gertrude Jekyll, who was a friend of Lutyens and was collaborating with him at the time on a house at Munstead Wood, 4 miles away, may have advised on the planting of trees and shrubs. James Veitch & Son, an old family firm which specialised in designing and planting gardens for the gentry, carried out the landscaping.

Under Paxton Watson's direction, two wings were added to the existing half-timbered manor house at the stupendous cost of £400,000. The end of the new west wing was adorned with a vast conservatory, which alone cost £10,000 (around £1 million in today's money). Designed to be 'fit for an oriental prince' (to use Wright's words), it was built of Bath stone with glass sides and a large central glass dome. At its centre was a fountain called 'The Three Fisherwomen'. Measuring 92ft by 42ft and filled with trees and exotic plants gathered from across the world by James Veitch's nurserymen, it was a palm court to rival those at London's Langham Hotel and Alexandra Palace, with a roof almost as high as the palm house at Kew. An orchid expert, Mr Goodbourne, was hired full-time to tend to and cultivate the flowers and plants in the conservatory and in Lea Park's reception rooms.

At the far end of the house – a walk of several minutes along more than 500ft of corridors adorned with hunting trophies, suits of armour and ceremonial swords – the end of the east wing catered for the Lord of the Manor's passion for astronomy, accommodating a domed observatory with a revolving copper roof through which he might observe the march of the planets across the heavens and study the mysterious canals on Mars. One of only a handful of private observatories in Britain, it was probably modelled in part on the Lick Observatory in California, and was the perfect place for a plutocrat to entertain his guests after dinner and before bedtime.

Between these two great embellishments were thirty-two bedrooms, eleven bathrooms, seventeen cloakrooms, seven reception rooms and numerous courtyards paved in white marble and beautified with Moorish arches. The most sumptuous of the upstairs apartments was the so-called bridal suite, formed of two rooms, each 74ft long and 54ft wide, in the shape of a capital L. It had thirty windows, and was adorned with moulded ceilings, tall mirrors, oriental carpets and an array of antique Chinese and Japanese furniture. The walls were hung with Japanese silk pictures patterned with foliage on an ivory background. The dressing table, all 32 square feet of it, was covered with a tapestry embroidered with the words 'Love Maketh a Feast With Most or Least'. Wright equipped the room with a piano, a harp, a zither and a Chinese gong drum, 6ft tall, which stood where the arms of the room met.

The largest of the downstairs rooms, at more than 2,600 square feet, was the cedar-panelled ballroom, with an oak and walnut dance floor capable of accommodating hundreds of people. Its furnishings included a pipe organ, a grand piano, crystal chandeliers and numerous armchairs and chaises longues. At one end of the room was a theatre, built at a cost of £16,000, with a fitted stage, dressing rooms, a drop curtain and a minstrel's gallery. The room deserved – nay, demanded – a ceiling to match its noble proportions, and was duly given one of appropriate grandeur. Taking its inspiration from the Sistine Chapel (Wright had become a lover of all things Italianate), it was decorated in chocolate and gold, and took a team of craftsmen more than two years to complete.

Statues, fine paintings, tapestries and furniture finished in gold leaf filled every remaining spare corner of the ground floor. The main dining room was 50ft long and had seating for scores of guests. A bank of cookers in the kitchens was capable of catering for up to 400 people at one sitting. A smaller family dining room was three-quarters panelled in oak carved by craftsmen brought in from Italy. Elsewhere on the ground floor were a drawing room panelled with brocaded silk, a library with carved oak mantelpieces, a billiards room fitted in carved oak with an arched ceiling, a small private hospital and – of all unlikely things – one of Britain's first private velodromes. Beneath the house were underground strongrooms with sliding steel doors where Wright stored those of his art treasures that were not on display.

In keeping with the properties of other plutocrats of the time, the house was characterised by overwhelming display aimed at showing the costliness of the building, not necessarily the beauty of its design. 'Royalty boasts nothing more luxurious,' commented Brisbane's *Truth* newspaper after its correspondent was allowed inside the house. A London architectural craftsman, John Thorp, on reading about Lea Park in a magazine, was so enraptured that he spent months building a stone model of the property to add to his replicas of St Paul's Cathedral and old London Bridge. Lord Reading's biographer, Derek Walker-Smith, wrote of the mansion: 'It would be no exaggeration to say that it was easily the finest private residence in the world … it was like an Aladdin's Palace.' The *Illustrated London News* cuttingly compared Wright to Mad King Ludwig of Bavaria, notorious for having abandoned affairs of state in favour of extravagant artistic and architectural projects. Other journals described the house variously as 'heavy without magnificence', 'a vast and shapeless mass', 'clever, Tudor style' and 'hideous'. Locally it was known as 'Wright's Folly'. The *Daily Express* was scathing:

Despite the fortune it has consumed, the great house at Lea Park is not pretty. It suggests that Mr Wright put half a dozen kinds of architecture into a hat, shuffled them, and then drew three, saying to his contractor, 'Make it so'. Nor does a one-storey stone laundry, sprawling at the back of the left wing, in full view of the principal drive, add to its beauty.

Wright was impervious to such criticism. None of his pampered guests had any complaints about the house and, besides, it was only one part of his grand design. It was in the grounds of Lea Park that he truly let rip, and here his creativity more than once blurred the lines between brilliance and madness. At a cost of £10,000, he had his men build a stone wall to enclose the 440 acres of parkland nearest the house – 'the finest wall in England', according to one newspaper. Another wall was built to enclose an eight-acre kitchen garden equipped with vast greenhouses. Next to go up was a stable block capable of holding fifty horses, a centrally heated equine palace thought by some to be more aesthetically pleasing than the house itself. There were separate stalls for every horse, along with a viewing space from which visitors could admire their mounts from the comfort of leather-upholstered oak settees shaded by palm trees. The electrically lit ceilings above the stalls depicted different aspects of the chase in moulded plaster – horses jumping ditches, top-hatted riders clinging to their mounts, harriers in pursuit of a fox. At one end of the stables was an equine hospital with gun-metal fittings, as neat and as clean as the apartments in the main house. As with other buildings on the estate, the entwined letters 'WW' were carved in stone above the stables' entrance. 'The whole thing was a blatant sumptuousness which must have embarrassed the horses,' observed one critic. The *Investors' Review* noted sourly that 'the only fault ever found with this stable was to the effect that it was so beautiful that the horses were overlooked'.

And then there were the lakes. Originally there had been two relatively small pools, fed by the stream that ran through the grounds. Wright had them transformed into three much larger bodies of water, which were approached by a series of terraces leading down from the house. To build them, he employed an army of labourers – around 600 by one estimate – who worked week after week, month after month, to reshape the landscape. Armed with a great oak stick, Wright stumped around among his workforce, a hulking figure usually dressed in black, directing them, encouraging them, and forever dreaming up new ideas. It became a standing joke that every time the navvies saw him wave his stick, someone would say: 'There goes another hundred pounds.' (A large mound made from the spoil generated from the landscaping of the gardens can be seen to this day on Witley Common.)

On one notorious occasion, Wright observed that a small hill would block the view from the house of one of his new lakes. 'Move it,' he demanded, as if directing an entry in a London and Globe ledger. Scores of labourers cut down the hill in slices, carted it away in barrows and rebuilt it in another part of the grounds. Given that the Lake View mine in Australia was in large part responsible for Wright's enormous wealth, it probably appealed to his sense of humour that the hill's removal gave him a panoramic lake view. To emphasise the point, he had the words 'Lake View' emblazoned on floor mats on the west-facing side of the palm court. Elsewhere on the estate an orchard was laid down. Wright inspected it and decided that he wanted it elsewhere. Veitch & Son duly obliged. To the contractors he was like a child playing with model trees and buildings on a toy farm. Not that they had any beef against their impulsive and unpredictable employer.

Demanding though he was, he treated them courteously and settled his bills promptly.

The labourers, too, liked 'Mr Whitaker' because he paid their wages on time and never talked down to them. He was a generous boss, and weekly earnings at Lea Park rose from fourteen shillings (70p) to twenty-one shillings (£1.05) during his tenure, much to the irritation of local farmers, for whom cheap labour became a thing of the past. It was said that throughout Wright's occupancy of Lea Park there was never any unemployment in the Witley area. The *Surrey Advertiser* noted: 'One would have to go back many years to find so small a number of persons in receipt of out-relief as when this gigantic work was at its height.' Men seeking work converged on Lea Park from all over the surrounding area, including Sussex. Some never made it, and it was not uncommon for the bodies of sick and starving men to be found on the wayside. One such was a labourer who died on his way to Lea Park and whose body was found lying outside the Star Inn at Witley. In his pocket were all his worldly belongings – a silver watch, two snares, a quantity of wire and two pennies. Those who were taken on were generally happy in their work. They warmed to Wright because he had a keen sense of humour and was prepared to dirty his hands. It was not unknown for him to remove his coat and wield a pick or a shovel himself, perhaps fancying himself back on the Snake River in Idaho. 'Put your back into it,' he said one day to a navvy. 'When I dug, I worked a lot harder than you're doing now.' 'Maybe,' replied the workman good-naturedly, 'but you were digging for diamonds...' Wright laughed and went on his way.

Months of back-breaking work resulted in the creation of three lakes on different levels – the square lake, the bathing lake and the big lake. The first fed water into the second via a cascade made from natural iron-stone block, marble edging and sea shells of Sienna marble. From the second lake the water flowed into the big lake through a great dolphin's head, and from there a turbine pumped it back to the first lake. Wright had taken a fancy to the dolphin's head when he saw it on display during a trip to Italy to enrol artists to decorate the house. It was carved from a solid block of marble and weighed at least thirty tons. He had it shipped to Southampton Docks, but the London and South Western Railway Company could not transport it to Surrey because it was too big to pass through their tunnels. Wright solved this problem by hiring a traction engine and having it hauled to Witley by road on a purpose-built flat-bed truck. More than once the roadway had to be widened to allow it to pass, and on one occasion, when it would not go under a bridge, Wright had the road dug out beneath the bridge to provide enough headroom for it to continue on its way. Transporting the dolphin from Southampton to Lea Park ended up costing more than the dolphin itself.

During the same trip to Italy, Wright had seen a fountain in the courtyard of an old palace. This too was brought back to his estate and placed near the dolphin's head. He obtained more art works from the Rome studio of sculptor Orazio Andreoni. These were transported to Witley along with a team of Italian masons and sculptors to position and install them. Soon gleaming Carrara marble statuary filled Lea Park's ground – a quartet of female figures in flowing robes representing the four seasons; a mermaid struggling with an octopus in one of the lakes; Venus, one hand raised to her flowing hair, riding a pair of winged horses surrounded by seven rock-climbing sea nymphs; water running through the hair of a beautiful female figure constructed of white marble.

The largest of the three lakes was the focus of Lea Park's grounds. Spread across some sixteen acres to the east of the house, it was bounded by holly, oak, fir and birch, all transported by Messrs Veitch from another part of the estate, with rhododendrons adding splashes of pink and purple. Wright had it filled with carp which, according to Harold Nicolson, were specially imported from an ancient lake at Azay le Rideau in France's Loire Valley, which was apparently the repository of particularly fine specimens. Among the lake's other adornments were a summerhouse, a pagoda, a pier, and a bathing pavilion and boathouse designed by Lutyens. The boathouse was home to a fleet of electric launches, sailing craft and rowboats in which Wright and his guests could set off on journeys of adventure. If they did not feel like wielding the oars themselves, boatmen were on hand to man the craft and show them the hidden sights. The first port of call was a water-filled subterranean passage on the far bank, its entrance all but concealed by trees and shrubs. Guests were encouraged to imagine themselves in the Blue Grotto at Capri as they floated along the darkened passageway and stopped at a flight of steps carved into the rock. Leaving the boats, they climbed into a cave bathed in blue light and filled with oriental decorations and statuary.* There was more to come. Much more. What really caught contemporary fancy, and has since been elevated to mythical status, was a domed, glass chamber, 18ft high, sitting like an igloo on the lake bed, completely underwater. A subaqueous smoking room, no less.

To reach it, one stepped into a small stone building beside the lake that sheltered the head of a spiral staircase. Descending the stairs, one passed through a wooden door into a 350ft-long underwater tunnel, wide enough for four people to walk abreast. Lit by electric lamps, and with a lancet-shaped roof, it led directly out into the lake. At the end of the tunnel lay Wright's dome-shaped pride and joy – what the press termed 'a submerged fairy room'. More than 200 panes of glass, each three inches

---

* The Lea Park grotto may have been partly inspired by Sir Frank Crisp's innovations at Friar Park, Henley, during the 1880s. Crisp, a wealthy solicitor, constructed a series of grottoes reached by waterways concealed beneath a sandstone replica of the Matterhorn. Beatle George Harrison bought and restored the property in 1970.

thick, and set between riveted ironwork, were used in its construction. It had a mosaic floor and was furnished with button-upholstered settees, chairs, small tables and palms. Perched on top of it was a statue of Neptune, which protruded from the lake's surface and was the only part of the structure visible from the land. An air vent emerged through Neptune's mouth and wisps of smoke were sometimes seen drifting out of this when Wright and his friends were down below enjoying cigars.

Wright's underwater smoking room at Lea Park as it is today. He called it his 'crystal cavern'.

Wright spent many happy hours in what he called his 'crystal cavern', reading the newspapers and reflecting on life over a brandy and soda or a bottle of champagne. Those invited to join him there were invariably enchanted. To ensure clear views through the glass, Wright hired divers to keep the dome free from algae. Spellbound guests were able to watch fish, and sometimes swimmers, disport themselves overhead. On summer nights their host might switch off the lights so that he and his friends could watch firework displays or simply gaze through the green curtain of water at the stars and moon. The effect from outside, with the ballroom lit up beneath the water, was equally spectacular. The *Royal Magazine* described it thus:

> It is a wonderful place – a fairy palace. In summer it is delightfully cool – in winter, delightfully warm, for the temperature is always fairly even. Outside the clear crystal glass is a curtain of green water – deep, beautiful green at the bottom, fading away to the palest, faintest green at the top, where little white wavelets ripple. Goldfish come and press their faces against the glass, peering at you with strangely magnified eyes. On summer nights one looks through the green water at the stars and the moon, which appear extraordinarily bright and large, for they are magnified quite ten times by the curved glass and the water.

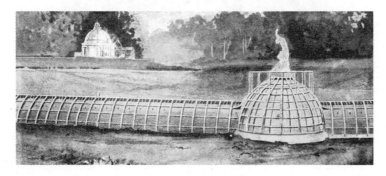

Artist's impression of the underwater room and connecting passageway before the lake was filled with water. The image appeared in the June 1903 issue of the Royal Magazine.

From the glass chamber, a short flight of steps led up to another sub-aqueous room with concrete walls and a curved ceiling supported on cast-iron columns. Lit by porthole-shaped skylights and equipped with a billiard table and card tables, this was the Lord of the Manor's secret gaming room, a place where the men could head off for some post-prandial fun. 'I bet I can beat you at billiards underwater' was one of his favourite opening lines to visitors who did not know of the lake's secrets. The ladies were catered for, too. From the gaming room, a spiral staircase led up to a cruciform-shaped stone viewing platform on the surface of the lake, not unlike a giant lily pad in appearance, where on summer afternoons Anna and her friends could take tea.

Wright relaxing in his underwater room… An image from the
Royal Magazine *of 1903, the year Wright fled to New York.*

The glass chamber was constructed while the lake was empty, and several anxious days followed its completion as it gradually vanished beneath the rising water. Costing £20,000, it was of necessity built with extreme care. Wright was warned it would flood within five minutes if a single pane broke. His estate manager at the time, a Mr Watkins, was a civil engineer by profession, and probably supervised the installation of his employer's unique and challenging project. The structure appears to have been in place by 1897, and showed up on the Ordnance Survey the following year. No record exists of who designed and constructed it, but there are various contenders. London and Globe was at the time involved in the building of the Baker Street and Waterloo Underground Railway (later called the Bakerloo Line). Most of the line's construction work was carried out by Perry & Company, whose chairman, Herbert Henry Bartlett, was an acclaimed designer, with both Tower Bridge and Waterloo Station to his credit. It is probable that he or a colleague had a hand in the underwater hideaway's creation. The walls of Lea Park's tunnels, including those of the passageway leading to the underwater chamber, were reinforced by iron rings used in the construction of the Metropolitan Line underground railway.

In subsequent years the glass chamber was often referred to in newspapers as an underwater ballroom, and occasionally as a music room. Wright did not build it as such, but he probably hosted dances there from time to time, and it was certainly used for this purpose by later owners of Lea Park. A young actress, Enid Clarke, attended a party there in the 1920s, and gave a description of it to her son, Rex Walters, which he wrote down for posterity:

> I was part of a touring company which put on a play in Lea Park's private theatre. After the performance we were led down a candle-lit walkway on the grass to the edge of the lake. From there we descended some steps and walked through a passage into a dream-like room under the water. We were served dinner by a staff of waitresses and butlers, and throughout the meal we could see the fish swimming around us on the other side of the glass. There was lighting both outside and inside the room, giving full effect to the ethereal atmosphere. At the end of the meal, the tables were moved to the side and music was played. I will never forget dancing the evening away, not beneath the stars, but in a phosphorescent water kingdom that was more magical than the stars by far.

CHAPTER EIGHT

LORD OF THE MANOR

Wright entertained on a scale that would have put a French monarch to shame. It was not just at Lea Park that he pushed the boat out. To celebrate his fiftieth birthday in February 1896, he reserved a Pullman carriage on the London and South Western Railway and took a party of business associates and their wives to Southampton. There they boarded a chartered steam yacht, *White Heather*, which had once belonged to Kaiser Wilhelm II of Germany, and embarked on an all-expenses-paid Mediterranean cruise. Wright laid on every conceivable luxury – uniformed stewards, first-class chefs, a fully stocked bar and a musical ensemble for dancing under the stars. As they sailed south for Nice and Malta, the assembled guests, who included Lord and Lady Loch, Sir William and Lady Robinson, Lord Edward Pelham-Clinton and General Gough-Calthorpe, swayed and spun to the romantic refrains of Dr Leo Sommer's Blue Hungarian Band and considered themselves blessed to be part of the great Whitaker Wright's inner circle.

The sea was one of Wright's passions. It was a hobby that ran in the family, for his young son was already showing a keen interest in boating, and his brother, JJ, had recently joined the Royal Canadian Yacht Club and was the owner of a steam yacht called *Electric*. Wright had acquired a taste for sailing in New Jersey. Now that he had seemingly limitless funds, he began to take an almost obsessional interest in the sport. Sailing journals described him as a 'most spirited and liberal yachtsman', although his enthusiasm probably had as much to do with social climbing as it did with any innate love of aquatic adventure. It had not escaped his notice that the Prince of Wales was also an ardent yachtsman.

During the summer of 1896, he attended regattas at Cowes, Ryde, Portsmouth and Nice, and at most if not all of these events he bought acceptance and popularity by donating generous prizes, in many cases handing them over personally to the victorious crews. They included a £100 trophy for a race between Nice and Malta, a £200 cash prize for the fastest cutter across the Channel, and a £300 trophy and £150 cash prize for the winners of the Royal Victoria Yacht Club's regatta at Ryde. At Valetta he helped the Governor of Malta to organise the island's first yacht races and was again lavish with prize money. The aloof sailing fraternity was no doubt wary of this brash newcomer, but could not afford to be churlish about largesse on such a grand scale. Before long, the Lord of the Manor of Witley was able to boast a new title – that of Rear-Commodore of the Royal Portsmouth Corinthian Yacht Club. He also became a member of five other yacht clubs – the Royal Cinque Ports, the Royal Dorset, the Royal Temple, the Royal Thames and the Royal Victoria. One of his greatest ambitions was to be accepted into the Royal Yacht Squadron, with all its prestige and privileges, including a dispensation to fly the White Ensign of the Royal Navy.

Wright's championing of the sport enabled him to mix freely with the upper echelons of society and brought him agreeably close to royalty. His guests on *White Heather* when she left Cowes for a pleasure trip to Normandy in August 1896 included not only the inveterate freeloaders Pelham-Clinton and Gough-Calthorpe, but an obscure Bavarian princess, Leopoldine von Wrede. The same month he took another step up the royal ladder when the German emperor's yacht, *Meteor*, won the 'Whitaker Wright Cup' at Ryde. Wright received a cable from the victor himself, the wording of which he made known to the press. 'I am most proud', wrote the Kaiser, 'to have won your cup, which I am told is a handsome one. I would be glad to have a photograph of it till the original graces my table.'

The following spring, Wright donated a 5,000-franc prize and a gold medal for the winner of a regatta in Nice. Among those who competed for it (unsuccessfully) was the Prince of Wales on his gaff-rigged cutter *Britannia*. Although Wright was never able to count himself among the prince's intimates, he was on good terms with the future King and regarded him as a friend. The two met from time to time at sailing events and on at least one occasion Wright was invited on board one of the prince's yachts while it lay at anchor off Cowes. According to an acquaintance of Wright, the politician and journalist T. P. O'Connor, they sometimes lunched together, and their paths crossed from time to time at charity dinners in London, notably when Wright made a substantial donation to the prince's Hospital Fund at a fundraising event at the Cecil Hotel. For his part, the prince, like so many other people who came into contact with Wright, would later regret his association with him.

In July 1897, when the building work at Lea Park was at its height, Wright shelled out £30,000 on a boat of his own, acquiring the 924-ton *Venetia* from bicycle tycoon Martin Rucker. Wright paid Rucker in

Lake View shares worth £4 each. Rucker, taking no chances, cashed in the shares immediately, but could have sold them at £23 apiece if he had hung on to them for a few more months. At 220ft long, the *Venetia* – 'a commodious steam yacht, fitted with every modern convenience and luxury' – had originally been built for Lord Ashburton, a member of the Baring banking family, and was manned by a crew of thirty-three. Happy to acknowledge his hedonistic lifestyle, Wright renamed her *Sybarite*, Sybaris being the ancient Greek city in Italy that was famed for its excesses and which was utterly destroyed in 445 BC. Wright had the vessel painted white for Mediterranean cruises and added numerous flamboyant touches, including the installation of two large cannon, which he liked to fire when out at sea. On one notorious occasion, he half-deafened Lord Dufferin, who happened to be standing nearby when one of the cannon went off. He also equipped *Sybarite* with one of the most expensive libraries afloat. Only the finest imprints would do, and to this end he acquired a collection of the Hundred Best Books as listed by the philanthropist and politician, Sir John Lubbock. He had each volume – the Bible, the Koran, *The Canterbury Tales*, *The Pilgrim's Progress* – bound in red leather with the words '*Yacht Sybarite*' stamped in gilt on the cover. One of *Sybarite*'s first ports of call was Bangor Bay in the north of Ireland, where she was placed at the disposal of the ever-grateful Lord Dufferin, who had yet to take delivery of his own yacht, *Brunhilde*.

Although there is no record of any members of the British royal family having visited Lea Park, foreign royalty was not immune to the Lord of the Manor's charms. 'He has a penchant for the company of crowned heads,' noted the American satirical magazine *The Wasp*. Both King Alexander of Serbia, and Leopold II, King of the Belgians, reportedly enjoyed Wright's hospitality in Surrey, and were entertained by

theatrical companies brought down from London to give private per-
formances. Roland Belfort recalled: 'He had a veneration of emperors,
kings and princes, and was proud of their flattering affability.'

Wright established another royal connection when he struck up a
friendship with Sir James Reid, personal physician to Queen Victoria
and medical adviser to the Prince of Wales. Reid was a spendthrift who
lived beyond his means, and in 1896 he sought Wright's advice on how
to make a killing on the stock market. Wright was more than happy to
help a man who moved in the highest royal circles. He bought and sold
a block of Lake View shares for him and presented the grateful doctor
with a cheque for £500. Subsequently the two men became close. Reid
stayed at Lea Park on numerous occasions and was invited on board
Sybarite at the time of his engagement to Susan Baring (of the same
banking family as Lord Ashburton). Reid recorded in his diary that,
with a glass of punch in his hand, he 'had long talks with Whitaker
Wright in the sunshine about shares etc., and he promised to do all he
could to help me'. In return, Reid agreed to become a trustee of Anna
Wright's estate. Like the Prince of Wales, and Edward Drinker Cope,
and Lord Dufferin, and Gough-Calthorpe, and all the others, Reid
would rue the day he became caught up in Wright's web.

Despite his exotic lifestyle, Wright claimed to be a 'home bird', and
often said he was happiest when walking around Lea Park in the evenings listening to the rooks in the elm trees. Usually he had a cigar on
the go (he always carried a silver cigar case, a silver cigar cutter and a
silver matchbox in his pocket). When not planning some new project
with his architects and contractors, or playing billiards or cards, he enjoyed a game of cricket on the lawn before heading off to his observatory
for a spot of star gazing. His interest in astronomy sometimes inspired
themes for his City speeches, as when he entertained the shareholders

of one his subsidiaries, the Nickel Corporation, with a whimsical theory about the origins of a 31-ton meteorite found by the US Navy in Greenland in 1894:

> Now, we profess not to know where meteorites come from, but I myself should not be surprised to find that this particular meteorite came from the planet Mars. Astronomers tell me that the lines on Mars are artificial canals of enormous width and length. It is a fair presumption, therefore, that they possess an up-to-date navy. [Laughter] Taking cognisance of our naval ambitions, and being our next-door neighbours in the planetary system, the wise men of Mars concluded to throw us a specimen of the material out of which they, in their advanced civilisation, construct their battleships. Hence this enormous meteorite, which they succeeded in throwing to us. Now, what do you suppose that meteorite was made of? It was nickel-steel – and our naval authorities cannot do better than accept the formula. And allow me to say that we can supply the nickel! [Laughter and cheers]

Back on *terra firma*, Wright shot and hunted in the grounds of Lea Park, although his age and increasing girth made him no more than an occasional and unenthusiastic rider. Ever hospitable, he kept up to twenty horses in the stable block for the use of his guests. He regularly welcomed the Chiddingfold Hunt onto his land, and hosted breakfasts for its members before meets. He also took a keen interest in farming. Lea Park's fruit and vegetables won him prizes at Royal Horticultural Society shows, and he built up a large flock of Southdown sheep. The £10 he won for three ewe lambs at an agricultural show in York – 'perfect little models', ruled the judges – probably gave him as much pleasure as many of the killings he made in the City.

Initially he was viewed with suspicion when he arrived in Witley, and there were concerns that he was destroying the character of the countryside. The *Surrey Times* ran a report headed 'Despoiling Hindhead Common', which stated that 'many residents of Hindhead are not a little annoyed, and certainly very much grieved, at the poor respect which the new lord of the manor is apparently showing for the natural beauty and adornments of Hindhead Common and the Punch Bowl'. The paper claimed that residents had seen Wright's workmen use an 'infernal machine' to dig up and remove holly bushes from the common, presumably to be replanted beside Lea Park's new lakes.

But the early doubts about him quickly dissolved. Over the years his improvements to the estate cost an estimated £1,115,000, and a large proportion of this was spent locally. Very few families in the neighbourhood did not benefit directly or indirectly from his lavish spending. 'Godalming district looks to Mr Whitaker Wright as one of the best friends it has ever had,' observed the *Investors' Review*. Wright often said that he would like to finish his works at Lea Park by the time of his son's twenty-first birthday in 1905, but the prospect of achieving that goal faded as he kept dreaming up new ideas. The local community raised no objections.

He was unfailingly generous with his money and seldom lost an opportunity to dispense largesse, especially if it helped the poor of the neighbourhood. (Did he perhaps worry that his long-dead father was looking down on him with a critical eye?) He built community halls at Witley and the neighbouring village of Milford and regularly opened up Lea Park's grounds for fundraising events. A Christmas bazaar he hosted in aid of the NSPCC included 'a display of Japanese and Spanish costumes, with music on a gramophone, and fortunes told by Madam Crystal'. At a garden party for 400 members of the Girls' Friendly Society, an organisation set up to protect young working-class country women who had left home to take up urban employment, he laid on a 'capital band'. According to the *Surrey Advertiser*, 'his generosity was unbounded, and the poorer classes of the community were the special objects of his benefactions'. Children at the village school recalled for years afterwards how his carriage and pair used to draw up next to their playground and he would throw them pocketfuls of loose change. He also gave generously to the church and was on good terms with the vicar of Witley, the Revd John Eddis, although it is unlikely that he ever confided to him that he too had once been a man of the cloth. On one occasion, during a meeting with Eddis, he offered to pull down 'this old church of yours' (Saxon in origin with twelfth-century wall paintings) and build a spanking new one in its place. He was apparently surprised when Eddis politely turned him down. A Witley resident, the play-wright Alfred Sutro, wrote of the incident: 'He probably marvelled at the vicar's short-sightedness in refusing his magnificent offer.' Notwith-standing Wright's Philistine propensities, Sutro liked and respected the Lord of the Manor and thought him 'a thoroughly good-natured man'. The *Daily Express* summed up the general feeling: 'Mr Wright is rated by the residents of Godalming as a veritable demi-god.' In time, this quiet corner of Surrey became one of the few places on the globe where he could be assured of a warm welcome.

Not that everyone in the locality admired him. One of Wright's Surrey neighbours, Francis Russell, the son of the former Prime Minister, Lord John Russell, wrote to him complaining that some of his diggers had failed to replace the topsoil where they had been quarrying for stone. When, after seven months, Russell had received no reply, he sounded off about the squire of Lea Park in a letter to his friend, Lord Dufferin: 'He might, if he cared about it, have helped considerably, without trouble or expense … He is, I think, the rudest person I have ever not met.'

Wright was fond of, and proud of, his family (although before the century was out he would succumb to the charms of at least one of the many alluring women who clamoured to be in his circle). He was devoted to Anna, who in turn loved Lea Park as much as he did and relished being Lady of the Manor. She took responsibility for the smooth running of the household and was said to have 'a wonderful gift for finance'. (The grounds themselves were administered by the estate manager, Yalden Knowles, a local magistrate and county councillor.) According to a Witley resident interviewed by the *Surrey Advertiser*, 'no one in distress ever approached her without having their necessities relieved … [S]he was a true lady; not half a lady, but a lady in the true sense of the word.'

The couple went to great lengths to keep their son and daughters out of the limelight, and little is known of their childhoods. John, a dark-haired, good-looking boy, became a pupil at Eton College in September 1897, joining Coleridge House under the supervision of housemaster John Montague Hare. He was good at sport, being a keen cricketer and an excellent rower. 'Soames and Wright immediately went off with a good lead, which they kept all through, and eventually won easily by ten lengths,' observed the *Eton College Chronicle* of a sculls race on the Thames. John's sisters, Gladys and Edith, who were aged ten and eight respectively when the family moved into Lea Park, were tutored at home by a German governess, Fraulein Scheurich. T. P. O'Connor, who met them briefly while a guest of Wright, described them as 'particularly intelligent and vivacious young people'. There was a veiled reference to them in Harold Frederic's novel, *The Market Place*, published in 1899, in which the central character, Joel Stormont Thorpe, who was based on Wright, has an Etonian son and two 'strikingly beautiful' daughters.

The family wanted for nothing. When time permitted, Wright

treated his wife and children to weekends at the Hotel Binder in Rue de l'Echelle in Paris. This was a favoured haunt of crowned heads and princes, and was conveniently close to the Avenue de l'Opéra, rated in guide books of the time as 'the handsomest shopping street in the world'. At home the family enjoyed a gilded existence with every conceivable luxury. Lea Park's annual running costs were estimated by the *Investors' Review* to be £50,000 (around £5 million in today's money), and to maintain what one newspaper called 'his life of insensate luxury', Wright employed no fewer than seventy-seven domestic staff. He himself hand-picked the key servants, such as his valet, Joseph Bishop, his footman, Henry Card, and his head gardener, John McHattie, who had previously worked for the Duke of Wellington and the Marquess of Lothian. He never asked for or bothered with references, but relied solely on instinct. 'I judge a man by his face,' he used to growl. 'I don't care tuppence what other people may say about him.'

He was a benevolent employer, entirely without pomposity, and the Lea Park household was by and large a happy one. Whenever he was able to do them favours, he did so. A young Irish curate whom he briefly employed as a tutor for his children mentioned that he was interested in music hall, and Wright promptly procured for him a post as a theatrical manager in Western Australia. He liked to tell his staff that he himself had started life as 'a footman and friendless', a claim that appears to have been a typical exaggeration but was intended to show that at heart he was 'one of them'. He held a lavish Servant's Ball each year, and every December he had cattle from the estate killed so that all his employees could be given a Christmas joint along with a plum pudding. In January 1898, he hosted two lunches for his retainers, one with twenty-four brace of pheasants, the other with forty rabbits. He was so casual and unguarded in front of his servants that he often let slip details of his business transactions. On the strength of these, several of them formed a syndicate to buy and sell shares. Wright was amused by their resourcefulness and teased the syndicate's members whenever the value of their stock fell. 'You are not looking well today,' he would say jovially. 'No, sir,' would come the downcast reply. 'We have not been feeling at all well lately.'

He took a lively interest in politics (he was a staunch Conservative) and was elected to the council of the British Empire League in 1897. On at least one occasion he hosted a Primrose League Fete at Lea Park, at which the local Conservative Member of Parliament, St John Brodrick, railed against the Liberals. Wright himself was capable of powerful oratory and perhaps liked to imagine himself in the House of Lords when he addressed shareholders, although in later years his tub-thumping rhetoric may have been a ploy to distract his listeners from the difficulties his companies were by then facing. A jingoistic City speech he made to shareholders soon after the outbreak of the Boer War had precisely this effect. In their wild applause his appreciative listeners forgave and forgot the unpalatable fact that profits and dividends were both down.

> I cannot refrain from congratulating ourselves on the success of our arms in South Africa, and especially on the dignified demeanour that has characterised our people not only in their reverses, but also in their successes. And, as good is the frequent outcome of evil, I am disposed to consider that possibly the greatest good that has come out of this unhappy war is seen in the welding together of our numerous colonies with the mother country into an empire stronger and more harmonious than any the world has yet seen. So long as our people, and with them our army and navy, are possessed of the dogged

determination that has recently been characteristic of the nation, all the waves of European malice and envy will break in vain on the rocks of liberty, justice and loyalty on which our empire is built.

By 1897, the once handsome and athletic young man who had forged his way through the Wild West had metamorphosed into a grossly overweight figure with a large head, small eyes and a bull neck. With a Viking's tolerance of alcohol, he drank steadily through much of the afternoon and evening, with a particular leaning towards brandy. The effect on his liver was such that he would often send for a tin of Carter's Little Liver Pills from the chemist's shop in Witley. He had a strong dislike of his own appearance and hated being photographed. When the *Magazine of Commerce* ran a portrait of him in April 1903, it claimed it was 'believed to be the only one extant taken by photography'. In this respect he was similar to his fellow burrower the 5th Duke of Portland, who built an elaborate network of tunnels and chambers beneath his estate at Welbeck Abbey, Nottinghamshire, during the 1850s and 1860s. The Duke not only hated being photographed, but so disliked his appearance that he threatened to sack any servant who set eyes on him.

There was, of course, a price to pay for Wright's privileged life at Lea Park. The threat of robbery, even kidnap, was ever-present, and he employed guards to protect both himself and his family from intruders. In a throwback to his Wild West days, he usually carried a loaded revolver. He kept several pistols in the house, concealing one in his pocket by day, another at his bedside by night. As the years went by, it may not have been only criminals he feared. He may have been worried about disgruntled shareholders too.

It was probably just as well that Wright's father was not alive to witness his eldest son's pleasure-seeking lifestyle. It would have filled him with unease and foreboding. More than thirty years earlier, the God-fearing minister had written a small book of devotion, *Our Father*, for the benefit of his flock. In it he related the strangely prescient story of a young lady who married a wealthy merchant:

He was engaged in a lucrative business, and the golden stream of wealth flowed in on him till he had amassed a large fortune. He went into the country and purchased a splendid residence; fine trees waved their luxurious foliage around it; here was a lake filled with fish, and there a garden full of rare shrubbery and flowers. Their house was fashionably and expensively furnished; and they seemed to possess all of earth that mortals could desire. The piety of the lady declined, and her heart became wedded to the world. 'A severe disease,' it is said, 'requires a severe remedy,' and that God soon applied. One morning intelligence came that her little son had fallen into the fish-lake, and was drowned. Soon afterwards, her only daughter, a blooming girl of sixteen, was taken sick of a fever and died. The only remaining child, her eldest son, who had come home from college to attend his sister's funeral, went out into the fields for the purpose of hunting, and was accidentally killed. The mother, in the extravagance of her grief, fell down, tore her hair, and raved like a maniac against the providence of God. Her husband afterwards fell a speedy victim to his accumulated afflictions, and she was left a widow and childless. At length she was led to reflection; she saw her backslidings and her rebellion, and wept the tears of repentance. Peace was restored to her soul.

Had Wright's father known of the tragedies that befell his son and his son's offspring in the wake of his rise to enormous wealth, no doubt he would have shaken his head sadly but knowingly.

CHAPTER NINE

ROGUE SPARK

Victorian self-confidence was reaching its apogee when Britain and her territories celebrated Queen Victoria's Diamond Jubilee in 1897. Across the country, and in the vast swathes of land coloured pink on the map, there were banquets, ox roasting, fireworks and the lighting of beacons. It was a golden age when optimism fired the air and the sun never set on the good Queen's empire. The mile upon mile of flag-bedecked British warships on display at the Review of the Fleet at Spithead that June were a testament to the country's global supremacy, numbering as they did more than the naval strength of all the other 'Great Powers' combined. In keeping with the times, it was a year of exciting technological advances. The Blackwall Tunnel, then the longest road tunnel in the world, opened for traffic beneath the Thames. Horseless taxicabs began operating in London, and Marconi sent the first wireless message over the open sea when he signalled 'Are you ready?' across the Bristol Channel. There was an overall feeing that things were going well – extremely well – for Britain and her empire. This buoyant mood naturally spilled over into the City. Market confidence was high, investors remained free with their cash and shares prices kept rising. The great gold-mining boom showed no sign of waning and, as one observer put it, the City of London was 'a Tom Tiddler's ground for company promoters'.

That same year, the *Financial Times* published a pictorial supplement entitled 'Men of Millions' to reflect the dominance of English-born entrepreneurs across the world. The twelve tycoons it featured were a motley bunch. They included diamond magnate Barney Barnato, company promoter Ernest Terah Hooley, financier Horatio Bottomley and mining magnate Woolf Joel. The newspaper made no predictions about what the future held for these men but, as it happened, many came to a sticky end. Barnato, suffering from delirium that led him to see banknotes which crumbled to dust between his fingers as he counted them, disappeared from a ship in the Atlantic in what was probably suicide but may have been murder. Hooley went bankrupt four times and served two prison terms, Bottomley spent five years in jail for fraud, and Joel was shot dead by a robber in his Johannesburg office.

Another magnate who featured prominently in the 'Men of Millions' supplement was Whitaker Wright – 'the Napoleon of finance'. Here was a man at the height of his power and influence. A man who seemed indestructible. He, surely, would not go the way of the others. If anyone was destined to buck the trend of bankruptcy and disgrace, it was the brilliantly successful managing director of London and Globe, a man described by the article as 'outstanding among international businessmen'. The weather during that dazzling Jubilee summer was fair and dry, perfect for evenings of gazing at the heavens from the Lea Park observatory. The stars seemed to be telling Wright that his future looked brighter than ever. But the stars, like the 'canals' of Mars, were all too capable of painting a deceptive picture...

Wright was greeted like a hero from a G. A. Henty adventure story when he gave his annual address to Globe shareholders that June. He could hardly make himself heard above the cheers as he listed the company's assets. They were, he said, worth a stupendous £7 million. One of Globe's most valuable acquisitions during the year, he declared, had been the Hannan's Treasure gold mine at Kalgoorlie, named after one of the three Irish prospectors, Patrick Hannan, who had found gold at the base of Mount Charlotte in 1893. Globe had purchased the mine on the cheap for £75,000. According to Wright, the gold at the site was now estimated to be worth £4 million, and the property was set to become a 'second Lake View'. And that was just the start. He went on to report that Globe's other acquisitions, such as Mainland Consols ('the mill is running splendidly and the mine is looking better than ever'), Paddington Consols, Wealth of Nations and Kalgoorlie's Golden Crown mine, were all performing exceptionally well.

Nor, he stressed, was Globe's prosperity based on solely gold. The company had recently spread its tentacles into the Pacific archipelago of New Caledonia, where it had bought 'the richest nickel mines in the world'. Within a year, said Wright, Globe 'could expect to hold the world's entire nickel supply', and with a 'moderate expenditure of capital' should be returning a profit of £200,000 a year from this venture alone.

It was heady stuff, and the press reflected the elated mood of the shareholders. 'Last year's dividend was equal to 70 per cent, and so well have the corporation's affairs been managed by its powerful board that it is the common assumption in the City that this year's return will be even better,' went one report. The London periodical *Truth* judged the company's progress to be 'very satisfactory', while the London correspondent of Perth's *West Australian* newspaper noted that Globe 'has achieved much success and magnificent prospects for the future'.

The *Daily Telegraph* concluded that Wright's name was 'a synonym for success and magnificence'. The mere fact that he was known to be interested in a venture acted as a powerful lever in the movement of prices. Apart from a handful of killjoys, no one was inclined to doubt the word or the ability of the man with the Midas touch. *The Economist* continued to voice occasional doubts, complaining of the boom in general 'that there has been incomparably more dishonesty in the short annals of Westralian mining than ever there was in the Transvaal'. It did not point the finger directly at Wright and nor did anyone else, at least for the time being. Only after several years did it become clear that most of Wright's boasts to Globe's shareholders that June morning had been far removed from reality, and that his crock of Australian gold was mostly a crock of bull.

True, the company's nickel venture in New Caledonia looked promising, but Wright had grossly overstated the value of many of his West Australian acquisitions, especially the much-vaunted Hannan's Treasure. Unknown to the shareholders, Wright's man on the spot, Charles Kaufman, had privately cabled him that the mine was a 'duffer' and warned him against buying it. Wright ignored his advice and purchased it anyway. Hannan's Treasure, like most of the other mines Wright had crowed about during that intoxicating shareholders' meeting, was destined to have a disappointing career, and within eighteen months it was on its last legs. Mainland Consols, after a promising start, fared little better. By the end of the century, it was languishing undeveloped, and was subsequently abandoned for several years.

Lake View and Ivanhoe were the magnificent exceptions. They kept the whole show on the road and helped to maintain Wright's reputation for surefootedness and foresight. Hadn't he always said that there would be lucrative results even if only one in twenty of his properties was successful? As his supporters pointed out, the proportion of tip-top mines in the Globe portfolio was well in excess of one in twenty, and its two star acquisitions appeared to contain inexhaustible wealth. Only in retrospect, in the words of New York's *Electrical World*, were Lake View and Ivanhoe seen as assets of 'marvellous richness but of doubtful enduring capacity'.

By now the initials WW were as familiar as those of the great cricketer W. G. Grace. According to an Australian newspaper, 'people who were themselves "big men" in the City looked up to this marvellous luminary, courted his word or nod, and told their lesser brethren that he was as unapproachable as the Grand Lama of Tibet'. He was even more revered than the cockney diamond king Barney Barnato, who was fond of saying that if he had proposed to make a tunnel from the Bank of England to Johannesburg, 'they would have snatched at the shares without waiting to hear a single detail of the scheme'. In Wright's case, recalled Roland Belfort, 'such was the glamour of his name that had he offered the ambient air for sale his propositions would have been clamoured for'. Belfort wrote that Wright

> was certainly the most striking personality and the most daring gambler that had ever mobilised the Stock Exchange, the press, the old nobility, and certain fascinating society beauties for his amazing manoeuvres ... He felt like a monarch; scattered his money freely, not only to satisfy his own grandiose yearnings, but among charities, churches and even foreign missions.

Government ministers and peers of the realm were among those who rushed to buy stock in his companies during that glorious Jubilee year. The First Lord of the Treasury and future Prime Minister, Arthur

Balfour, was in the former group. Baron Sudeley and members of the celebrated Spencer-Churchill family were in the latter. Even the royal family was said to have benefitted from Wright's financial prowess. It was rumoured that the financier had engineered a £25,000 windfall for the needy brother of the Prince of Wales, the Duke of Connaught. It was even said – whisper it softly – that the future King himself had made a handsome profit from one of Wright's enterprises. Whether or not these rumours were true was anyone's guess, but they were widely believed. Wright did nothing to dispel them – he had never been a bedfellow of truth and accuracy – and as likely as not he started them himself. Not that anyone, in public at least, went so far as to question his integrity. Richard Haldane (later Viscount Haldane), who as a young barrister carried out legal work for Globe, recalled:

> The company, although speculative in its business, was very honestly managed by Whitaker Wright, who was at this stage showing himself not only a great man of business but, as far as I could discover from my experience of suits which I conducted for him, for the time a thoroughly honest one.

To the world at large it seemed that the presiding genius of London and Globe could do no wrong. He became a major contributor to charitable causes, and at the start of the Jubilee year gave £250 of his own money and another £250 of Globe's to the Indian Famine Fund. Here, it was evident, was a man who, on top of his many other attributes, had a social conscience. Outside his office, wrote Belfort,

> beautiful, fascinating adventuresses, with designs on the great man, sat side by side with sisters of mercy, eager to plead the cause of charity.

City men mingled with financial magnates, fretting at being kept waiting, bishops and deans came for backing and other subscriptions. All worshipped at the shrine of the idol that made millions.

A fellow promoter, Henry Osborne O'Hagan, called him 'this meteor who flashed across the paths of finance'. New York's *Albany Review* described him as 'a born fighter – a modern struggle-for-lifer glorifying in the fierce combat of the field financial'. T. P. O'Connor recalled:

> I don't think I met him more than twice, but he was such a striking personality that I feel as if I had known him well. He really made a very favourable impression on me. Though he was of good height, he gave an impression of a shortish man, but it was because of his extreme stoutness, of his chunky shape, of his short neck. It was also a 'pouchy' face. There were big bags under the eyes; there was a huge pouch under the chin, wide and protuberant rather than deep. The head was a 'pouchy' head – that is to say, it was small, round, thickset – and the neck was short. Yet, though this was the exterior of a man of fierce and almost brutal strength, the impression he gave was not unpleasant. The jaw was massive and suggested the rigidity and strength of steel. The face was resolute – I would say frowning except that there was also an element of good nature in the expression. One felt that, though he might never spare a fool when there was a fight, yet he might be genial and even generous to those who were outside the struggle and the fury of his life.

Buoyed by the success of the revitalised Globe, Wright floated a second holding company, Standard Exploration, with a capital of £1.5 million in February 1898. Despite its name, it undertook no exploration. Its object was to bring together a number of mining and exploration companies, such as the Thames Hauraki Goldfields in New Zealand and the Deep Leads of Victoria, under one umbrella. Its board members included the ever-compliant Pelham-Clinton and Gough-Calthorpe and, as with Globe, its shares were heavily oversubscribed. Not everyone was impressed. A journalist wrote of the Thames Hauraki mine: 'Their timbering is careless and makeshift, and their drives are wretched things.' This was perhaps not surprising given that Standard spent only £80,000 of its capital – barely 5 per cent – developing the mining properties it had brought together. The balance was available for stock and share transactions by Wright to be used at his total discretion. For the first time since launching his career in London, he came in for some stinging personal criticism in the press. *The Sketch* declared:

> Of all the Whitaker Wright prospectuses we have seen, the Standard Exploration just about takes the banner. The company collects some less than a dozen of the greatest crocks in the Westralian market, puts them into a golden basin, throws in a few figures to solidify the lump, and then asks a million-and-a-half for the lot.

The British financial journal *The Statist*, while not singling out Wright by name, seems to have had him in mind when it wrote:

> What is perhaps the most unpleasant feature about West Australian promotions is the list of companies offering entirely undeveloped, or but little developed, properties at extravagant prices, having regard to the amount of work done. In great part the extravagance of the prices arises from the greed of the intermediaries in contracts. Promoters still resort to the practice of issuing companies in what is

termed a private manner; in other words, without essential facts being made public.

Some viewed Wright and his ilk as a blight on the British way of life. *Blackwood's Edinburgh Magazine* identified a 'restless unsettling spirit of speculation all through society' which was destroying the traditional Victorian values of thrift and providence. It warned that 'even commercial circles are becoming infected by it; and if the credit of British commerce is to maintain the high level of the past, this organised gambling under the mask of finance must be checked.' In the same vein, the *National and English Review* was undoubtedly thinking of Wright and Dufferin, among others, when it wrote in 1898 of 'ingenious money-spiders who can corrupt half the City, including men whose wealth and position ought to place them above temptation'.

Neither Wright nor his star-struck shareholders cared tuppence – to use one of Wright's favourite expressions – about this carping from the sidelines. The success of the companies was there for all to see. In 1898 alone, Lake View yielded nearly 4 tons of gold worth around £500,000. The Ivanhoe also came up trumps, having been correctly forecast to produce up to £1 million in gold annually. The artist James McNeill Whistler bought fifty £2 Ivanhoe shares and saw them climb steadily in value. 'Tell the Financier [Whistler's broker] I am delighted with his news about the Ivanhoes,' he wrote that year to his publisher friend, William Heinemann. 'Whenever he thinks it time to sell out, he will say.'

Raymond Radclyffe, a *Financial Times* journalist who travelled through the goldfields of Western Australia and New Zealand between 1896 and 1898, was unstinting in his praise for Wright. He wrote that he had 'no hesitation in saying that Lake View and Ivanhoe are probably two of the greatest mines in the world'. In words that might have been scripted by Wright himself (and possibly were, as will become clear in the next chapter), he enthused in his book *Wealth and Wild Cats*:

> These great mines ... are a standing tribute to the acumen and ability of Mr Whitaker Wright, who superintended the negotiations for their purchase ... no man in the City of London has a higher reputation for financial ability and business integrity. He is something more than a mere financier, and is no 'juggler with millions'. His practical mining experience on the goldfields of the United States, Mexico and South America has been of the highest value to himself and those associated with him in his ventures ... he has made it a rule only to purchase mines after diligent inquiry and careful test by the best mining engineers available. As a result he has succeeded in securing the two greatest mines in Western Australia.

In the same book, Radclyffe provided a vivid illustration of the huge sums to be made from the Australian goldfields. In Coolgardie, he encountered a young entrepreneur from Adelaide who had just purchased a lease for £100 from a miner he had met in a bar. The new owner teamed up with a stockbroker, and within two days they had floated the mine with a capitalisation of £100,000, each keeping 45,000 of the £1 shares for themselves. On the train back to Adelaide, the young man fell into conversation with another passenger who gave him a cheque for £90,000 (which was met) for his shares. In the space of a week he made the modern equivalent of around £10 million. The actual property, which Radclyffe visited later that week, consisted of one trench, 10 yards long and about a foot deep, with no sign as yet of any gold.

Happy though he was that the public kept throwing money into his lap, Wright knew he could not afford to be complacent. Even before the Jubilee year had drawn to a close, he realised – even if the shareholders did not – that he could not rely on the goldfields to prop up his companies for ever and that he needed to diversify Globe's holdings. Casting around, he alighted on a stalled plan for a new London underground railway between Baker Street and Waterloo. The company behind the scheme had won government permission to construct the line as far back as 1893, but had struggled to find finance in an uninterested market. Not that it was an inherently unsound proposition. At the time there were three underground lines running east to west beneath the centre of London but none travelling from north to south. The suggested new line would rectify this, and incorporate stations at several key locations, including Oxford Circus, Piccadilly Circus and Trafalgar Square, with trains running every three minutes. One of its suggested benefits was that West End businessmen would be able to use it to reach Lord's Cricket Ground after work for the last hour of play. To ensure a wide mix of passengers, it was planned that there would be both first- and second-class seats, at maximum rates of 2d and 3d a mile respectively.

With his penchant for subterranean ventures, Wright took the opportunity in November 1897 to commandeer the languishing company, install his own board of directors and breathe new life into the project. One or two Globe board members questioned if it was a sensible move, but Wright ignored them. With some justification, he described the railway as a potential gold mine which, once completed, would produce handsome profits for the indefinite future. He foresaw that the line would carry at least 50 million passengers a year. Probably he also anticipated a knighthood in gratitude for what he hoped would be seen as a public-spirited effort to improve life for the city's travelling public. Play his cards right, and there might even be a seat in the Lords. (Ernest Terah Hooley had been given to understand that a contribution of £50,000 to Conservative Party coffers would secure a baronetcy in the Queen's Diamond Jubilee honours.)

The railway was a big commitment. The new line was to be one of the capital's first deep-level tubes, which entailed tunnelling deep beneath the streets rather than using cheaper cut-and-cover methods. Costs included the purchase of four hydraulically powered 'Greathead' tunnelling shields, numerous workshops and a small power station for temporary lighting and power in the tunnels, not to mention the weekly wages of hundreds of workmen. Under-river digging necessitated the use of compressed air, and a decompression chamber had to be purchased to prevent workers from succumbing to the diver's condition of 'the bends'. Large bubbles of air sometimes escaped, creating turbulence on the surface. In a bizarre incident, one created a 2ft waterspout, which obstructed a competitor in the London Watermen's traditional Doggett's Coat and Badge and cost him the race.

The total cost of the railway's construction was estimated at £1,615,000 – equivalent to around £165 million today – with no prospect of a return on outlay for several years. (The line would not open until 1906.) With Wright calling the shots, the contractors, Perry & Company, began work on the first stage of the project – a tunnel beneath the Thames linking Waterloo with Trafalgar Square – in August 1898. Wright billed it as the 'most important of any of the electric railways … passing through the most important shopping centres, and within easy reach of many theatres and other places of amusement'. To his irritation, the press was lukewarm about the project. *The Sketch* declared chauvinistically: 'Ladies may patronise the new line to some extent – no doubt they will. But as time is of very little consequence to them, as a rule, will they not stick to the bus that takes them to the very door of the shop that they want to visit?'

It was not only the press that lacked enthusiasm. As in the past, so did the public, and investors could only be persuaded to part with £700,000. This was nothing like enough, and Globe had to dig deep into its liquid capital, to the tune of nearly £800,000, to keep the venture alive. In due course this strain on its resources started to tell, and when the company needed cash at the critical moment, none was forthcoming. Wright would later admit that Globe's involvement with the railway had been 'unwise', and that it was Lord Loch who had talked him into taking on the project. Lord Loch was not in a position to refute this claim because he had since died. Whether or not the peer had been the driving force behind the plan, or whether it was Wright himself, the Baker Street and Waterloo Railway was to be the rogue spark that met dry leaves and started a conflagration that would eventually engulf Globe and its allied companies.

It was probably towards the end of that Jubilee year – as he made plans for a post-Christmas sailing trip to the Mediterranean with his family – that Wright began to hear the first disquieting rumblings from his ledgers. He can have had no inkling at this stage that his career was in danger of ending up like those of the other financiers who had featured in the *Financial Times*'s 'Men of Millions' article, but it would not be long before a raft of problems began to press in on him, perhaps suggesting a Freudian dimension to his womb-like sanctuary beneath the waters at Lea Park.

CHAPTER TEN

KING OF THE HILL

For now, however, Wright still had plenty more tricks up his sleeve. In the wake of his 'Westralian' successes, he set his sights on Canada, specifically on the so-called golden city of Rossland, high up in the Monashee Mountains of British Columbia, where a Jurassic-era volcano had once spewed thousands of tons of pulverised rock and minerals into the surrounding valleys. The discovery in 1890 that this ancient volcanic material was rich in gold ore had sparked a rush, and by 1898 the south slope of Rossland's Red Mountain was home to scores of active mines. The *Daily Mail* called Rossland 'the greatest gold-copper mining camp on the face of the earth'. The most famous and valuable of its mines was the mighty Le Roi – the 'King of the Hill'.

Wright's interest in the 'golden city' was sparked largely by the Hon. Charles Mackintosh, a former Lieutenant-Governor of the Northwest Territories and one-time Mayor of Ottawa. Mackintosh judged that given a large enough injection of capital Rossland's mines could rival those at Coolgardie and Kalgoorlie, and in September 1897 he travelled to England to entice investors. 'You have tried South Africa and Australia,' he declared at meetings with City moguls. 'Now give Canada a chance.'

Mackintosh was keen to win over Wright in particular. In his full frock coat and embroidered shirt, and with his impeccable social skills, the Canadian cut an imposing figure. He was, according to the *Toronto Telegram*, 'warm-hearted, amiable and altogether likeable', and Wright took an immediate shine to him. Greeting him like a visiting prince, he wined and dined him at Lea Park and feted him with Lord Dufferin and Lord Loch at a banquet in London's Savoy Hotel. Satisfied that here was an opportunity not to be missed, Wright launched the British America Corporation (Brit-Am) with a capital of £1.5 million. The company was modelled on the same lines as Globe and Standard Exploration, its objective being to acquire mining interests in Alaska and British Columbia, especially in Rossland, and where possible to float them as separate ventures. The juicy prize Wright had his eye on in particular was the famed Le Roi. In the year ending October 1897, the mine had yielded nearly £50,000 in dividends for its current owners. Here, he suspected, was Canada's answer to Lake View and Ivanhoe. The game was on again.

Wright made Mackintosh Brit-Am's resident director in Canada, not for his knowledge of mining (he had almost none) but because, in the time-honoured fashion, his name and antecedents gave the new company an added sheen of respectability. Lord Dufferin, who knew even less about mining than Mackintosh, was appointed Brit-Am chairman, and to show his faith in the company he threw caution to the wind and bought 20,000 £1 shares. Wright named himself as vice-chairman. The share-buying public, as ever, rushed into his arms, and the 1898 flotation was the high point of his career. In the space of four years, his two original holding companies with a combined capital of £400,000 had blossomed into three companies with a capital of £5 million. At the same time, the army of accountants and clerks working under his direct control at 43 Lothbury had swollen to more than a hundred.

Flush with Brit-Am's money, and under instructions to snaffle the Le Roi at all costs, Mackintosh returned to Canada and travelled to Rossland in a private railroad car on the newly opened Red Mountain Railway. There he scouted for suitable properties and acquired a number of mines – the Josie, the Great Western, the Poorman, the Nickel Plate, and the Columbia and Kootenay – but not yet the Le Roi. Brash and articulate, he was the perfect frontman for the new enterprise. Banging the drum for Brit-Am at a banquet in Rossland, he told local dignitaries that the company would 'prove how rich British Columbia is in mineral wealth'. When Brit-Am shareholders gathered in London in January 1898 for their first meeting, they applauded as Wright read from a cable Mackintosh had sent him:

> The British American Corporation has secured and holds the keys to a majority of the golden treasure houses of British Columbia. We will practically control the mineral resources of this province. We can look forward to the future with unabated confidence ... on the present appearance and prospects we will have four Le Rois.

These words may have lifted the hearts of the shareholders in London, but they were treated with derision in Canada. The *British Columbia Review* dismissed the cable as 'unworthy of serious consideration' and commented that 'of his many excellent social qualities we are well aware, but there is no mining man in Canada but would laugh at the idea of "Charlie Mackintosh" having any idea of the value of an ore body'. The *British Columbia*

Mining Record commented: 'It is certainly fair to question whether he [Mackintosh] has sufficient training or experience to enable him to purchase mines to the best advantage … [W]as there ever such a preposterous document as the prospectus of the British America Corporation?'

These and other publications were right to be sceptical about Mackintosh's competence. Among the claims made in Brit-Am's 1898 prospectus was that he had indeed negotiated to buy the Le Roi mine, and that it promised 'a minimum profit of £20,000 a month'. Subsequently, a company circular issued in Lord Dufferin's name on 19 May reiterated the claim: 'I have pleasure in informing you that this corporation, after prolonged negotiation, has now purchased for cash the famous Le Roi mine.' The circular went on to assert that the mine had been bought for the bargain price of £400,000. On the strength of this, the value of Brit-Am shares rocketed. Everyone looked forward to another Lake View-style bonanza.

But there was an embarrassing complication. The claim that the Le Roi now belonged to Brit-Am was hokum. True, Mackintosh had indeed written out a cheque for £400,000, but it had been returned by the owners as not enough. (The owners were split about the merits of the deal.) Not only that, but at the time the prospectus was published earlier in the year – with its assertion that Le Roi would make the company at least £240,000 a year – the mine's owners, far from agreeing a sale, had not even known that Brit-Am was interested in buying the 'King of the Hill'. A director of the Le Roi Mine and Smelting Company, Colonel Isaac Peyton, stated later: 'To my mind it looked much as if the people who drew up the prospectus used the name of the Le Roi Mine to attract the attention of the English investing public.'

As it happened, Colonel Peyton and his fellow directors were keen to sell the Le Roi, but not before they had played for time to get the best

possible price, a delay that provoked Mackintosh into starting litigation
to secure a deal. In the meantime, the false claim in the prospectus and
in the 19 May circular did considerable damage to Brit-Am's reputation
and to Wright's standing in the City. It also caused great embarrassment
to Lord Dufferin, who, on Wright's instructions, reluctantly repeated the
assertion that Brit-Am now owned the Le Roi when he addressed the
annual shareholders' meeting that summer. Wright himself remained
silent when challenged by the press to admit that the Le Roi was not yet
in Brit-Am's hands, but several newspapers were determined to make
him and Lord Dufferin squirm. In August, the *Pall Mall Gazette* commented: 'The shareholders of the London and Globe, who have taken
so much stock in the British America Corporation, are to be pitied. The
Le Roi mine, which was to pay them a dividend this year, is caught up
in litigation, and is not now shipping ore.'

Two months later, the *Sketch* put the boot in:

When Lord Dufferin said Le Roi had been purchased most people in
the City shook their heads and whispered to each other what a pity
it was to see so distinguished a figure made a cat's paw of. Of course,
Lord Dufferin believed what he said but this only shows on what un-
reliable information he was induced to make his speech. Mr Wright
loves a game of bluff, but this time it has not come off.

The Economist, never a fan of Wright, was equally scathing, commenting
that the business had 'arrived at a burlesque stage now, if it had not done
so before'. It went on: 'It is inconceivable that any self-respecting prudent investor should regard the latest scheme evolved from the fertile
imagination of Mr Whitaker Wright as worthy of serious consideration
and pecuniary interest.'

In the event, it took Mackintosh nearly a year of complicated ma-
noeuvring, along with three lawsuits, to complete the deal. He ended
up shelling out not £400,000 for Le Roi but £800,000. The sale was
finalised on 22 November 1898, at which point another unfortunate
problem emerged. It became apparent that the mine's former owners
had ravaged the pit for valuable ore during the months before the sale,
removing, smelting and selling deposits worth around £175,000. In the
process they left the workings in an unstable condition and in immediate need of costly repairs. To make matters worse, the price of Rossland
ore had dropped far below its 1895 peak of $36 a ton. The mine's new
general manager, Bernard MacDonald, was shocked to discover that
ore coming out of the Le Roi was netting $12.50 a ton, while mining,
smelting and shipping costs were totalling $15.14 a ton. In other words,
the mine was operating at a loss of $2.64 a ton.

The fact that the whole venture was in danger of foundering on a
reef of duplicity and incompetence did not appear to bother Wright.
He judged, correctly at first, that mere ownership of the Le Roi, and
the prestige it brought to Brit-Am, would bring investors running
and inflate the value of his stock. Like Lake View and Ivanhoe, its very
name set pulses racing. In a typical ploy, the following year he told Brit-
Am shareholders that it 'appears we own a mine which may probably
prove more valuable even than the Le Roi mine, and a third mine of
perhaps equal worth', adding that it was not 'expedient' as yet to give any
more details. Those details were never forthcoming (the mines almost
certainly did not exist), but Wright's alluring words about 'a new Le Roi'
had the desired effect of keeping the share price buoyant.

Wright again highlighted the mine's potential when he floated the
Le Roi Mining Company as a separate concern at the end of 1898.
He claimed that the Le Roi's ore would increase in value as the work

went deeper into the bowels of Red Mountain, an assertion that was denounced by *The Economist* as 'purely fallacious'. Several publications urged caution. The *British Columbia Review* complained that the Le Roi prospectus resembled a 'collection of choice panegyrics on a new soap'. The *British Columbia Mining Record* said those who bought on the basis of the prospectus were forced to invest 'blindly'. But investors were not in a mood to listen to the purveyors of doom, as Wright knew would be the case. Within three days of the subscription books being opened, there were two and a half times more applications than available shares. This though the prospectus was overloaded with superlatives and devoid of specific facts.

Even now, the Le Roi's problems were far from over. Once the purchase price of the mine had been taken into account, there was only £50,000 left in working capital. This was not enough to initiate a vigorous programme of development to find new high-grade ore bodies in Red Mountain's network of veins. The *Mining Journal* complained that 'time after time it has been pointed out that an inadequate working capital is the most serious possible drawback to the successful prosecution of any mining proposition, and how the modest sum of £50,000 can be expected to suffice for the demands of so large and, it may be conceded, promising a company, is not apparent'. Wright did not let such matters concern him. When the share price needed an upward nudge, he deployed the simplest of tactics. In November 1900, he began a groundless rumour that the Le Roi was on the point of declaring a bumper dividend with the result that the share price jumped from £5 to £9, so allowing him to make a quick personal killing. The vaunted 'bumper' dividend did not materialise. It was the same old story as it had always been.

The success of the Le Roi flotation spurred Wright into launching yet another motley collection of Rossland mines under the unimaginative but alluring name of Le Roi No. 2. Brit-Am and Globe pocketed £550,000 out of Le Roi No. 2's initial capital of £600,000, leaving the new concern – like its namesake – with only £50,000 in working capital. This time investors were not so confident about handing Wright their cash, and rightly so, for the company's ore shipments fell far below the enormous tonnages that had been promised. One of the few winners, of course, was Wright himself. He subscribed for 5,000 shares in Le Roi No. 2 and sold them at their peak for £75,000, so netting a personal profit of £50,000. Again, the same old story.

To acquire properties for Brit-Am, Wright went to Rossland himself and, as was his way, he greatly impressed those he met there. A. H. Tarbet, owner of the Center Star mine, for which Wright made an unsuccessful bid, would recall that he exuded plausibility:

> He was absolutely devoid of any of the elements of a crook or even of an irresponsible promoter. He was broad-minded and had an intensely interesting personality. He was a very large man and distinguished looking. He possessed a great fund of information and was an interesting talker. In all his business transactions with which he was acquainted he was absolutely honest and above any suspicion whatever.

Uncritical assessments of Wright such as this were no longer universal, however. To begin with, the grumbling was muted, and those who harboured doubts about him tended not to advertise their thoughts widely. A London banker, Gaspard Farrer, had written privately the previous December:

> Mr Wright has plenty of means and plenty of following, for the time-being. I am afraid I am a sufficient sceptic to believe that both

the parent company and its offshoot the British American Corporation will, in a few years, reach the same ending to which all other similar companies have attained. For the present all is 'couleur de rose.'

Just before the Le Roi fiasco hit the headlines, a London magazine, *The Critic*, directly challenged Wright's business methods, calling him 'a past master in the art of arranging figures' and an 'apostle of mystification'. In particular, it highlighted the practice of artificially stimulating a company's capital by buying large numbers of shares and then, as demand exceeded supply, cashing them in for personal profit and depressing the price in the process. The following September, *The Sketch* suggested that Wright had dangerously overstretched himself: 'From Baker Street to British Columbia, and thence to Western Australia, seems a pretty far cry, and how the directors can manage so many irons at one time without considerable danger of burning their fingers we cannot see.'

An anonymous contemporary of Wright wrote in the *British Columbia Review* in the autumn of 1898 that

his success had made him somewhat egotistical – not more so, perhaps, than is to be expected in a man who has fought the battle of life with the unaided strength of his own right arm and brain. This quality, however, has made him many enemies whose opposition he is too apt to belittle.

As usual, Wright let such criticisms wash over him. The good times continued to roll, and very few investors had yet woken up to the fact that the fortunes they had poured into his flotations were not going to earn them a glittering return.

In the long term, ownership of the Rossland mines, as with the 'Westralian' mines, would prove to be a bad deal for most of the investors,

who waited in vain for the handsome dividends they had been promised. More problematically for Wright, when trouble hit other parts of
his empire, the Le Roi was not in a position to compensate for the
losses. The only real Rossland victors were Colonel Peyton and the Le
Roi's other former directors. Congratulating themselves on having sold
their mine just as it was going barren, they retired to their clubs and
began to look for new opportunities.

If the whiff of skulduggery attached itself to Brit-Am's purchase of
the Le Roi mine, the stench of corruption surrounded Globe's payments to a financial journalist earlier the same year. Bartrick Baker, the
City editor of the *Pall Mall Gazette* – 'notoriously impecunious and
not over-sober', according to a fellow journalist – called frequently at
Globe's Lothbury offices in the hope of picking up titbits of news. That
was not all he was after. He was also on the lookout for ways of lining
his pockets.

One afternoon, he managed to collar Wright in person. According to
Wright's version of what happened (almost certainly highly sanitised),
Baker pleaded: 'You know, we poor devils of the press earn but little in
our profession, and you City financiers always have sound information.
Won't you give me a tip to some good investment?' Wright recom-
mended he buy Lake View or Ivanhoe shares, and in due course Baker
received a cheque for £406 from Globe as his profit from the purchase
and subsequent sale of Ivanhoe stock.

The editor of the *Pall Mall Gazette*, the aptly named Sir Douglas
Straight, reacted with fury and embarrassment when details of the
transaction leaked out. He was in no doubt that the arrangement was
nothing more than a bribe to a crooked journalist in return 'for favourable notices of Globe or to avoid adverse criticism'. His fears were
confirmed when it emerged that Baker had previously accepted cheques

from Globe amounting to £2,568 (some £250,000 in today's money). Equally embarrassing, a note in Wright's handwriting which praised Globe, and which subsequently appeared word for word in the *Pall Mall Gazette*, was found in Baker's desk. Unable to sack Baker, who had since died, Straight vented his anger on Wright, displaying derogatory placards about him in the City and using the columns of the *Pall Mall Gazette* to condemn his behaviour as 'scandalous'.

Wright, perhaps wisely, refrained from suing for libel. Instead he persuaded the Globe board, including Lord Dufferin, to issue a statement saying that any transactions with Baker had 'occurred in the ordinary course of business, and were absolutely justifiable in themselves'. The statement added that Wright's motives for passing on the tip to Baker, which he did 'partly from good nature and partly with the desire of being rid of Mr Baker's importunity', were 'unimpeachable'. In a separate letter, Wright observed lamely that the *Pall Mall Gazette* would be wise to observe the 'good old' Latin saying '*De mortuis nil nisi bonum*' – 'Do not speak ill of the dead.' His protestations cut no ice with the *Pall Mall Gazette*. The paper responded:

> To us this proceeding, twist and turn about it as you may, is absolutely improper and indefensible … [T]he glamour of Mr Wright's adventurous personality may blind his co-directors and possibly even the shareholders of some of his companies; but all his ingenious phrases and indignant protests cannot disguise the true nature of his transaction.

Other newspapers joined in the attack, further denting the reputations of Globe and its directors. The *Daily Chronicle* called the affair 'an amazing revelation as to what passes for honesty in the City'. The *Westminster*

Gazette said the arrangement appeared 'undignified, not to say disgusting'. The *St James's Gazette* declared: 'This is very near corruption, very near indeed,' while *The Star* accused Globe of 'an abnormally low standard of morality'. The company's aristocratic directors were also drawn into the row. The London-based *Globe* newspaper challenged them to resign: 'Surely, Lord Dufferin, Lord Loch and the other directors will not accept the position of being directors of a bucket-shop company … there is yet time to cut the Gordian knot.'

The censure of the peers did not end there. In August 1898, above the caption 'Noblesse Oblige', *Punch* cartooned coroneted sandwich men parading the streets with boards advertising the Rainbow Gold-mining Corporation, the Will o' the Wisp Syndicate and the Bust Tyre Company. *The Times* commented that 'the strangest and one of the least satisfactory things in the whole business' was that Dufferin and the other board members should have accepted Wright's version of events about the payments to Baker without, apparently, any misgivings. Dufferin in particular, who had only just taken up his position as Globe chairman, was mortified. *The Sketch* added to their lordships' discomfort:

The question which the *Pall Mall Gazette* has raised, and which Mr Whitaker Wright has not thought fit to answer, is not one that can be passed over in silence. The honour of such men as Lord Dufferin and Lord Loch demands an answer to the question that a company of which they are directors bribed the City editor of the *Pall Mall Gazette*.

Bribery it undoubtedly was, but not in a way that crossed the boundaries of the law. The arrangement between Wright and Baker was known in the trade as a 'press call'. It involved the promoter of a new company offering journalists a 'call' on its shares; in other words, the right to buy them at a guaranteed low price. If, by his praise, the company floated well, the journalist stood to make a good profit. It was a subtler way of buying influence than a direct bribe, but it amounted to the same thing.

Wright had first come across the practice when he was in America (and almost certainly put it to good use there). In the States, it had been considered an essential tool in the mining promoters' armoury for years. Mark Twain happily admitted in his book *Roughing It* that as a journalist he had regularly swapped favourable newspaper coverage for mining shares. He claimed that he could have made $20,000 a year out of the practice if he had possessed more business sense, and argued that it was no different to a man walking up the street with a couple of baskets of apples and giving some to a friend. Wright had found out the hard way what could happen if newspapermen seeking hard cash were rebuffed. In 1883, the *New York Mining and Financial News* had demanded $250 a month from him to publish announcements of Lake Valley dividends. Wright had refused – and paid the price when the paper published a damning report about Lake Valley's prospects.

In England, 'press calls' had been pioneered by crooked financier Ernest Terah Hooley, and the practice was widespread by the mid-1890s. The British periodical *Nineteenth Century* complained that there were a large number of 'reptile journals' which would praise a company – and, if required, condemn a rival one – in return for favours. Not without reason did Alfred Harmsworth, the future Lord Northcliffe, complain in 1903 of 'the tradition that Grub Street is not a thoroughfare for respectable wayfarers'. Charles Duguid (who had been Baker's predecessor at the *Pall Mall Gazette*) referred to the practice in his book *How to Read the Money Article*, published in 1901: 'The pen is mightier than the sword, and sometimes, unfortunately, the purse is mightier than the pen. The writer of the money article, from the highest to the lowest, is subject to the frequent temptation of those financiers who would have him withhold his criticism or praise his wares.'

For all of Wright's protestations about his relationship with Baker, he was an enthusiastic practitioner of press calling, and it emerged some years later that he had put aside up to £30,000 a year for transactions with newspapermen. At least nine senior journalists were on his books, including Douglas MacRae, the editor of the *Financial Times*, who made a personal profit of at least £4,000 from press calls associated with Wright's companies, and two members of the *Financial Times* staff, a Mr Coward and a Mr Filby. (The financier's relationship with the *Financial Times* may help to explain the somewhat excessive praise of Wright by the journalist Raymond Radclyffe in his book *Wealth and Wild Cats*.) Horace Voules, the editor of the satirical magazine *Truth*, and his City editor, L. M. Brousson, were also on the take and resigned their positions when their financial arrangements with Wright were revealed in 1902. Others who were implicated included C. E. Rose of the *Daily Mail*, and journalists from the *Financial News*, *The Citizen* and the *Australian Mail*. In an instance which came to light later, shares in a Globe subsidiary, Loddon Valley Goldfields, were sold to the owner of the *Financial News*, Harry Marks, for £84,562 on 26 November 1898 and repurchased the next day for £93,537. It also emerged that some newspapers charged fees of between five guineas and twenty-five guineas to attend and report meetings of shareholders. The higher the fee, the greater the number of column inches.

Not that the shareholding public was much fussed by the revelations about 'press calls'. They tended to take the view that if that was what it took to run a successful business, then so be it. As an official report into Wright's activities published in 1903 pointed out: 'So long as profits were made, it mattered not to them how they were made.' Wright's empire continued to reward most of its investors with handsome dividends during 1898, and by and large they were happy for the managing director to act as he saw fit. Nonetheless, the Le Roi debacle and the *Pall Mall Gazette* scandal inevitably damaged his reputation. With his halo fading, he was given a rough ride at the 1898 Globe shareholders' meeting, where he was accused of producing a 'meagre and insufficient report'. Word was starting to go round in the City that 'the Napoleon of finance' might not be all he was cracked up to be.

But Globe's Napoleon had more exciting things to think about than a few disgruntled shareholders. Around now, just when he needed to concentrate all his energies on preventing the fissures in his operation from widening into chasms, a huge new distraction upended his life. During a trip to France, he fell head over heels in love with a Parisian woman and embarked on a full-blown and all-consuming extramarital affair.

CHAPTER ELEVEN

EMPTY SHELL

Eight days before Christmas 1898, a portly figure carrying a child's doll strode into Witley Village Institute accompanied by a phalanx of prosperous-looking City friends who were staying with him at Lea Park. A Christmas bazaar was being held in the hall in aid of the Children's League of Pity (an offshoot of the NSPCC) and Whitaker Wright wanted to spread some seasonal largesse. As he wandered around the stalls with their displays of plum puddings, mince pies and children's toys, villagers pressed in on him to shake his hand and wish him a happy Christmas. Almost everyone there had at one time been directly or indirectly employed by him, and they were genuinely pleased to see him in their midst.

After a while, the local vicar, John Eddis (he who had turned down Wright's offer to replace the ancient church), called the villagers together and announced that the Lord of the Manor intended to hold a charity auction. Wright stepped forward and held aloft the doll he had brought with him from Lea Park. He explained that it had belonged to one of his daughters and had cost him 7s 6d (a little under 40p). What, he asked, was the bid for it? There was some good-natured cat-calling as a villager offered a shilling, followed by applause as the figure rapidly rose to fifteen shillings. Not good enough, said Wright jocularly. He expected the bids to be in pounds, not shillings. By now most of the villagers had dropped out of the bidding, but Wright's City friends entered into a friendly and spirited competition. Their offers went up in multiples of £1, then £5, then £10. Finally, to the astonishment of the spectators, the bidding reached £350. 'Sold to Mr Labouchere,' declared Wright, handing the doll to Frank Labouchere, a director of one of his Canadian subsidiaries. The bazaar's organisers could not believe their good fortune. The doll had fetched the modern equivalent of £35,000.

The incident was the talk of Witley for weeks afterwards. Labouchere, it transpired, was not as generous as he appeared, for it emerged that Wright had tucked a certificate for 500 Le Roi shares into the doll's dress, enabling its new owner to make a profit from his purchase. But, for the villagers, such a detail was of no consequence. One way or another, the Lord of the Manor had engineered a colossal windfall for their bazaar, and had once more demonstrated his value to the community.

Wright was patently in a charitable mood that Christmas. A week before the bazaar, he had given generously to the Lord Mayor of London's fund for a college to be built in Sudan in honour of General Charles Gordon. His £500 donation topped the subscriptions list. During the following year, many other causes gained from his beneficence. He gave £100 to help the victims of a hurricane which ravaged the West Indies in August 1899, and a week or two later he donated £500 to a fund opened by the Lord Mayor of London for refugees from the Transvaal. Anna was equally generous with her cash. She gave £500 to a fund for widows and orphans of soldiers killed in South Africa, and won the gratitude of Winston Churchill's mother, Jennie, by donating £100 to her 'American Ladies Hospital Ship Society' to help pay for the conversion of the SS *Maine* into a Boer War hospital ship.

These five donations alone, spread over the course of just twelve months, amounted to around £175,000 in today's money. Knowing that such munificence could only enhance his reputation among the investing public, Wright ensured that these and his many other charitable gifts were publicised. The large sums he gave away suggest that he still felt financially secure in the face of mounting evidence that all was not well within his empire. Despite the problems with the Le Roi and the underground railway, his personal position had never looked healthier. On top of his £6,000-a-year salary as managing director of the three holding companies, he raked in a large share of their profits – 5 per cent of all money paid in dividends – and owned several hundred thousand shares in Globe and its many offshoots. Estimates of his personal wealth in the late 1890s varied, but he was thought to be worth not less than £3 million, the equivalent today of well over a quarter of a billion pounds.

As the end of the century approached, the private spending spree he had embarked upon three years earlier with the purchase of Lea Park showed no sign of abating. In January 1899, contractors finished work at his new London abode at 18 Park Lane. The six-storey mansion had originally been built in the 1880s at a cost of £40,000, and had belonged until recently to the late Prime Minister, William Gladstone. Wright bought it in 1897 and gutted it. He hired the original architect, George Lethbridge, to redesign the interior, adding a wood-panelled billiards room, an oak staircase, mosaic and parquet flooring, elaborate ornamental plasterwork and two lifts. Standing next to Londonderry House, the magnificent residence of successive Marquesses of Londonderry, No. 18 was one of the finest private houses in the capital by the time the work was complete. Here Wright indulged his new passion for all things French by filling it with Louis XV and Louis XVI furniture, including a copy of Louis XV's famous Bureau du Roi, which alone cost him £2,000. Paintings from the French Rococo period – Watteau, Boucher, Fragonard – adorned the walls, while his sailing trophies graced the drawing-room shelves.

Residential properties in that part of London were generally seen as the preserve of statesmen and aristocrats, and eyebrows were raised at the appearance in Park Lane of this brash newcomer from the world of commerce. A couple of years earlier, the gold and diamond magnate Barney Barnato had built a vast house close by on the corner of Park Lane and Stanhope Gate. Not everyone was pleased that this illustrious thoroughfare separating Hyde Park and Mayfair was becoming populated by mining plutocrats – 'discoverers of nuggets', as Disraeli called them. 'At the bottom of their hearts,' wrote Hippolyte Taine in his *Notes sur L'Angleterre* in 1870, 'the English believe or are tempted to believe that a manufacturer, a merchant, a monied man, obliged to think all day about gain and the details of gain, is not a gentleman.' This attitude clearly still prevailed in Park Lane in the 1890s, and it was said that some of Wright's fellow residents looked down on him because the buttons on his tweed jacket were not made of leather. The *Gloucester Citizen* observed of his purchase of No. 18: 'Pity the perplexities of the neighbouring nobles who have not yet been able to make up their minds whether they ought to "know" the intruder.'

The haughty denizens of Park Lane notwithstanding, Wright spent four nights a week in his new residence, travelling the 4 miles to Lothbury each morning by horse-drawn omnibus or on the underground railway. Nothing would induce him to ride in a hansom cab, more than 10,000 of which plied for trade in London at the turn of the century.

Their fragility and their tendency to go at a furious pace resulted in frequent accidents involving death or serious injury. The diamond magnate Woolf Joel had been badly hurt in a hansom accident in 1896, although he was greatly consoled when he won £16,000 in half an hour while recuperating at Monte Carlo. Joel's mishap was probably the chief reason that Wright was so vehemently opposed to this means of travel. If alternative transport was not available, he preferred to walk. Whether he ever splashed out on a new-fangled automobile is not recorded, but the fact that among his friends was a Mr Moffatt Ford, whose Motor Car Company supplied petrol-driven vehicles to the gentry, suggests he did.

Once at his Lothbury headquarters of a morning, he was constantly on the move. Visitors described the offices as a 'gigantic money-making factory', with telegraph instruments clicking, telephones ringing, and an army of clerks on several floors poring over ledgers. Wright always appeared busy, hurrying breathlessly from room to room, granting interviews in any corner that was available or while walking between offices. During busy periods he snatched meals in the company dining room, but whenever possible he went out at lunchtime on intelligence-gathering missions. One of his regular haunts was the City Athenaeum in Angel Court off Throgmorton Street, a 'club for financial men' known by everyone as the 'The Thieves' Kitchen'. Here, according to the *Financial News*, brokers' clerks ran in and out executing the commissions of their masters, and the rooms after lunch 'would be noisy with the rattle of dominoes … and what sums used to pass across the dominoes tables at the end of the game!' Another of Wright's lunchtime favourites was the newly opened Hotel Cecil in the Strand, which was owned by the notorious Jabez Balfour (yet another financier who would serve time in jail). The hotel was a hang-out of American mining promoters, and Wright liked to keep tabs on what they were up to. Fastidious about his appearance, he usually took the opportunity to slip into the Cecil's basement to have his hair trimmed by Harry Jones, the head of the hotel's renowned hair-dressing salon.

After work, if he was not entertaining lavishly at home or attending a masonic meeting at the Freemasons' Hall in Great Queen Street (he was a member of Columbia Lodge, No. 2397), he enjoyed nights on the town, as often as not with an informal 'syndicate' of fellow financiers, all of whom knew each other and liked to mix business with pleasure. This select group of twelve or so multimillionaires – which included Wright's fellow mining promoter, Horatio Bottomley, and the flamboyant American financier Charles Tyson Yerkes – met regularly in the oak-panelled sitting room of Belle Livingstone, a 23-year-old New York showgirl known as 'the Belle of Bohemia'. Discreet, beautiful and wealthy, Livingstone loved the company of rich and famous men (the Prince of Wales was among her admirers) and they in turn were bewitched by her exuberant personality, her flirtatious manner and her 'poetic legs'. Her apartment on the ground floor of the Walsingham House Hotel in Piccadilly had three entrances, and Wright and the rest of the syndicate were able to go in and out without drawing attention to themselves. Livingstone explained in her memoirs: 'Often it was enough for two or three speculators to be observed in conversation to cause important rises or falls in stocks in which they were concerned, so an apartment like mine, offering easy entrance and quick exit, was an ideal haven of safety for quiet talks.'

Livingstone was useful to the syndicate in many ways. When they needed attractive young women to entertain 'suckers', she was happy to lay on a gang of her showgirl friends. In return for her favours, the syndicate treated her well. On one occasion, Wright and his friends hosted a dinner for her at Willis's Rooms in St James's and presented her with a string of pearls. There is no evidence that his relationship with the showgirl was anything other than platonic, but he had an eye for the ladies and revelled in the company of captivating women. He was often the guest of honour at soirées hosted by society ladies such as Daisy Greville and the writer and poet Mrs Alice Meynell. He enjoyed their attention, and often flirted with them, but as the end of the century approached, his thoughts became focused on just one woman – a married Parisienne named Rosalie.

Details of the affair were revealed thirty years later in a magazine article by his friend Roland Belfort. According to Belfort (who did not divulge the woman's surname), the two met during one of Wright's brief visits to the 'City of Light'. Rosalie had run up heavy gambling debts, and dared not tell her husband, who had money problems of his own. Faced with social ruin, she 'wheedled' Wright into financing her extravagant way of life in return for sexual favours. Belfort, who enjoyed a colourful turn of phrase, wrote: 'Seductive, alluring, her eyes gleamed with the fire of passion … [S]he revealed to him a glimpse of a paradise of which he had never dreamed.' For his part, Wright was not only smitten, but believed his passion to be fully reciprocated:

> Struck by this *coup de foudre* he wooed her with characteristic ardour. Before he met Rosalie his mind was concentrated upon his financial affairs, but the souvenirs of his Paris visit were so bewitching he could not always banish them from his mind. Sometimes he felt impelled to abandon all and return to Paris. He quite thought his hour had arrived. His happiness was reflected in his face. Love had transformed this portly, flabby-faced financier. There was a glorious flame in his eye. Absorbed by this fierce passion, he forgot the City – the market, his wife, his children, his embarrassments – everything.

Belfort had little doubt that Rosalie was cynically using Wright as a cash cow, and that beneath the surface allure she was cold-hearted and treacherous, and probably had other lovers. But it would have taken a brave man to tell that to Wright. She made regular trips to London, where he showered her with money and cancelled most of his appointments to be with her. It is more than likely that the distinctive French feel to 18 Park Lane was down to her influence. He even had a private staircase built at Lothbury so that she could enter his office unobserved. On one occasion, when Lord Dufferin called on urgent business, he was told: 'Mr Wright can see no one.' The peer, suspecting the reason for Wright's unavailability, left the building 'angry and worried'. Belfort wrote: 'Wright had arrived at that age when a vigorous man commanding money feels the last urge of romance. The tide of time was flowing against him … no longer young, he yearned for something more exciting than domesticities.'

All this hard living and frantic juggling of time made for a long week and an ever-increasing girth. On Friday evenings – if he had been unable to engineer an illicit weekend with Rosalie – Wright boarded a train at Waterloo Station and settled himself in the corner of a first-class apartment. He was usually asleep within minutes. A carriage and pair would be waiting for him when he alighted at Witley eighty minutes later and, having dispensed tips to the station staff, he would set off for Lea Park to spend Saturday and Sunday with his family and to indulge in more hobnobbing with the great and the good.

Whether or not Anna knew of his affair is impossible to know, but at the very least she probably had her suspicions. In her fatalistic way, she may have considered that giving him free rein to indulge his passion was a price worth paying for her gilded existence. Socially, the couple moved in ever more elevated circles. An age was dawning in Britain – even in aloof Park Lane – when money was able to buy a position equal to that of good birth. As Edward VII's grandson, the future Edward VIII, observed: 'Although I was too young to realise it, I was seeing the birth of a new era … High office or ancient lineage were no longer the sole criteria of status.' The previous year, in recognition of her charitable work, Anna had enjoyed the ultimate social accolade of being presented to Queen Victoria during a ladies' reception at Buckingham Palace. When this corporal's daughter from the back streets of Philadelphia wanted her photograph taken, she went to Speaight Limited of London's Regent Street, which numbered the royal family and most of England's aristocracy among its clients. On summer weekends, she might find herself taking tea with Lady Dufferin, Lady Loch and other high-ranking women on the viewing platform of the estate's 'big' lake. The annual 'county ball' she hosted with her husband was described by the Surrey press as 'a great event throughout the countryside'. Eton College was another means for her to mix with society's top drawer. By 1899, the Wrights' son, John, was a third-year pupil there, and his parents made a point of attending the school's annual Fourth of June celebrations, held in honour of King George III's birthday. There, on the banks of the Thames, they watched the famous procession of boats and mingled with the likes of Prince and Princess Adolphus of Teck, the Duke and Duchess of Newcastle, the Earl and Countess of Dudley, and Lord and Lady Iveagh. Like her husband, Anna had come a long way.

Wright himself yearned to be seen as a man of the same breeding and ancient lineage as the grandees with whom he mixed. Among the books he kept in his library at Lea Park was a two-volume history of Cheshire published in 1880. This contained details, which he bookmarked, of a wealthy family called Wright, who had lived for more than a century at Mottram Hall, a Georgian mansion just 6 miles from his father's Macclesfield birthplace. There was nothing to link these landowning Wrights to the humble Macclesfield Wrights, but it is not hard to imagine the Lord of the Manor of Witley showing the Mottram Hall page to his illustrious guests and telling them that this was where he hailed from. Given his capacity for self-delusion, he probably believed this fanciful notion of his origins himself, and no doubt embellished it over the years. (Intriguingly, Mottram Hall had three lakes, and perhaps served as a partial model for Lea Park.) One way or another, Wright managed to gain the full acceptance of the country's elite. Sidney Felstead, the biographer of Sir Richard Muir (who would represent Wright in court), observed that 'the aristocracy looked upon Whitaker Wright as a desirable addition to their most select and exclusive circles, and if all had gone well with him he would certainly have found himself in the peerage within a few years'.

Heading for a peerage and cavorting with a mistress… Wright in the late 1890s.

The work on 18 Park Lane, the continued expenditure on Lea Park and the wooing of Rosalie were not Wright's only extravagances in 1899. The same year he placed an order with the acclaimed naval architect George Lennox Watson for a 100ft racing yacht capable of taking on all comers. His instruction to Watson, whose other clients included the Prince of

Wales, the Kaiser, the Vanderbilts and the Rothschilds, was to design a vessel impressive enough to earn him membership of the exclusive Royal Yacht Squadron and, ideally, to compete in the America's Cup. Such was his ambition to achieve glory in the sport that even before the keel had been laid he appointed a professional yachtsman, Charlie Bevis, to be the skipper of his new plaything, and hired another experienced sailor, Percy Thellusson, to be his yachting secretary and adviser. The latter resigned the secretaryship of the Royal Victoria Yacht Club in order to work full-time for Wright.

And so the lavish spending went on, as did the affair with Rosalie. Over drinks in London not long before the end of the century, Wright told Belfort that he saw life as one huge gamble:

I have always been a fighter – and a gambler. And had some knock-down blows, cruel blows. I have seen life as a mule driver, baggage man to a western outfit, mining labourer, broker, financier, promoter. And I've enjoyed every job. To me life is a gamble, a hustle, a fight with fate. Not so long ago I was trying to find fifty dollars. Tonight I entertain a prince, a bunch of dukes and some of society's smartest society women. Next week I shall be racing my yacht against the Kaiser's *Meteor*. After that I shall be discussing with my architect the £1 million house he is building for me in the country. In a few months I may be hunting for £50. A mad gamble, I tell you.

Belfort wrote that he envied Wright 'his pluck, his luck and his sporting temperament':

Endowed with a nimble brain, served by a strong will, a passionate energy that nothing could tire, a varied experience of men and cities,

Wright appeared to be a man born to dominate ... He had gone through the mill and he had gloried in it all. He enjoyed the delicate attentions, the flattery, the hubbub created by his sensational exploits. He lived in a whirl of feverish excitement, seldom missing a chance. He decided a deal with intuitive rapidity, took a risk pluckily, faced a loss with a smile.

As it turned out, Wright's observation that there might come a time when he found himself hunting for £50 was not so wide of the mark. Belfort never guessed from his friend's ever-confident demeanour and flamboyant purchases that he was a troubled man and that his hydra-headed business operation had become dangerously fragile. It was not only the Rossland mines, the cash-guzzling underground railway and the press criticism that were causing him concern. To compound the existing problems, he was bamboozled early in 1899 into making a disastrous error. Ironically, it involved his cherished Lake View Consols.

At his City office, Wright was in the enviable position of being the first person in London to receive cables from the mine superintendents in Australia. He released their reports to the press when he thought it advantageous to do so, but sometimes withheld details so that he could trade on inside information. A cable from Lake View's general manager, Henry Clay Callahan, caught his eye at the start of the year. 'Old Cal', a grizzled American otherwise known as the 'King of Kalgoorlie', claimed his men had encountered a phenomenally rich patch of ore at 300ft. The Duck Pond, it seemed, was about to produce yet another cascade of golden eggs.

Keeping the news to himself, Wright immediately went on a spending splurge, using his own money and that of his companies to buy up all the Lake View shares he could. For a time all went well, and when

Lake View Consols soared from £9 to £28, he congratulated himself on a canny move. Once again, the Wright magic appeared to have reaped dividends. But his euphoria was short-lived. It turned out that the Lake View boom was based on bogus information, and that Callahan, who was in league with an American mining magnate, Henry Bratnober, was up to his neck in skulduggery. Engaged in insider trading of his own, he had grossly exaggerated the extent of the ore find in order to push up the share price to Bratnober's advantage. To keep the charade going for as long as possible he barred access to visitors, made misleading claims about the quality of the equipment, and 'gutted' the mine while investing nothing in exploration. At one stage, to maintain the illusion, he took to 'salting' ore samples.

Bratnober cleaned up (he and his sidekicks reportedly made £1 million from the scam), but not Wright, who discovered too late that he had been taken for an expensive ride. Instead of the predicted increase in production, Lake View's gold output fell from a peak of 30,000 ounces a month to just 10,000 ounces. Within five months, its riches had been all but drained. A dash to sell Lake View stock began in Adelaide, where speculators had a better idea of the mine's condition than anyone in London. Picking up early rumours about its imminent depletion, they offloaded shares by the thousand. They were relieved to get out when they did. As the penurious state of the mine became ever more obvious, dividends of £1 a quarter were revised to five shillings (25p) a quarter and the share price plummeted accordingly, at one point sinking to £11. A warning by *The Economist* that, in the absence of more reliable information, Westralian mining shares 'would remain a medium for gambling rather than investment' fuelled the rush to dump stock.

Caught on the hop, Wright's response was to keep buying Lake View shares in a bid to maintain their value, manipulating the price in the face of strong selling. His problem was that most of Globe's spare cash had already gone on the new underground railway, and in his bid to corner the market he was forced to raid the coffers of Standard Exploration. He even used £300,000 of his own money – cash, he later claimed, he had been going to settle on his children – to fund the spree. His plundering of Standard's reserves greatly alarmed Lord Loch. The peer brought the matter to the attention of Lord Dufferin, who in turn raised it with Wright. Wright was in no mood to be placatory. His testy response to Dufferin may have reflected his own growing unease. He wrote to him:

> I will do everything in good time and I claim to know best when that time is. Lord Loch is making a great mistake to fidget about it. Everything is going our way at present. Of course I can't do impossibilities. My object in writing to you is to show you that there is no need to worry about the Standard. When my colleagues fidget, it only adds to my burden.

But Lord Loch was right to be worried. The price of Lake View Consols kept falling, and by the autumn of 1899 Globe and Standard Exploration had jointly lost more than £1 million in trying to prop them up. Direct criticism of Wright was muted (only he knew the extent of the losses) but the grumbles about his empire in general began to grow in volume. Rankled by Lake View's poor performance, shareholders started to question the competence of the board in letters to the newspapers. The *Freeman's Journal* went on the attack, declaring that 'the manner in which the affairs of the group generally have been managed of late has rather sickened many operators in the market'. *The Investors' Review* thundered that it was a humiliating spectacle to behold men of the repute and standing of the Marquis of Dufferin and Ava and Lord Loch openly lending their names and influence to what is neither more nor less than a system of rigging markets so that privileged parties may, if they can, unload shares upon an innocent public at hollow prices.

Meanwhile, Le Roi shareholders were also restless as they waited for the much-vaunted Rossland gold mine to make a satisfactory profit. The *Sporting Life* commented in September: 'The strength of the Whitaker Wright crowd seems powerless with the sagging tendency of Le Rois, for they were down again today … one gets a bit tired of waiting for the promised rise.'

Yet, despite the brickbats, and in the face of all the difficulties, Wright not only contrived to keep the show on the road but managed to end the financial year on a triumphant note. No matter that the Lake View shares he had bought at £23 were now worth £8. In its accounts for the year ended 30 September 1899, Globe announced profits of £483,000 with a cash balance of £534,455 in the bank. On the face of it, everything looked rosier than ever, and he wrote to Lord Dufferin on 9 October that the balance sheet was 'excellent'. Addressing Globe shareholders at their annual meeting three weeks later, Wright said the Lake View mine 'is just as good as ever it was' and added that 'you hold shares in a corporation about which you can feel perfectly easy in your minds'. As ever, his persuasive manner and his abilities as a public speaker, honed to perfection in his days as a Methodist preacher, inspired confidence and sparked rounds of applause.

At the same meeting, Lord Dufferin was equally reassuring. Ever trustful of Wright, he had accepted the managing director's word that attempts by rivals to 'bear' the company were 'most unfair', and that any resulting difficulties had now been overcome. In his chairman's report, written for him as usual by Wright, he told the shareholders that Globe's impressive cash balance was 'one of the best witnesses we can point to in support of the success of our operations'. He added that the 'corporation was never in a sounder condition than it is at present … a conclusion that has no doubt been reached by all of us after the inspection of the balance sheet'. So healthy was the group's position, he asserted, that a dividend of 25 per cent or even more could have been declared on the strength of it. However, good sense must prevail and, as in previous years, the financial policy of the company dictated a more prudent 10 per cent.

If there had been doubts about Globe's prospects at the start of the meeting, they were dispelled by the end of it. The shareholders left happy, and some went straight to their brokers to increase their holdings on the basis of what they had been told. Typical of them was 71-year-old Benjamin Nicholson, a Gosport magistrate and retired master shipbuilder. He was so impressed by what he had heard that he immediately coughed up £1,500 for another 1,000 Globe shares. Neither he, nor any of the other shareholders, nor Lord Dufferin, nor anyone else on the board for that matter, had any idea that behind the scenes Wright had been frantically cooking the books. Globe's 'sound condition' was an illusion. In reality, the company was an empty shell, and its collapse was now all but inevitable.

CHAPTER TWELVE

FIN DE SIÈCLE

How had the illusion been achieved? Though the mechanics were labyrinthine, the strategy was simple. Wright had been robbing Peter to pay Paul. In the final days before the accounts were published, he had conducted a string of paper transactions between Globe, Standard and Brit-Am. This ensured that first Globe, and later the other two companies, appeared to be healthily in the black each time one of them came under the microscope. Under Wright's direction, assets, liabilities, cash and shares were shuffled backwards and forwards with the speed and cunning of a three-card trick. All three companies, for instance, found the same 'nest egg' of £250,000 available as an asset when they published their balance sheets. Deals initiated by Wright as managing director of one company were given the nod by himself as managing director of another. Page after page of company ledgers were filled with inky credits and debits, all at the bidding of the same man. It was a consummate piece of window-dressing.

Other unorthodox devices were used to boost the bottom lines of the trio of companies. Securities were quoted at above their balance sheet value; Brit-Am conveniently allowed Globe to retain its share of a joint venture; Globe sold Standard a large holding of Lake View shares at nearly three times their market value; Wright lent Standard £40,000 of his own money. Irregular manoeuvre followed irregular manoeuvre.

The immediate effect was to turn a Globe loss of £750,000 into a fictitious profit of nearly half a million pounds. As soon as Globe's 1899 accounts had been published, the deals were reversed to enable Standard and Brit-Am to show a profit as well. The dividends the companies paid were purely artificial. In each case they were made possible only by pillaging the funds of the sister companies. Wright's fellow directors were blissfully unaware of this gargantuan sleight of hand. Some of the transactions were made without their knowledge. They nodded through others like pecking hens in the sure belief that their esteemed managing director had everything under control. Who were they to question the actions of the Napoleon of finance? And who were the shareholders to doubt the robustness of the balance sheets? Blinded by wishful thinking and the juggling of figures, Globe's investors had no inkling that the company was effectively bankrupt and that its only hope of survival was built on a castle of contingencies. Maintaining their faith in Wright, they continued to back the board and carried on buying shares.

Wright himself, ever the optimist, hoped his actions would tide things over until Lake View Consols rose in value or the Baker Street and Waterloo Railway came up trumps, so allowing him to put the companies back on an even keel. Failing that, he hoped, like Dickens's Mr Micawber, that 'something will turn up'. He was whistling in the dark. Even as he and Dufferin doled out their 'good news' to Globe's shareholders in October 1899, yet another problem was unfolding. For the first time in more than forty years, Britain had become enmeshed in a full-scale conflict.

The Boer War, the opening shots of which had been fired in Natal exactly one week before Globe's annual meeting, took most of Britain by surprise. The hostilities were to drag on for two and a half years and would cost the country £210 million. It was the most expensive war Britain had fought up to that time and the bloodiest since 1815. Nearly 350,000 British troops and more than 100,000 colonial forces were sent to South Africa. Some 20,000 never returned. Like a vast weather system sweeping across the country, the war unsettled the financial markets, deflated the share values of mining companies generally, and shrank the likelihood of a comeback for Wright's over-capitalised empire.

On a personal level, the war occasioned a tragedy for Lord Dufferin. His eldest son, Archie, a lieutenant in the 17th Lancers, had been posted to South Africa at the start of the conflict. The day after the fateful Globe shareholders' meeting, he emerged unscathed from a skirmish at Elandslaagte in northern Natal, and shortly before Christmas a proud Lord Dufferin read accounts of his son's valour in the press. A few weeks later, however, Archie's luck ran out. He was shot in the head during a Boer attack on Waggon Hill and died four days later without regaining consciousness.

For all his stoicism, Dufferin never recovered from the blow. He received the news while in Ireland and sought solace by designing a window in his son's memory and erecting a granite Celtic cross looking south to the distant land where he had died. Globe's affairs inevitably receded in his mind. In failing health, and beginning to have considerable misgivings about Wright's business methods, he decided it was time to cut and run. The shock of losing his son apart, he was finding it increasingly gruelling to be chairman of a company whose complex workings he struggled to understand. Several times during the ensuing months he told Wright that he wished to stand down, but the forceful managing director was having none of it. He assured Dufferin that the three holding companies and their subsidiaries were in sound shape, and that the good times would return once the public realised that the underground railway was a profitable concern. There was a risk, Wright told him, that his sudden resignation would destroy confidence and bring the whole edifice crashing down. The ailing Lord Loch had announced his intention to resign from the board in October, and the departure of a second director so soon afterwards might be misinterpreted by the shareholders. Dufferin, ever honourable, reluctantly agreed to stay on. His decision provided a respite for the struggling companies, but it did not stop the whisperings. By the end of 1899, the City was rife with rumours that Wright was in trouble. The *Globe* newspaper commented: 'We wish we could believe that Mr Wright's forecast about substantial Lake View dividends in the future was likely to be true. The market is disgusted with the whole matter, shareholders are disgusted with the gambling tactics resorted to, and the ordinary investor wisely holds aloof.'

On 29 December, Dufferin received an agitated note from Lord Loch, who had spoken to Wright over the Christmas break. Loch revealed that to prop up the Lake View shares Wright had 'raised upward of two million!!! He said he had pledged everything he had.' Once again Dufferin took up the issue with Wright, and as before he was told that there was no cause for concern. Seeking to give the impression that it was business as usual (and to raise more ready cash), Wright floated another company, the Nickel Corporation of New Caledonia, with a capitalisation of £750,000. As with his previous ventures, there was a brisk take-up of shares, but the adverse comments continued. *The Sketch* declared on 8 January:

Mines of all sorts are weak … the Westralians are still the worst
market, and the erstwhile strongest group, viz the London and Globe
(or Whitaker Wright group), is now the weakest. It seems very unfair
that the controllers of Lake Views should have allowed people to buy
them at £23, only to let the price down to £11 or so … it must be a long
time before the public will feel inclined to handle West Australians
again to any great extent.

The attacks on Wright became increasingly personal. Only eighteen
months earlier, the press had hailed him as a genius. Now an all-out
assault by the *Daily Express* effectively laid the blame for most of the
country's ills at his door. Even the financially illiterate Gough-Calthorpe
complained privately to Lord Dufferin that he thought some of the
companies did not have enough working capital. Not that Wright gave
any hint that he was rattled. Though the hoped-for revival in Lake View
shares stubbornly refused to materialise – by June they were trading at a
fraction over £10 – he continued to act as though all was well. The building work at Lea Park continued apace, and in May he hosted a lavish
party there to celebrate the relief of Mafeking. Lesser mortals might
have laid on a brass band or a fireworks display to mark this momentous
military victory; Wright rounded off the festivities by arranging for a
battery of guns to fire a salute from the top of Charterhouse Hill in
Godalming.

The same month, his new yacht, *Sybarita*, was launched on the Clyde,
and was delivered to him at Cowes. In June, he entered her for the
North German Regatta Club's annual race in Keil Bay, a distance of
31 nautical miles. Proving exceptionally fast in light winds, she won
the prized Emperor's Cup, beating Kaiser Wilhelm II's yacht, *Meteor*,
into second place. At one stage during the race, *Sybarita* inadvertently

obstructed the royal yacht, much to the Kaiser's annoyance. In what some may have seen as a maritime metaphor for Wright's business activities, she was given the benefit of the doubt and was allowed to continue without penalty. The Kaiser afterwards boarded *Sybarita* with his younger brother, Prince Henry of Prussia, and congratulated Wright on his victory. Wright (who perhaps took the opportunity to show off his fluent German) was elated to have two of Queen Victoria's grandchildren on board his new toy. The trophy he won – a model of the Kaiser's primary imperial yacht, *Hohenzollern* – was solid-silver evidence of his royal connections, and he put this and other mementoes of *Sybarita's* victories on display at 18 Park Lane. Later in the year, the Prince of Wales himself (about to become King Edward VII) watched a race in the Solent between *Sybarita* and Sir Thomas Lipton's *Shamrock*. Afterwards he boarded *Sybarita* at Cowes and took tea with Wright in the saloon. The financier doubtless considered the visit to be one of the high points of his life.

For most of the rest of 1900, this friend of royalty continued to maintain an image of success and prosperity to the world at large. It was enough to fool some of the most powerful men in the land. In October, the news editor of the *Daily Mail*, R. D. Blumenfeld, attended a lunch at the home of the *Daily Mail*'s owner, Alfred Harmsworth (the future Lord Northcliffe), in London's Berkeley Square. Blumenfeld asked his dining companions who they thought was the richest man in the world and afterwards jotted down their responses in his diary. The American ambassador, Joseph Choate, suggested it was probably the steel baron Andrew Carnegie. If not him, then the oil magnate John D. Rockefeller. Harmsworth himself thought the Czar of Russia was richer still. A fourth diner, Kennedy Jones, Harmsworth's business manager, said he believed there was one man richer than all of them: Whitaker Wright.

Whatever the accuracy of this assessment, it was certainly the case that in the dying months of the nineteenth century the Lord of the Manor of Witley had few rivals for the title of 'Richest Man in Britain'. Only Wright himself knew just how close to the precipice he now was.

Like a circus rider who has to stand on the backs of several galloping horses at once, he maintained a precarious hold on his empire's finances for the first nine months of the year. Unknown to the rest of the board, he won the promise of a £250,000 loan from the Rothschilds to prop up the business, but they withdrew the offer upon inspecting the books. An American financier also backed out of a deal to inject cash after the five-hour time gap between London and New York held up the transaction. The delay was just long enough for the American to have second thoughts. On top of this, Wright had a spectacular falling-out with his man on the spot in Australia, Charles Kaufman. During a visit to London, the latter claimed he was owed £22,000 as his profit from the sale of a block of Lake View shares, and reportedly drew a gun on Wright in a bid to make him pay up. The dispute was only resolved after nearly a year of costly litigation. Problems were piling up, but Wright's continuing affair with Rosalie meant that he failed to give his companies his fullest attention. Roland Belfort for one was convinced that he did not have his eye on the ball: 'Just at this critical moment, when he needed all his strength, mental and physical, he was abandoning himself to a dream of love, while the market was slumping disastrously.'

Wright's continued 'bull' attempts to boost the value of Lake View Consols and beat the stock market 'bears' eventually brought matters to a head. Early in October, the company accountant, George Worters, presented him with a draft balance sheet which showed a cataclysmic loss of £1,645,748 for the year ended 30 September. It should have been clear to Wright at this point that Globe was irretrievably done for. The proper course of action would have been to throw in the towel, break the news to the shareholders, and put Globe out of its misery. But winding up the company and slinking off like a wounded animal was against all his instincts. Instead, he launched a desperate new bid to keep Globe alive. The methods he used were even more convoluted than those of the previous year.

He began by changing the accountant. Out went Worters, and in came one Henry Malcolm, a malleable individual who had been his personal clerk at Lea Park. By law the company accounts had to be presented to the shareholders within three months of the accounting date. To buy time, Wright put off the balance-sheet date to 5 December and, as before, embarked on numerous inter-company transactions to make Globe appear solvent. In one deal, he arranged for Globe to sell some worthless shares to Brit-Am for £350,000. In another, the board of Standard (only he and one other director, Sinclair Macleay, were present at the meeting) agreed to pay £1,392,600 to Globe for 105,102 Lake View shares. Numerous other exercises in creative accountancy were added to the mix. The value of mining shares held by Globe was shown as a re-markable £2,332,632, 0s 1d, the final penny being an artistic touch to add plausibility. To boost its cash balance, Globe borrowed £75,000 from one of its subsidiaries, Victorian Gold Estates, and obtained a two-day loan of £25,000 from a firm of stockbrokers, for which it paid £500 in interest. In what was later explained away as an 'oversight', liabilities of £119,769 were omitted from the Globe accounts altogether. With these and sundry other manipulations, the balance sheet ended up showing an apparent profit of £463,673. Malcolm persuaded an auditor, James Ford, that all the manoeuvres were above board, and the accounts were signed off just in time for the annual meeting of shareholders. Every transaction was reversed a few days later.

To the outside world, there was still almost no hint of the brewing trouble. A handful of shareholders wrote to the *Financial Times* expressing concern about the hold-up in publishing Globe's accounts, but the paper assured them that there was probably a 'good reason for the delay', adding that 'at any rate it is not at present a heinous fault. What a time the writers' cooks must have if their dinners are even half an hour late.' But one or two astute observers could see the writing on the wall. An Adelaide sharebroker, H. L. Conran, wrote to his accountant, Alfred Saunders, on 23 November: 'Whitaker Wright has been buying Lakes, and he is playing a desperate game ... this will be his last effort, as the mine is looking very sick.'

Globe's shareholders were still prepared to look on the bright side. To begin with, the atmosphere was tense when they met at Winchester House in Old Broad Street for their annual meeting on 17 December. They had heard rumours that no dividend was to be paid. The delay in the publication of the accounts had hardened suspicions that the company was in difficulties. One shareholder, the Revd Randle Feilden, the elderly rector of Mugginton in Derbyshire, was keen to make his feelings known. He did not have sufficient expertise to question the figures in the balance sheet. He had, however, heard tales of the mansion in Surrey and its rooms beneath the lake. He felt that a man who entertained his friends underwater was not to be trusted, and he stood up to denounce what he believed to be a misuse of invested funds.

In this atmosphere of suspicion, the trusty Lord Dufferin was duly trotted out to address the meeting. To begin with he was met with hisses and frequent interruptions as he sought to blame the company's difficulties on the Boer War. His opening remarks, according to *The Times*, were made 'during the prevalence of some disorder in the body of the hall'. Struggling to make himself heard, he said:

We are passing through not only a period of great public anxiety, but one of severe financial depression owing to the South African war. Securities of every kind have depreciated in value with unwelcome rapidity ... the nominal expenditure on the war of nearly £100 million is but a drop in the bucket compared with the indirect losses it has occasioned.

'What's that got to do with us?' interrupted a shareholder. Patiently and courteously, Dufferin soldiered on, sticking studiously to the script supplied to him by Wright:

Our own company has been unable to escape from the consequences which were bound to flow from these untoward circumstances. It has been our unpleasant lot to have to write off a far greater loss from depreciation than anyone could have anticipated. In face of these difficulties the directors have applied themselves with renewed energy to replace the affairs of the company on their normal prosperous footing. As a result they are enabled to present a balance sheet with a very substantial sum standing to the credit of the profit and loss account.

With these words Dufferin began to win over the crowd. Even the doubters started nodding in approval. As *The Times* reported, his 'scholarly, elegant and persuasive' style ensured that the mood quickly settled. When he explained that the building and equipping of the Baker Street and Waterloo Railway had absorbed a great deal of funds, and that this had compelled the directors to advise that no dividend would be declared, there were shouts of 'hear, hear'. The directors, he went on, knew it was unpleasant to pay no dividend, but this was 'the only honest course to follow'. For good measure, he added: 'The directors are the first and principal sufferers, not only as large shareholders, for there being no dividends there are no fees.'

In a further masterstroke, he managed to distance the current Globe board, and Wright in particular, from the difficulties associated with the new railway. It was, he said, the late Sir William Robinson and the late Lord Loch (Loch had died in June of that year) who had wanted to diversify the company's activities. 'Though the railway does not strongly appeal to your managing director, whose experience naturally lies in another direction, he and the other members of the board acquiesced in the recommendation of the then chairman and Lord Loch.' The notion that Wright had acquiesced to anything, let alone the massive railway venture, was absurd, but the dead directors were not in a position to argue. Wright looked on sagely as Dufferin declared that the company was in talks with a syndicate that was keen to buy out the unwanted investment.

Putting on a brave face in front of the shareholders cannot have been easy for Dufferin. He for one had incurred enormous financial losses. The 5,000 Globe shares he had bought three years earlier were now worth less than half the £7,500 he paid for them. His shares in Wright's other companies had also sunk in value. Though he must have suspected that Globe was in bad shape, he made it clear that he had no intention of 'deserting the ship'. He told the meeting that 'only a sense of duty has prevented me from bowing before advancing years and declining health and relinquishing my post'. In a final flourish, he declared of the managing director (in words scripted by the self-same managing director): 'Never have I seen any man so devote himself, at the risk of his health, and at the risk of everything that a man can give to business of the kind, as Mr Whitaker Wright. We ought to be deeply grateful to him.'

Dufferin's speech had the desired effect of calming the meeting.

When it came to Wright's own turn to address the shareholders, he had less of an easy ride and was constantly interrupted. But, in the words of the *Daily Mail*, he was 'at his best and strongest' when quelling a disturbance, and he too began to win the audience to his side. He blamed many of the current difficulties on 'a conspiracy of financiers who are trying to wreck the company and depreciate its shares'. Batting off complaints about the lateness of the balance sheet, he forecast that Globe would soon be paying dividends again once the underground railway had been sold. 'There will be no Christmas box,' he said to sympathetic laughter, 'but I hope there will be an Easter offering.' As for himself, the man who had spent much of the summer on board *Sybarita*, and much of the rest of it in the arms of Rosalie, declared:

> In the whole of my life I have never worked so hard in the interests of the shareholders as during the last year. I offer to give all I possess to any man who could come forward and say that I have made any private gain out of any enterprise on which the company has been engaged.

As usual, his honeyed words were almost hypnotic in their influence, and at the end of his speech he was greeted with cheers from the floor. The meeting formally adopted the report and ended with a vote of thanks to the chairman and the directors. Once again, Wright had engineered a triumph. The bulk of the shareholders left Winchester House full of Christmas cheer, proud to be investors in such a sound and well-managed concern. John Millard, of Brenchley in Kent, was typical of those who were there. Taken in by the distorting mirror of the accounts, and impressed by what he had heard, he immediately instructed his broker to buy another fifty Globe shares. Dufferin recorded in his diary that it had been a 'very successful meeting' despite the lack of a dividend and the disturbances of a minority of 'bears'. Even the press criticism was muted, if not supportive. In its City Notes two days later, *The Sketch* commented: 'Why there should be such universal distrust of the Globe group and its numerous offspring, nobody seems quite to know, but there is a vague feeling of uneasiness in connection with all the Whitaker Wright concerns.'

The respite was all too brief. Globe's failure to pay a dividend unnerved the market, and the next day stock market 'bears' began off-loading Lake View shares by the thousand, knocking another £3 off the share price. The following week Dufferin heard that another of his sons, Freddie, who was serving with the 9th Lancers in South Africa, had been severely wounded in the chest at Gelegfontein. Here, at last, was a reason to be shot of the Globe nightmare without adding to the panic on the Stock Exchange. He immediately resigned the chairmanship of Globe and booked a passage to the Cape to be with his son. Wright, aware that his departure would remove one of the company's last fig leaves of credibility, was appalled. According to Dufferin's nephew, Harold Nicolson, he told the peer that 'to leave at this moment would be to act with great disloyalty and to jeopardise the savings of many fatherless children, motherless daughters, widows and children'. The wretched Dufferin, torn between filial loyalty and public duty, withdrew his resignation and cancelled his voyage. (Freddie eventually made a full recovery.)

In a last-ditch bid to stave off disaster, Wright went on another Lake View Consols buying spree, funding it with £500,000 borrowed from a group of London stockbrokers he later referred to as 'the syndicate'. To close observers of his actions, he was like a man carelessly dropping matches beside a powder keg with a mixture of vainglory and reckless-ness. The security for the loan was a block of Lake View shares, which the group acquired at £11 a share, with an understanding that they would not sell until the price rose to £17. The *Financial Times* advised its readers to hold on to their shares and await developments, but Globe was too far down the line to be saved. Wright continued to buy up all available Lake View shares, but the price did not rise as he had hoped. He eventually discovered that the syndicate was selling its holdings and that he had been buying back his own shares. At an angry meeting on 27 December at 18 Park Lane, he accused the syndicate of 'ratting' on him, but by then it was too late. At the end of the Christmas break, Globe was subject to claims on the Stock Exchange of £968,000, a sum it could not possibly pay. No more sugar-coating was possible. On 28 December 1900, the company announced its insolvency and the shutters went up.

Word of Wright's downfall had travelled ahead like the compressional wave that precedes an earthquake, detectable only by special equipment. The Adelaide sharebroker H. L. Conran was one of those who had seen it coming. Earlier in the day he had written to his accountant: 'Whitaker Wright, I expect, has not been able to pay. I only hope he gets wiped out altogether, as I do not care about playing a game with a man who cheats.'

The crash, on the last day of trading of the nineteenth century, was a true *fin de siècle* moment and spread panic in the stock market. Both Lake View and Globe shares nearly halved in value. Twenty firms of stockbrokers, unable to meet their obligations because of non-payment of their accounts, were drawn into the vortex and declared defaulters. Some were ruined. Others survived only after suffering enormous losses. One firm alone lost £365,000.* The *Pall Mall Gazette* described the scene:

---

* One of the Stock Exchange victims was reportedly on his honeymoon at the time of the crash. Another was commanding a battalion in South Africa.

Then, with white faces, the brokers came flying back from their banks with the news that the cheques of four-five-six firms had been returned to the payees! All the returned cheques emanated from firms closely connected with the London Globe division. One of them, the news of whose trouble caused the greatest astonishment, was a firm of old-fashioned brokers, whose name has been to conjure with for solidity.

In a book about the Stock Exchange published the following year, the journalist Charles Duguid wrote that 'the very hand of Barker, the waiter [Stock Exchange attendant], shook like an aspen leaf as, amid death-sentence silence, he announced failure after failure'. With masterly understatement *The Times* commented that 'the last settlement of the century has certainly terminated in a deplorable manner'.

It was not only the professional wheeler-dealers who were knocked for six on what the press dubbed 'Black Saturday'. Employees of Globe and its offshoots, most of whom had known nothing of Wright's machinations, found their future careers blighted by the distrust that now attached to them. Hundreds of small investors were ruined by the debacle, and thousands more suffered heavy losses. Some, like Baron Sudeley, weathered the storm. Others did not. A London solicitor, distraught at losing his retirement nest egg, absconded with his clients' money. The Edinburgh newspaper editor Sir William Nicoll told the story of a highly respectable Scot he knew who, having worked hard all his life to provide for his family, entrusted his savings to one of Wright's companies. 'When the crash came he went straight home, burned the family bible, never entered the church again, would make no effort to save himself, and sank at length to the poorhouse.'

The *Financial Times* – usually a friend to Wright – condemned his activities as 'reckless, indiscreet and blameworthy', but there was not universal sympathy for those who had lost money. *Blackwood's* magazine shed no tears for Globe's shareholders, who 'were wilfully blind and helpless in the hands of their manipulator'. An American newspaper pointed out that Wright 'could not have succeeded without the cupidity and credulity of his victims'. The *Derry Journal* said the victims of the collapse had only themselves to blame: 'When people blame the law for failing to protect them against the financiers of the Whitaker Wright stamp, the law is entitled, in a way, to retort on them, that fools who rush with their eyes open into every snare spread out before them defy protection.'

A lucky few counted their blessings. Among those who had bailed out in time was Wright's aristocratic friend, Daisy Greville. Three months before the crash, 'Babbling Brooke' sold all her stock in his companies, reportedly realising a profit of £160,000. There were rumours in the City – impossible to prove – that Wright had tipped her off about the approaching disaster. Dufferin's son-in-law, Sir Ronald Munro Ferguson, was another who escaped with a profit, having bought and sold a block of Lake View shares just before Christmas, at a time when they briefly rose in value. Wright himself had also disposed of the vast majority of his shares before the collapse, although in his case this was scant consolation for the horrors to come.

On New Year's Eve, three days after Globe went belly up, a gale-force wind blew over an upright sarsen at Stonehenge, breaking its lintel. The event was widely seen as symbolic of the disaster in the City and as an omen of worse to come. With military reverses in South Africa adding to the gloom, it was held by many that the self-confidence of the nineteenth century crumbled in its last three weeks. A Thomas Hardy poem, 'The Darkling Thrush', published for the first time on 28 December, captured the sombre mood:

The land's sharp features seemed to be
The Century's corpse outleant,
His crypt the cloudy canopy,
The wind his death-lament.

Perhaps the most horrified person of all – even more horrified than Wright himself – was Lord Dufferin. 'Unknown to me and to all his colleagues, Mr WW has engaged in a gigantic gamble in Lake Views which has broken down and the company will have to be wound up,' the shocked peer wrote to Munro Ferguson. To his friend, Lord Rose-bery, the former Prime Minister, he wrote: 'I am half-ruined, and all through the folly of a man who, without the consent or knowledge of his colleagues, embarked on a gigantic gamble … and lost us nearly a million of money. Up till then our affairs were stable and prosperous.' Harold Nicolson wrote of the disaster:

For my uncle, who had spent his years in the full blaze of imperial sunshine, the clouds that gathered in the twilight seemed to darken the whole sky. It was with deep despondency that he watched the clock upon the mantelpiece tick out the last few seconds of the nineteenth century. The whole scheme of things for which, for seventy-three years, he had laboured so ardently, appeared, within a few days, to have dissolved in shame and ashes. He looked forward to the new century with a dread which had about it something of presentiment.

Dufferin was a well-read man and may well have wished that he had taken heed of Adam Smith's words in *The Wealth of Nations*, written more than a century earlier:

Of all those expensive and uncertain projects ... which bring bankruptcy upon the greater part of the people who engage in them, there
is none perhaps more perfectly ruinous than the search after new silver
and gold mines. It is perhaps the most disadvantageous lottery in the
world, or the one in which the gain of those who draw the prizes
bears the least proportion to the loss of those who draw the blanks:
for though the prizes are few and the blanks many, the common price
of a ticket is the whole fortune of a very rich man.

CHAPTER THIRTEEN

LYNCH THEM!

Even now, Wright refused to accept that the game was up. Putting on a brave face, he determined to carry on, seeking a path through the valley of angry creditors and shareholders, with cannons to the right and left of him. To defuse criticism and to calm nerves, he issued a statement claiming that Globe's assets were sufficient to pay more than twenty shillings in the pound. Vowing to keep the show on the road, he announced plans for a shareholders' meeting early in the New Year at which he would reveal his proposals for restructuring the company and making it profitable again. 'If the creditors and shareholders stand by the directors in the present emergency, neither are likely to suffer any ultimate loss,' he declared.

By staying in control and taking positive action, Wright hoped to side-step the further calamity of a compulsory liquidation, the scrutiny of the Official Receiver and a public examination. It was a route that most shareholders favoured, too, even if it required them to advance more funds. Word went around that the company could be 'reconstructed' successfully with only a 'moderate' injection of new equity capital. Globe shares, which had fetched forty-five shillings (£2.25) in 1897, changed hands on the stock market at six shillings (30p) in the belief that the company might yet be rescued.

Lord Dufferin agreed to remain in London to chair the meeting, although he fully expected to be 'torn to pieces'. He was already the subject of a grim City jest – 'When was Whitaker right?' 'When he took a duffer in.' A sailing friend, Launcelot Rolleston, wrote to him: 'Personally I never believed in that confounded Whitaker Wright since he let off that cannon in your ear, and always felt a degree of anxiety as to your trusting him.'

Too mortified to show his face in public before the meeting, Dufferin hid away in his London hotel. In correspondence, he described Globe's downfall as 'an indescribable calamity which will cast a cloud on the remainder of my life'. In his darkest moments he accepted that he had found himself 'entangled with a set of people, all of them engaged in a fraudulent conspiracy, all of them in WW's pocket'. Letters he received from distraught shareholders asking him to do everything in his power to mitigate the effects of the crash added to his misery. His sense of personal responsibility for 'our poor broken Phoenix' led him, despite his own losses, to offer some of them compensation from his own 'de-pleted resources'. One of his first actions after the collapse was to make arrangements to sell his beloved yacht, *Brunhilde*.

A close friend, Jacob Luard Pattisson, assured him that 'throughout all circles, both City and social, the blame has been put upon the right horse and not a word except of friendly regret towards yourself that you should have been drawn into such a catastrophe'. Dufferin drew scant consolation from such words. He was particularly upset at the effect of the crash on his wife, writing to her:

You have been everything to me in my prosperous days and they have been many; and now you are even more to me in my adversity. But what I feel so dreadfully is that *your* life should be thus suddenly over-shadowed, just as we thought to enjoy the evening sunshine of our days in our happy home.

The brickbats of an unsympathetic press also tormented him. Harold Nicolson described the criticism he endured as 'an agony to the soul'. The *Investors' Review* was among the publications which saw no excuse for his actions, calling his speeches at company meetings 'a disgrace to his understanding and an insult to the public'. *The Economist* thought it regrettable that 'one who has in many highly responsible positions rendered valuable services to his country should in his later years have so far demeaned himself as to become, for a monetary consideration, the passive tool of a scheming financier'.

It was thus with some trepidation that Dufferin arrived at the Cannon Street Hotel on 9 January 1901 for an extraordinary general meeting of Globe. Shareholders began trooping in two hours before-hand, and by the time the proceedings started at midday some 2,000 people were packed into the hall and galleries. There were hisses as well as cheers when Dufferin and Wright took their seats, but the audience listened to the peer in respectful silence. In an emotional speech, he spoke of his 'deepest mortification' and declared that, while there might have been errors of judgement, the board had at all times acted honestly. He urged the shareholders not to let their 'most able managing director' assume full responsibility for what had happened, adding of Wright that he 'had never met anyone more devoted to the service of those with whose interests he was charged'. Diplomat to the last, Dufferin thanked the shareholders for 'the patience and generosity with which they had listened to his observations'. Much to his surprise, he sat down to cheers. 'Anything more generous than the conduct of our share-holders you cannot imagine,' he wrote to his friend Sir Richard Garnett. 'They received me as if I had been Lord Roberts [Commander-in-Chief of the Forces]. One is proud of such an incident for the sake of human nature.'

Next it was Wright's turn. Employing every oratorical trick in the trade, he set out to win the day through sheer force of personality. Offering to take full responsibility for the collapse, he went on to point the finger at pretty well everyone but himself. His culprits included the Lake View management for producing a false report about the mine's prospects, the 'bears' who had dragged down share prices, the Boer War for creating a lack of confidence, and above all the so-called syndicate which had gone back on its word after he had tried to rescue Globe after Christmas. 'Some members of the syndicate are gentlemen, but others are unmitigated knaves,' he growled.

The audience liked his defiant tone and they liked it even more when he launched an all-out attack on the press. The newspapers, he complained, had a lot to answer for. Globe's directors had been 'basely attacked by the gutter press' and he himself had been accused of setting up a 'palace of delight' at the company's expense, when in fact he had bought both his houses before the corporation was formed. (Technically this was true, but most of the expensive renovations and additions to 18 Park Lane and Lea Park, including the underwater smoking room, had been carried out *after* the company's formation.) 'The treatment the company has received at the hands of many newspapers during the last ten days is not English, nor is it cricket in the truest sense of the word,' he thundered. Only the other day, he added to loud cheers, his Surrey neighbour, Arthur Conan Doyle, had declared that the chief danger confronting the new century was 'the uncontrolled supremacy of an ill-conditioned, excitable and sensation-mongering press'.

But there was good news, too, he told his audience. Globe's directors, he claimed, were close to reaching an arrangement with the creditors. Those owed money would release the company from all its obligations on payment of £485,000. This could be raised by selling Globe's interest in the underground railway, in which an American consortium was already showing a keen interest. If the shareholders were prepared to trust him, all would be well. 'I do not believe we have a bad egg in the basket,' he assured his listeners. 'With a long pull, a strong pull, and a pull all together, our good ship will soon be off the rocks and sailing once more in smooth water.' As a measure of his good faith, he added, he had advanced Globe £250,000 of his own money 'to tide over their troubles'.

By now Wright's tub-thumping words had won over almost the entire audience. 'We are not afraid of investigation,' he went on. 'We have not a single transaction to cover up – everything is open to the light of day.' He said he had thought about calling in the Official Receiver, but creditors and shareholders alike had beseeched him not to do this because it would mean – perish the thought – that the shareholders would receive nothing. He proposed to adjourn the meeting for five days. By then, he said, all Globe's debts would be settled and he would be in a position to announce a scheme of voluntary liquidation followed by reconstruction 'to ensure future prosperity'. He finished his tour de force by pledging 'his health, his strength, his life, and as far as might be his private fortune, to carry the enterprise to a successful issue'.

Like Dufferin, he sat down to cheers. His magic had not deserted him. Fired up by Wright's speech, one person after another let loose torrents of indignation against the so-called wreckers who had apparently conspired to damage Globe. Dipping into the Wright book of maritime metaphors, one shareholder said that if the managing director's advice was heeded, he was sure 'the good ship will be steered to a haven of rest'. When a Mr Seal called for an independent inquiry into the company's affairs rather than 'throw more money into the sea', he was shouted down. The *Financial Times* observed that the meeting was marked by a 'rather surprising spirit of harmony'. The *Chicago Herald* commented admiringly:

> With his back to the wall he [Wright] faced small armies of clamour-ing shareholders. They came away full of admiration for the fighting qualities he showed. They were shouting with him, cheering his points, and promising vengeance on those to whom he pointed as the authors of their joint undoing.

A Witley tradesman who had sunk most of his savings into Globe was typical of the shareholders who were won over by Wright's oratory. He had taken the train to London intending to vent his anger on the financier. Instead he joined in the cheering. He told the *Daily Express* afterwards: 'I felt sorry for Mr Wright instead of myself. I don't blame him now. He never wanted his friends to invest in his companies, and I am sure there isn't the slightest resentment against him in Witley.'

The press in general was less inclined to be generous. Wright's old enemy, the *Pall Mall Gazette*, said of the meeting that 'there were gen-eralities on assets, much skilful handling of an audience, various vague promises as to the future and that was all'. The *Daily Mail* said the directors' attempts to avoid a compulsory winding-up 'is a little too transparent, and is the usual device of directors of companies when there is something to hide'. The London correspondent of the *Chicago Tribune* observed that 'the wreck of darkness is as thick as ever'.

The press was right to be suspicious. It was all very well for Wright to pledge 'his health, his strength, his life, and as far as might be his private fortune' to save Globe, but there was precious little evidence of what this meant in practice. 'Where is Mr Whitaker Wright and what is he doing?' asked the *Investors' Review* in exasperation later that month. 'He seems to be busy giving balls at his palace near Godalming. The "servants' ball" was on Tuesday last, and the "county ball" is next week.' The death of Queen Victoria on 22 January provided the press with a distraction, but the carping resumed in February. The *Engineering and Mining Journal* commented: 'Mr Whitaker Wright airily assured his audience that voluntary liquidation and reconstruction would be the simplest thing in the world if they only supported him. Since then, however, we have heard nothing from him.' When census-takers arrived at Lea Park in March, they recorded that a governess, a cook, a lady's maid, six housemaids, two kitchen maids, a butler, two footmen and a coachman were still living with the family in the main house, and that an army of other retainers occupied the outlying cottages and lodges. This though there was still no sign of the promised reconstruction plan and not one Globe creditor had received a penny in cash. A Globe shareholder wrote to the *Daily Colonial*: 'It is indefensible that a man like Jabez Balfour should be in prison [the portly financier and owner of the Cecil Hotel was serving fourteen years for fraud], while the parties responsible for the London and Globe frauds should be revelling in luxury.' *The Times*, losing patience, led calls for all three of Wright's holding companies to be compulsorily wound up.

Over the ensuing months, Wright's empire lurched from crisis to crisis. Next to collapse was Brit-Am, which suspended operations in May. The company was heavily in debt and had just £157 in the bank. During a meeting of shareholders, Wright and his fellow directors were met with groans and hisses as they took their seats, along with cries of 'The same old game!' and 'Aren't you ashamed to face us?' Brit-Am's chairman, Sinclair Macleay, had to shout to make himself heard. He claimed that the company's failure was the result not of mismanagement but of 'complications … in which liability is claimed against the corporation for the same shares in several directions'. Wright seconded Macleay's proposal for voluntary liquidation and reconstruction, but was given a rough ride. 'Now for the promises!' someone sneered. There were jeers and hisses when, once again, he tried to absolve himself of responsibility for the crash and blame it on 'the treachery and default of members of the Stock Exchange'. Investors were tiring of his excuses, and one branded the company's conduct 'a disgrace to the commercial world'. A more cautious speaker urged the meeting not to be 'led away by any spiteful feeling towards the directors' and said that a compulsory liquidation would 'wipe his shares off at once'. To which someone hit back: 'They are wiped off already.'

Once more, Wright managed to talk his way out of trouble. He advised shareholders not to 'cut their own throats and rush hastily to a decision which they might regret afterwards'. His reconstruction plans, he said, would be announced shortly, and the millstone of the Baker Street and Waterloo Railway 'was practically sold' for £500,000. To the surprise and regret of the financial press, he persuaded the meeting to vote for voluntary liquidation rather than for a compulsory winding-up, although he added that the new company would have to do without him. 'Nothing under the sun would ever induce me to be a director again in any company in the City of London.'

Opinion against Wright, however, was hardening. More and more people were coming to the view that he was a spent force. 'We do not believe', said *The Times*, 'that the real interest of creditors, shareholders or the public will be served by allowing Whitaker Wright to raise five shillings, or any other sum per share, and continue to carry on this moribund and mischievous concern.'

The next month, Standard Exploration hit the buffers with liabilities of £362,000. Events now took a dangerous turn for Wright. Investors petitioned for Standard to be compulsorily wound up in July, and the Official Receiver, George Barnes, became involved for the first time. Wright sensibly stayed away from a meeting of creditors and shareholders at which speakers referred in 'vehement language' to the conduct of the company's business. Pelham-Clinton and Gough-Calthorpe, who reluctantly showed their faces, were hissed for their troubles.

The Official Receiver painted a grim picture when he addressed the meeting, telling his audience that it had been 'no light task to unravel the tangled skein of affairs'. The company's books, he said, lacked crucial information and did not reflect the true state of play. Assets claimed by the directors to be worth £1,160,000 were based on 'quite impossible estimates'. Fourteen mines valued on Standard's balance sheet at £767,000 were earning no income. Some had been starved of funds and were effectively worthless. Most of the shareholders' money had been lost in Stock Exchange speculations. Dividends doled out had not been earned, but had been paid by means of loans from Wright and other companies. Of particular concern, he added, was the to-and-fro transfer of funds the previous year between Globe and Standard – 'threads perpetually crossing and re-crossing'. These were manoeuvres for which he had yet to receive a satisfactory explanation.

It was a damning litany, and it shocked the shareholders. One said the revelations would 'stagger humanity'. Another asked: 'Are the rest of the directors still at large?' When told they were, he shouted: 'Lynch them!' At his home in Ireland, Lord Dufferin was kept abreast of events.

Apprehensive about the way things were going, he wrote to his daughter: 'Not yet in the dock, but outlook is very unpleasant.' When Barnes published his full report on Standard Exploration the following month, the *Pall Mall Gazette* commented: 'Shareholders in that lamentable undertaking will read it with interest, and will probably kick themselves once again for their folly in accepting Mr Whitaker Wright as a guide on a short cut to fortune.'

It was the same sorry story in the rest of Wright's empire. Shares in the Le Roi Mining Company, once worth £23, slumped to 12s 6d (62.5p). Stockholders were furious when they gathered for their annual meeting at the end of August. 'Where is Whitaker Wright?' someone shouted. 'On the telephone,' came a reply from the platform. Wright was indeed on the telephone, handing in his resignation and advising the shareholders to elect new directors. Those present were not placated. They spent most of the rest of the meeting making derogatory comments about their former managing director. Despite the widespread anger, few people at this stage foresaw that Wright would ever have to account for himself in a court of law, although there were plenty who thought that he should join Jabez Balfour in jail. Commenting on the shortcomings of the legal system, *The Times* declared: 'It would seem that the penalties of the law, however terrible they may appear on paper, can be no real deterrent to the rogue. The chances are, particularly if his frauds have been bold, large and uncomplicated, that he will never be prosecuted.'

In October, fresh back from a family holiday in Bilbao, Wright finally unveiled his reconstruction plans. Even now he still believed the sinking ship could be salvaged. With Standard in receivership, his main proposal was to combine Globe and Brit-Am with a capital of £2 million, half of this to be in new shares. But it was too late. He had lost every vestige of credibility. Four days later, the disillusioned Globe shareholders rejected his proposals and voted for compulsory liquidation. Brit-Am followed suit. For Wright, it was a crushing if inevitable blow. By now he was starting to feel the pinch personally and one by one his outward trappings of wealth disappeared. He vacated the Lea Park mansion in September and moved into a rented house, Tigbourne Court, a mile south of Witley. A handful of staff stayed on at Lea Park to keep the place ticking over, but the property quickly acquired a neglected look. The scaffolded south wing remained unfinished, and wooden cases containing marble statuary from Rome lay unopened on the lawn.

Next to go was 18 Park Lane, which Wright sold to a German mining millionaire, Friedrich Eckstein. In its place he acquired rented rooms at 2 Whitehall Court. He sold his yacht *Sybarita* to an iron and steel tycoon, Myles Kennedy, and his steam yacht *Sybarite* to George Jay Gould I, an American railroad baron. For all his belt-tightening, he was still wealthy by most people's standards. He and Anna retained several domestic staff and continued to send their son to Eton. But if he entertained hopes that he had turned a corner, they were about to be dashed. The Official Receiver continued to comb through Globe's paperwork and delivered more shocks when he addressed shareholders in December. The company, he revealed, had unsecured creditors of £1,142,000. Half its estimated assets of £424,000 were made up of claims against Brit-Am and Standard which could never be realised, and much of the rest was in overvalued shares. Vast sums had been dissipated in failed speculations. Barnes described the infamous 1900 balance sheet as a 'work of art' and said the managing director had inflated if not manufactured assets to make Globe appear solvent. Wright stayed away from the meeting, pleading illness. 'We learn with unfeigned regret', scoffed the *Pall Mall Gazette*, 'that Mr Whitaker Wright is suffering from influenza and the complications which so often accompany it ... he would have been so useful at the Globe corporation meeting.'

The way was now clear for a full public examination of Wright and his fellow directors and functionaries. The proceedings at the London Bankruptcy Court in Carey Street – described by one journalist present as 'a sordid, gloomy, Dickens-like room' – began in January 1902 and must have stirred uncomfortable memories in Wright of his appearance before the Halifax Bankruptcy Court more than three decades earlier. He kept resolutely quiet about this little-known aspect of his past, and it was never revealed during the hearings. One by one the board members of his companies were exposed to humiliating interrogations by the Official Receiver. Brit-Am's Sinclair Macleay conceded that he was an 'ornamental' director who was largely ignorant of the company's activities. The board, he said, had little to do except sign certificates. Asked to name one thing he had done to protect the shareholders, he said:

> I never questioned anything the managing director did. Whitaker Wright is a man of very great financial ability and the board always had every confidence in his integrity. In the majority of cases the directors were never asked to do anything but confirm the resolutions relating to transactions that had already been carried out.

Gough-Calthorpe, a director of both Globe and Standard, was disarmingly frank about his near-total ignorance of financial matters. He conceded he had been present on 16 November 1899 when Wright transferred £250,000 from Globe to Brit-Am but had supposed 'that the Globe was so rich it could afford to do anything'.

Official Receiver: Were the reasons for the transfer explained to you?

Gough-Calthorpe: I don't suppose I would have understood what was happening even if it had been explained to me. It was a matter of City finance.

Official Receiver: But you were a director of a company engaged in City finance. Had you any idea of your duty?

Gough-Calthorpe: As far as I could ascertain it was to sign my name many thousands of times on share certificates.

Official Receiver: You did not guide the policy of the company in any way?

Gough-Calthorpe: Oh dear no!

George Worters, Globe's former accountant, confirmed that the directors were kept in the dark about Wright's transactions. Asked if they ever saw the company books, he replied to mocking laughter from the gallery: 'Not to my knowledge. They may have seen the outsides.' Questioned as to whether he did anything to protect the shareholders, he responded: 'I never interfered with the managing director.'

For his part, Wright continued to maintain that he was innocent of any wrongdoing, and that all his actions had been standard business practice. At the start of his evidence, he tried to win sympathy by claiming that he had been 'seriously ill' for the past six weeks, but this cut no ice with the Official Receiver, who was persistent and aggressive in his questioning. Wright followed his usual ploy of blaming everybody but himself for what had happened. He could not, he said, be held responsible for errors made by his accountants, or for the misleading reports about the Lake View mine, or for the problems created by the Boer War. Asked by Barnes if he agreed that Globe's assets were 'increased artificially' between 1 October and 5 December 1900, he said he strongly objected to the use of the word 'artificially'. It was his duty, he insisted, to present the best possible picture of Globe's financial position, and if that meant the transfer of assets from one company to another, that was a matter for him. Questioned about a liability of £150,000 which was missing from the balance sheet, he pointed the finger at Globe's new accountant. Henry Malcolm, he claimed, had 'overlooked the contract notes for £100,000 and put them together with contract notes for £50,000 in a drawer and forgot about them'. He added disingenuously: 'I cannot be responsible for other people's mistakes.'

Official Receiver: You seem to think a good many things do not matter.
Wright: Nothing matters when you are right and straightforward.

If Wright's armour was dented by the grilling, he was far from crushed. One of the problems for the Official Receiver was that he was unable to launch all-out attacks on the two most vulnerable positions: the balance sheets of 1899 and 1900. Surprisingly, the publication of a false balance sheet was not illegal under the Companies Act, so that any accusation that Wright had shamelessly cooked the books carried little weight. Barnes, however, did score points on the issue of so-called press calls, and succeeded in making the transactions between Globe and numerous newspapermen look tawdry and underhand. 'Will you swear that you have not paid between £8,000 and £9,000 to certain newspapers – tantamount to bribery – to puff every company you have promoted?' asked Barnes. Wright hit back, saying he strongly objected to the word 'bribery'. Journalists, he maintained, would not take an interest in a company's prospects and progress unless they owned some shares. Barnes had the last laugh by pointing out that their interest could not have been very profound since they had often only held on to the shares for a single day.

If Wright made a significant mistake during his evidence, it was in alleging that Lord Dufferin, who was seriously ill and was not required to attend the hearing, was party to the decision to buy up large numbers of Lake View Consols. Dufferin was so incensed by this claim that he wrote to the Official Receiver from his sick bed, all but denouncing Wright as a criminal.

> I beg to state that Mr Whitaker Wright neither consulted me beforehand nor confided to me his projects in respect of the [Lake View] operations, by the first of which the company lost £700,000, and by the last one nearly a million, and that they were entered upon without my knowledge and consent. I trust it will not be necessary for me to add that I should have considered myself highly criminal if I had knowingly consented to the shareholders' money being gambled away in such a manner.

In a letter to Wright himself, he was more conciliatory, and perhaps over-generous.

> I called upon you last Sunday in order to bid you goodbye, as I shall not be over in London much now. I need not say that I have deeply sympathised with you in your present troubles, and I am very sensitive of the manly and straightforward part you have taken in exonerating your colleagues of all responsibility in regard to the unhappy collapse of our company.

In the words of Harold Nicolson, Dufferin then went back to Ireland 'broken in fortune, in reputation and in health'. His 25,000 shares in five of Wright's companies, valued in 1899 at more than £72,000, were worthless. Gone were many of his treasured possessions, including his yacht, his Italian pictures and his ancestral candelabra. Even after these large-scale economies he was left, to use his own understated words, 'very much to leeward of my normal financial status'. The inglorious end of his great-grandfather, the playwright Richard Brinsley Sheridan, who went bankrupt and died in poverty, cannot have been far from his mind. Three weeks after his return to his Clandeboye estate, he died of stomach cancer. In the opinion of his 1905 biographer Charles Black, his one 'ruinous mistake' after a lifetime of exemplary public service 'sapped his strength' and 'hastened his death'. Another contemporary biographer, Sir Alfred Lyall, told the industrialist Lord Rendel that 'it is impossible to palliate it [Dufferin's involvement with Globe] for every friend Lord Dufferin had seemed to have poured in warnings, and yet Lord Dufferin was obstinate'. The *Saturday Review*'s verdict on his final years could hardly have been more damning:

> Lord Dufferin could not have been on the board of the Globe for six months without discovering that he was perfectly incompetent to control or even to understand Whitaker Wright's actions. Yet he went on doing what he was bid, and speaking another man's words. *As the prompter breathed, the puppet squeaked.*

When Wright's companies were finally wound up, the Official Receiver's report revealed the full scale of the disaster – namely that assets worth £5 million had been irretrievably lost in the space of two years. Gross assets Wright had valued at £7 million were found to be worth £1.5 million at most, while debts were close to £3 million. All forty-one of Wright's companies, with an aggregate capital of £22,355,000, had failed or gone into liquidation. At the final reckoning, the most that could be retrieved for Globe creditors from the smouldering corporate ruins was one shilling (5p) in the £1, while Standard creditors received barely half that. Brit-Am creditors were paid a slightly more generous 2s 6d (12.5p) in the £1. For the 50,000 shareholders, there was nothing. They lost every penny of their investments. The official receiver concluded: 'I feel quite satisfied that there is not a single one of the directors who really knew what was going on except Mr Whitaker Wright ... They ought to have known, but one and all seem to have relied upon somebody other than themselves.'

Still insisting that he was an innocent man who had been grievously wronged, Wright embarked on a lawsuit with the aim of recovering £1 million in damages from the 'syndicate' he blamed for causing Globe's collapse. 'It is well known that I was the victim of treachery at the Lake View mine, traitors there having entered into a conspiracy with certain operators in London,' he declared. It was a last, desperate throw of the dice. The nine-day trial was heard before the Lord Chief Justice, Baron Alverstone, in June 1902, and Wright lost. After the case, the man once dubbed the Napoleon of finance was slated by the *Auckland Star* as the 'Napoleon of unsound finance ... far too hot for everyday consumption'. But at least, to widespread annoyance, he was still free...

CHAPTER FOURTEEN

THE NET CLOSES IN

Wright hoped that the Official Receiver's report would be the end of his troubles, but he reckoned without the anger and determination of John Flower, a stockbroker who had lost money in the Globe crash. Flower & Co. were one of the firms that had foundered on 'Black Saturday'. The head of the business, a strong swimmer amid the flotsam and jetsam of the Wright wreck, was not prepared to forgive and forget. Flower had sat through the Official Receiver's public examination and, like many others present, he had hoped and expected that Wright would be arrested as soon as the proceedings were over. When that failed to happen, he took matters into his own hands, and in the summer of 1902 began a relentless campaign to have Wright prosecuted.

To begin with he made little headway. Wright's 'sin' of capitalising at £22 million mining properties worth less than one twentieth of that amount, and palming off the securities on the public with rosy prospectuses, was not in itself against the law. The Attorney-General, Sir Robert Finlay, studied the case but refused to sanction a prosecution. Though sympathetic, he said that legal proceedings could not be undertaken with any confidence under the Companies Act as it then stood. It was a criminal offence to issue a fraudulent prospectus, but, as the Official Receiver had already made clear, it was not at the time an offence to issue a false balance sheet. Sir Edward Carson, the Solicitor-General, supported his view.

As it happened, many in the City had no great wish to see the blood-hounds of the law let loose on Wright, probably because he had done nothing they had not done themselves, if on a lesser scale. They argued that he had neither created the market exuberance which led to the surge in stock prices, nor was he responsible for the inevitable downturn. Besides, they said, the shares of Globe and its subsidiaries were never regarded or proclaimed as gilt-edged. The people who sank money into Wright's ventures did not belong so much to the investing public as to the speculating public. They had known the risks.

Rather than pursue Wright through the courts, some City men pre-ferred to concentrate their efforts on seeing what, if anything, could be salvaged from the disaster. One group of brokers asked Herbert Hoover, a brilliant young geologist and mining engineer from Iowa, to inspect some of Wright's Australian mines with a view to getting them up and running again. Hoover thought that most were a lost cause, but he and his team secured access to several abandoned mines in the state of Victoria and began pumping water out of them. The operation proved difficult and costly, and in due course the clients accepted Hoover's advice that they should waste no more money on the venture. Hoover's work for the brokers greatly enhanced his reputation in the industry and he went on to have an illustrious career. Mining made him a multimillionaire, and in 1929 he was elected President of the United States. Unwittingly and indirectly, Whitaker Wright had set him on the path to greatness.

Wright himself drew some comfort from the fact that not everyone was baying for his blood. He made plain his feelings about Flower and the others who were crying foul – 'squealers', as he called them – in a 1903 newspaper interview:

It's all luck in these mining operations. Not one mine in a hundred pays. Anyone who knows anything and goes into mining speculation ought to know there is more than an even chance that he will lose. If he wins, he wins heavily on the other hand. And yet here is part of the British public investing in the most risky securities in the world, and then when the slump comes they look on their speculative counters as if they were special deposit banks. All old financiers know that waves of prosperity advance like the waves of the incoming tide, and that then nothing can stop prices from advancing, nor can any human power check the recession of the wave when prices tumble. These circles of rising and decreasing values no man can control ... I could not stem the tide of depression which followed the Boer war. I failed to accomplish the impossible. I gave up a fortune in the attempt, but I could not stand alone against the entire London Stock Exchange ... Would that I had never left America. When Americans speculate and lose they never squeal. In all New York I do not think a speculator could be found like those in London, who cannot take their medicine.

But by now Wright's opinions counted for little, and there was a growing feeling among the public and in the press, if not in the City, that he should face criminal charges. Backed by the powerful voice of *The Times*, Flower kept up the pressure. For the rest of 1902, he got nowhere, and in December he received a letter from the Treasury stating that fresh papers he had sent to the Attorney-General 'contain nothing to alter his conclusion that this case is not one which should be taken up by the Director of Public Prosecutions'.

Wright's reprieve was short-lived. At the start of 1903, Flower formed a four-man committee with the aim of raising funds to pay for a private prosecution. The group consisted of himself, the journalist and polemicist Arnold White (who had invested and lost £600 in Globe), solicitor Percy Simmons and another stockbroker, R. C. Powers. The basis of their offensive was that the Companies Act allowed plaintiffs to instigate criminal charges at their own expense, provided they could convince a High Court judge that they had a viable case. It was the committee's contention that while the two questionable balance sheets might not fall foul of the Companies Act, they *did* contravene the Larceny Act of 1861, which made it an offence to make a false statement with intent to deceive or defraud.

As well as raising cash to fund a prosecution, Flower and his team collected affidavits from firms which claimed to have been defrauded. They also persuaded leading lights on the London Stock Exchange to sign a petition demanding that Wright be brought to trial. Not everyone gave their support. Some felt that pressing for a private prosecution smacked of vindictiveness, while Globe creditors feared that criminal proceedings would use up what little cash was left from the collapse. Despite these doubts, Flower's campaign gathered pace.

On 16 January, the committee convened a public meeting at Anderton's Hotel in Fleet Street. It had already raised £1,400 towards a trial and wanted to increase this to £5,000 to avoid dipping into Globe's surviving funds. There was a large turnout, and speaker after speaker rose to condemn Wright. Flower declared that Globe's shareholders were victims of one of the most 'terrible, heartless and gigantic swindles that this age has ever known … they had a board of blind or "dummy" directors;

auditors who were careless or indifferent to what they signed; and an unscrupulous managing director acting in collusion with the skilled accountants within the walls of the office.' The highlight of the evening was an incendiary speech by Arnold White. A conspiracy theorist *par excellence*, he gave currency to a rumour that the government was reluctant to prosecute because 'great names were involved in the scandal'. Wright and his co-directors, he contended, had avoided charges because they were threatening to drag members of the royal family through the mud if the case went to court. Specifically, he said, they were prepared to blacken the names of King Edward VII and his brother, the Duke of Connaught. White was careful not to attack the King and his brother personally, and stressed that he had no evidence that they had ever invested in Wright's companies. Be that as it may, he asserted, Globe's former executives would try to embarrass them in the courtroom regardless.

The suggestion that Wright was effectively blackmailing the government was pure conjecture, and almost certainly nonsense, but White succeeded in planting an unsettling seed. Up and down the country people began to wonder if he had hit on the real reason why there had been no prosecution. The accusation, baseless though it was, caused considerable embarrassment to the establishment. The King himself was stung, and let it be known through friends in the newspaper industry that there was 'not a vestige of truth in the insinuations to the effect that he or any member of his family was in any way financially interested in the Whitaker Wright schemes'. Word also went out on his behalf that his social contact with Wright had been minimal. One specific rumour, that he and Wright had been on board Sir Thomas Lipton's yacht, *Shamrock II*, when it was dismasted off Cowes in 1901, was categorically denied in the press by 'friends of the King'. Other meetings between Wright and the King could not be so easily denied.

Soon afterwards, White exploded another bomb by revealing that the Prime Minister, Arthur Balfour, had been in possession of 1,000 Globe shares. His clear implication was that the premier's ownership of Globe stock had played a part in the Attorney-General's refusal to authorise a prosecution. Again, this was pure innuendo. There was no evidence whatever to suggest that Balfour had influenced Finlay's decision. Nonetheless, the disclosure added to the growing suspicion that the government had engineered a cover-up. This dark and damaging talk of conspiracy began to filter out beyond Britain. Even the *Calcutta Weekly Notes* weighed in:

> The whole affair has been so mysterious and the action of the Prime Minister and of the Attorney-General so completely at variance with the simple facts as to the law of England and the canons of common sense and plain justice, that it is only natural to suppose that there is something behind the Whitaker Wright case which the Government desire to suppress, but which in the interests of public justice should be revealed.

On 17 February 1903, Flower ratcheted up the stakes when he won an application to have his case for prosecuting Wright heard before a High Court judge. In legal circles, his chances of winning consent for a trial were thought to be slim. The courts had never before overridden the Attorney-General in this way, and a number of creditors, notably those of the Nickel Corporation, hired lawyers to oppose the application on the grounds that it was a waste of Globe's few remaining resources. Flower might have failed but for one lucky circumstance. The case came into the list of Mr Justice Buckley. The 57-year-old judge probably knew more about company law than anyone at Bar or on the bench.

His massive work, *Buckley on the Companies Act*, was a bible for law-yers. According to the *Daily Mail*: 'Sir Henry Buckley to look at is the embodiment of a cold, unemotional lawyer ... [H]e has inherited from his father, a vicar, the grave clerical manner as well as the clerical face.' Crucially, Buckley was known for his independence of mind. All involved could be confident that the finer feelings of the King and the Prime Minister would not have the slightest bearing on his ruling. The hearing began in chambers at the end of February, but was adjourned until the following month after Buckley insisted it should be heard in open court.

Two days later, Wright suffered another body blow. With matters coming to a head, the combative Liberal MP George Lambert stood up in the House of Commons to lambast the Attorney-General's failure to sanction a prosecution. Denouncing Wright's 'financial jugglery', 'ma-nipulation' and 'fraud', he protested: 'Here is a company which issued a report showing a profit for the year of £463,000, and twenty-three days afterwards they collapsed and were unable to meet their liabilities.' He demanded an immediate change in the law and, like White, insinuated that the reason Wright had not been charged was because 'certain exalted personages have been mixed up in these matters'. He declared:

There have been aristocratic gentlemen mixed up in this affair. I am very sorry for it, but if men with noble names allow themselves to be connected with companies they must take the consequences of their action. If they use their names as bird-lime for the unwary investor they must take the responsibility, as they draw the salaries. Either these directors are much-maligned men or they deserve punishment, and I ask the Attorney-General to allow a jury of twelve British men to decide that question ... By failing to prosecute in this case the Attorney-General is taking a grave responsibility ... If this had been a bank manager, or a bank clerk with a salary of £100 a year, the law would have been upon him at once. There ought to be no difference.

The Attorney-General rejected Lambert's accusation. He conceded that Wright's inter-company transactions had been 'indefensible' and that 'everyone must feel in their nature they were most reprehensible', but he insisted that it was simply a deficiency in the law which prevented him from authorising a prosecution. He added that there was 'not one vestige of truth in the rumour' that the government was protecting people in high places: 'Be they aristocratic or plebeian, it would not make the slightest difference in my decision in regard to the matter of a prosecution.' Amid jeers from opposition MPs, Sir Edward Carson, the Solicitor-General, rose in support of Finlay. Acknowledging that there were deficiencies in the law, he declared: 'It is said that Mr Whitaker Wright published a false balance sheet. I believe that he did. I think it is an admitted fact that this was done; but will anyone get up and say that a man ought to be prosecuted for issuing a false balance sheet?'

Next it was the turn of the Prime Minister himself. Balfour made no reference to his own Globe shares, but Arnold White's revelation had clearly needled him, and he distanced himself from the company's machinations with an outspoken attack on their architect. Professing his 'deep and profound indignation at the fraudulent transactions in which Mr Whitaker Wright has been engaged', he described the financier's behaviour as 'scandalous and painful'. He promised a swift change in the law 'to make such practices impossible', adding:

Nobody can have even a most cursory knowledge of those transactions without being conscious that if these are things which can be done in a great commercial centre like London, in connection with a vast transaction like that of the London and Globe, and can be done with impunity, a great fault lies somewhere.

The Prime Minister's attack on Wright failed to appease Arnold White. He promptly wrote an open letter to Balfour headed '*I Accuse*', charging him with 'betraying your imperial trust by sheltering the guilt of the wealthy and fashionable, and sacrificing little people to the miserable interest of your incompetent administration'. His letter, which was sent to every major London newspaper, charged Finlay and Carson with deliberately misleading the Commons. 'To allow Whitaker Wright to shelter himself behind the King's ermine may be convenient to the Government,' he fulminated, 'but it is not convenient with the interests or traditions of Englishmen.'

Inflammatory though it was, White's letter attracted little attention. Instead, it was the actions of Wright himself that were about to make the headlines again.

CHAPTER FIFTEEN

ON THE RUN

Amid the growing furore, Wright made a determined effort to appear untroubled. He told friends repeatedly that he had nothing to hide and nothing to fear from prosecution, and that if charged he fully intended 'to face the music'. He continued to go regularly to his office in the City, spending weeknights at his new Whitehall apartment and weekends at Tigbourne Court. Only Anna (and possibly Rosalie) knew that he was becoming increasingly unnerved by the incoming fire. The breaking point had come when the Prime Minister stood up to denounce him in the Commons on 19 February.

Balfour's comments were widely reported in the next day's newspapers and spurred Wright into a dramatic course of action. Realising that public opinion had moved decisively against him, and that a private prosecution was looking increasingly on the cards, he fled the country. The morning after Balfour's broadside, he armed Anna's lady's maid with a cheque for £500 and despatched her to the Godalming branch of the Capital and Counties Bank, where he had an account. On her return to Tigbourne

Court, she handed him gold coins to the value of £200, and three bank-notes, each with a denomination of £100. The total was broadly equivalent to ten years' wages for one of his farm labourers. The next day, Wright and his valet, Joseph Bishop, were driven to Godalming Station where they boarded a train for Southampton. They went to some lengths to avoid drawing attention to themselves or to give the impression that they were going abroad. To enable them to travel with a minimum of luggage, Bishop arranged for Wright's seven leather trunks, all unlabelled, to be sent on ahead. The stationmaster at Godalming was an admirer of Wright and assured the two men of his discretion, no doubt in return for a generous tip.

On reaching Southampton they stayed with friends of Wright for three days before taking the night boat to Le Havre on 24 February. From there they went by train to the French capital and booked into Wright's favourite Parisian hotel, the Binder. Bishop had reserved two rooms in advance by telegram, and they signed in unobtrusively as 'J. Wright' and 'J. Bishop'. (Wright, who had signed in as 'Whitaker Wright' during previous stays at the hotel, was no doubt aware that the names of all foreign visitors were routinely passed to the police.)

How long Wright envisaged staying abroad at this stage, and how he saw his life unfolding in the longer term, is unclear. With diminishing funds and his tarnished reputation, he would have struggled to stay on the run for ever. For the time being, however, he simply marked time in Paris while he waited to see if he was to face criminal charges, and probably took the opportunity to find solace in the arms of Rosalie (he was not, after all, short of ready cash). Cut off from his family, and suffering from insomnia, it is possible that he was on the verge of a nervous breakdown. At one point he asked Thomas Cook's to send him an English-speaking guide to show him the sights of Paris, and one Arthur Dryon duly arrived to spend the day with him. The two men got on well – so well that Dryon accepted Wright's invitation to join him on a yachting trip to Norway. Since Wright no longer owned a yacht, this seems to have been an offer without much substance. At any rate, Dryon did not hear from him again.

Each time Wright returned to the Binder he checked to see if there were any telegrams from Anna. There usually were. They were often coded, and were sometimes addressed to Bishop in an apparently deliberate attempt to keep Wright's name off the messages. On 6 March, his tenth day in Paris, Anna sent ominous news. John Flower's application before Mr Justice Buckley for a direction to prosecute Wright under Sections 83 and 84 of the Larceny Act of 1861 was in full swing in London. Although the judge had yet to make a ruling, the outcome looked certain. 'Case to prosecute settled today – all looks bad,' she wired.

The telegram propelled Wright into a flurry of activity. He cabled Anna (in Bishop's name) telling her to send his 22-year-old American-born niece, Florence Brown, to France with a further £500 in cash and to wait for him at Le Havre. (Florence, known to the family as Florrie, and her sister, Gertrude, were the daughters of Wright's Philadelphia-based sister, Matilda. After their father, James, abandoned the family, they crossed the Atlantic and lived with the Wrights in Witley while they completed their education.) Apparently anxious that no incriminating documents should fall into the wrong hands, he added: 'No more letters are to be forwarded to me.'

On Saturday 7 March, Wright went to the Saint-Lazare railway terminus in Paris and returned by train to Le Havre. There he parted company with Bishop and met up with his niece. Together they went to the offices of a local shipping agent, Compagnie Générale Transatlan-tique, where he used one of his £100 notes to buy two first-class tickets for New York on the French liner *La Lorraine*. The tickets were issued in the names of Monsieur and Mademoiselle Andreoni.

Wright would claim in court the following year that all his actions since 20 February – the night trip to France, the unlabelled luggage, the coded messages, the telegrams in his valet's name – had innocent explanations, right down to the booking in the name of Andreoni. There was nothing suspicious about that, he would say. It was not, he protested, an alias he had plucked from the ether to avoid detection, as some unkind people had suggested. It was simply that the CGT shipping clerk at Le Havre was called Andreoni and that his name had mistakenly appeared on the tickets. Possibly so, but given Wright's free-and-easy relationship with the truth, and given the suspicion that he simply seized on the first name that came into his head, it may be relevant that the sculptor responsible for some of Wright's favourite works at Lea Park, including the rock-climbing nymphs, was named Orazio Andreoni.

Whatever the reason for the wrong name appearing on the tickets, and whether it was Wright's or the clerk's doing, he did not immediately correct the error. He and Florence boarded *La Lorraine* at 3 p.m. that Saturday, and only after the ship had sailed two hours later did he write down their correct names on a standard form given to the passengers for the use of American immigration officials. Asked by the purser why the names did not tally, he said there had been a mistake, and the booking was duly changed to 'Mr J. W. Wright and Miss F. Brown'. The incident caused a good deal of speculation among the crew, although no one on board recognised Wright or suspected his true identity. (Very few images of the camera-shy Wright had ever appeared in the press.) The general view was that the two mysterious passengers were in the throes of an illicit affair.*

The couple occupied the most expensive suite on the ship, Rooms

---

* In a subsequent newspaper interview, Florence came up with a different version of how the tickets were obtained. She said Wright had been unable to secure first-class accommodation and paid a couple called Andreoni to swap cabins.

116, 118 and 120, consisting of a private dining room and two deluxe bedrooms on the port side. Between them they had no fewer than fourteen items of luggage. They seldom left their quarters and had all their meals sent up to them. Wright informed the crew that Florence was suffering from seasickness and did not feel up to eating in the dining saloon (this though the weather was good and the sea relatively calm). Florence appeared briefly on deck four days into the voyage but was not otherwise seen in public. Wright himself took a brisk walk along the deck each evening and smoked a cigar. Unlike his niece, he mingled with the other passengers. He engaged in conversation with them and handed out cigars, but never gave any clue as to who he was.

After a week-long crossing, *La Lorraine* dropped anchor off the Sandy Hook peninsula, south of New York City, early on the evening of Saturday 14 March. There she was obliged to wait overnight until a berth became available in the harbour the following morning. Again, although he would deny it later, Wright gave every impression of being a man on the run, trying to persuade the crew to hail a tugboat or other small vessel so that he might be taken ashore there and then. The purser told him that this would not be possible and that he must stay on *La Lorraine* until she berthed.

Unknown to the stout fugitive, events back in England had proceeded apace. *La Lorraine* was already far out into the Atlantic when, the previous Tuesday, John Flower had finally won his battle to have Wright prosecuted. Mr Justice Buckley directed the Official Receiver 'to institute and conduct against Whitaker Wright a criminal prosecution' on the grounds that 'he unlawfully did make, articulate and publish a statement of accounts he knew to be false, with intent to deceive and defraud the members, shareholders and creditors'. Buckley made it clear that he did not blame the Acts of Parliament for the previous failure to prosecute

Wright. Rather, it was down to the people using them. 'The apathy of the public in setting the Law in motion has – I will not say encouraged – but has at least failed to repress grievous frauds which have been committed and have too often gone unpunished.' He said the case clearly fell within the scope of the Larceny Act of 1861, and he took a gentle dig at the Attorney-General for having failed to start the ball rolling. His ruling made front-page news. A cartoon in the *Colonial Goldfields Gazette* depicted Wright as a disgraced schoolboy, with 'monitor' John Flower handing the birch to schoolmaster 'John Bull', who says threateningly: 'Now, Sir, I want you to explain how you came to get these sums wrong.'

Anna's photograph in The Tatler *in March 1903 belied
the impression of someone who was feeling the pinch.*

The ruling was welcomed by the press, which had been increasingly warming to Arnold White's view that the government was trying to protect 'people in high places'. A warrant for Wright's arrest was issued, and a court officer tried and failed to serve the summons at both Whitehall Court and Tigbourne Court. When it emerged that Wright had not been seen at either address for at least three weeks, the Official Receiver's lawyers announced angrily that it appeared he had absconded.

Newspaper reporters descended on Tigbourne Court, where Anna, in a rare interview, protested that it was 'too cruel' to suggest her husband had bolted. He had, she claimed, gone to the Nile Valley via Paris 'fully five weeks ago', his doctors having advised him that a rest was imperative. His one desire was to 'do something for the unfortunate shareholders', and the worry had told severely on his health. She had not heard from him, she said, since he had left Paris.

He is in the interior of Egypt just now, and I don't suppose he will know anything of what has happened until he hears from me. He has told me if ever there was any trouble he must recover his strength to enable him to fearlessly meet the charges brought against him.

Laying it on thick, she insisted that there had been no secret about his departure from England.

Everything was quite open. He is not the man to run away from anyone. He is a most honourable man. Think of how he stood up in court for ten days last year and answered all their questions. He told me that while in Egypt he will have the opportunity of looking into some mines there, and may be able to do something for the people who have lost money.

In a flurry of self-pity, she added: 'What do people expect of him? Lea Park has been mortgaged and is gone for ever. The yachts have been sold. I have been one of the heaviest losers of this. I lost £45,000 and I have nothing left but the furniture in this house.'

It was a show of bravura of which her husband would have been proud. Mesmerised by her good looks, her charm and her soft American accent, one journalist wrote of her 'undoubted belief in her husband and her touching, woman-like loyalty and strength'. To Wright's enemies, all it proved was that Anna was as adept at lying through her teeth as her spouse. The general consensus was that Wright had done a bunk and that Anna had connived in his vanishing act. To conspiracy theorists like Arnold White it went further than that. To him it was plain that the government had helped to engineer Wright's disappearance because it was desperate to avoid embarrassing revelations in court. 'The London and Globe is the biggest scandal in England for 200 years,' he thundered at a public meeting in London shortly after Wright vanished. 'Smart society dares not face his revelations. The reputations of too many people are in his possession.'

That no one appeared to have any idea of Wright's whereabouts was a considerable embarrassment to the powers that be. On the day that Anna was holding forth to the press, the Irish Nationalist MP Swift MacNeill rose to his feet in the House of Commons and asked the Home Secretary, Aretas Akers-Douglas, why Wright had not been placed under police surveillance as soon as Mr Justice Buckley had made his ruling. (It was not known at this stage that Wright had already left the country when Buckley announced his decision.) 'I will not go so far as to suggest that the Home Office connived at Whitaker Wright's escape,' said McNeill, 'but they neglected their duty.' Akers-Douglas replied testily that every effort would be made to bring Wright to justice. His dander up, he walked straight from the Commons to Scotland Yard and demanded to see Sir Edward Henry, who had been appointed Commissioner of the Metropolitan Police just seven days earlier. His mood did not improve when a duty constable asked him the nature of his business. 'I am the Home Secretary,' declared Akers-Douglas. The constable stood his ground. 'We have plenty of maniacs calling themselves that,' he retorted.

Eventually an inspector sorted out the confusion, and Akers-Douglas was taken to see Sir Edward, who immediately ordered a full-scale manhunt. The officer he put in charge of the search was Detective Inspector John Willis, who was based at the Old Jewry in the City of London. With fourteen years of police service behind him, Willis was widely regarded as one of the cleverest young officers in the force. Slightly built, smartly dressed and sporting a neat moustache, he could easily have passed for one of the City businessmen whose activities he regularly investigated. Earlier in the year, he had been widely lauded for his 'greatest coup yet': the capture in Blackpool of 'Redgrave, the Barnet lease-forger'.

Willis and two other officers, Detective Inspector Henry Phillips and Sergeant William Gough, hotfooted it to Witley. Gough went to see the stationmaster at Godalming, who, fiercely loyal to the Lord of the Manor, refused at first to co-operate but eventually conceded that Wright had caught a Southampton-bound train three weeks earlier. Willis and Phillips decided to try their luck at Tigbourne Court, but gleaned nothing from Anna other than what she had already told the press. Her husband, she insisted, was in Egypt and uncontactable. The police officers had no way of knowing that Wright was now just two days out of New York on *La Lorraine*. For all Willis knew, he might be anywhere in the world. The detective ordered a watch on several ports in the south of England in case his quarry was still in the country. A dozen officers headed for the coast armed with a sketch of Wright which had appeared in the *Sphere* newspaper. They concentrated their inquiries on two of Wright's known haunts, Cowes and Southampton. Rumours abounded at both locations. There was talk of a mysterious yacht laden with luggage observed departing from Cowes in the middle of the night. A boatman who had once conveyed Wright to *White Heather* was convinced he had seen him on Southampton Pier the previous week.

The yachting fraternity suggested he had sailed to Rome, to Marseilles, to Queenstown in Ireland, to Alexandria. There was even talk that he was holed up in the ice house at Lea Park.

In the end it was the resourceful Willis who homed in on the vital clue. He went to the Capital and Counties Bank in Godalming and learned that Wright had been supplied with gold and banknotes the previous month. He cabled the numbers of the three £100 notes to the Bank of England, which informed him that one of them, No. 75,775, had been used at a shipping office in Paris seven days earlier and returned to London through the usual clearing channels.

It was by now Saturday morning and *La Lorraine* was twelve hours off Sandy Hook. Willis called the Paris agents of Messrs Michael Abrahams, solicitors for the Official Receiver, and asked them to make urgent inquiries at the shipping office. Later in the day, a Paris solicitor, J. H. Saville, wired back the information that a man answering Wright's description had booked passages for himself and a lady to New York on *La Lorraine*.

Ship-to-shore wireless telegraphy was still in its infancy in 1903. It would be another seven years before it was famously used in the arrest of the London cellar murderer Dr Hawley Crippen while he was fleeing to Canada with his mistress on the SS *Montrose*. With time running out, Willis's only option was to cable the New York police and ask them to arrest Wright as soon as *La Lorraine* docked. He went straight to the top, addressing the cable to New York Police Commissioner Francis Greene. He provided him with a detailed description of the wanted man, which was broadly accurate except for his age. (Wright had recently turned fifty-seven.)

Absconder, charged on warrant with fraud to a large amount, Whitaker Wright, manager of London and Globe Finance Corporation of this city. Aged fifty years, height 5ft 10 or 11in.; complexion florid; hair and moustache dark; large head: small eyes; receding forehead; weight about 252 pounds; wears gold-rimmed glasses with gold chain attached; speaks with a slight American accent. Usually dressed in frock-coat suit and silk hat. Please arrest if possible and wire Commissioner of Police, London.

In his suite on *La Lorraine*, Wright had no idea that the police were closing in on him, or that his famed good luck was running out fast. Had he landed in Rhode Island, Massachusetts, or been able to dash from New York to any one of twenty-three other states, he could not have been arrested or have faced extradition proceedings. The fraudulent activity of which he had been accused was only a crime in nine states of the Union, and it was his misfortune that New York was one of them. The final turn of the screw was *La Lorraine*'s overnight stop off Sandy Hook. It gave the New York police just enough time to pick up Willis's message and board the vessel as soon as she berthed on Sunday morning. Two officers, Detectives Moody and Leeson, hurried up the gangplank and made their way along the saloon deck. Peering through an open cabin door, they saw the unmistakeable figure of Wright sitting at a desk. He was, it transpired, composing a telegram to the Lafayette Hotel in Philadelphia requesting the 'best two rooms and bath in the house'. He was dressed in a dark suit and was wearing tan shoes. Florence was already on the deck with the luggage, waiting for her uncle to leave the ship with her.

'Mr Wright?' asked Leeson as he and Moody entered the cabin.

'That is my name,' came the reply.

'Well, if you are Whitaker Wright you are under arrest.'

'What!' Wright rose to his feet, clearly surprised, but he remained calm. Excuses, protestations and pleas came thick and fast. He told the detectives he could not understand why he was under arrest because he believed that 'the matter – a business transaction – was all settled in the British Parliament'. His name, he assured them, would be quickly cleared. He said he would go with them willingly but would like to leave the ship 'with as little noise as possible'. He would be grateful, he added, if the newspapers were not tipped off that he was being held. It was not as if he had done anything wrong, he pointed out. Rather, it had all been a misunderstanding. As the detectives escorted him from the suite, he offered a final mitigating thought: 'I am', he declared, 'a friend of the King.'

CHAPTER SIXTEEN

GOT HIM!

The New York authorities were not prepared to take any chances with their high-profile prisoner. As Wright was escorted down *La Lorraine*'s gangplank, reinforcements arrived in the shape of two Pinkerton detectives and two marshals from the Department of Justice. Hustling him into a horse-drawn police wagon, they took him under armed guard to police headquarters in Mulberry Street. Detectives Moody and Leeson's only concession to their captive was to let him tell Florence in person that he was under arrest. This he did in a brief, whispered conversation on *La Lorraine*'s deck. Fighting back tears, Florence stood with her face in her hands as her uncle was led away.

At police headquarters, Wright was questioned by the chief of the NYPD Detective's Bureau, Inspector George 'Chesty' McClusky, whose nickname reflected his loud clothing and swaggering manner. The *bête noire* of confidence men and crime bosses, and the scourge of the city's *mafiosi*, McClusky carried out a search of Wright's wallet. To his considerable surprise, it yielded forty-six £10 notes, ten £5 notes and two £100 notes, the total of £710 being roughly three times McClusky's annual salary. He confiscated the lot and ordered that the prisoner be taken to Tombs Police Court in Lower Manhattan. There, later that morning, Wright appeared before Magistrate Barlow charged with being a fugitive from justice. McClusky was on good terms with the press, and it was no doubt thanks to a tip-off from him that the court was swarming with reporters.

Wearing an overcoat to keep out the chill of a March morning, Wright said nothing at the brief hearing. His only reaction was to smile dismissively on hearing himself described as a fugitive. As was routine in extradition cases, bail was refused. The magistrate signed an order handing him over to the prison service and ruled that the £710 should remain with the police on the grounds that it might be part of the money alleged to have been obtained fraudulently. Sunday was normally a quiet day for news, and the duty reporters could hardly believe their luck at seeing the world's most notorious financier standing in front of the bench. Any hopes that Wright had entertained of minimal publicity were dashed. Moody and Leeson provided detailed descriptions of the arrest to anyone who would listen, and the capture made front-page news around the world. The New York *Sun*, in an early example of a punning headline, proclaimed: 'GOT WHITAKER RIGHT HERE … LONDON'S FUGITIVE PROMOTER NABBED ON LA LORRAINE'. The *San Francisco Call* was one of many newspapers that embraced the Arnold White school of thought: 'Britain's aristocracy is shaken … J. Whitaker Wright's arrest likely to result in revelations in which even the Royal Family may not be spared.'

Back home, *Punch* took a more whimsical stance. It satirised the financier's arrival in New York by listing the publications of 'the well-known author, Mr Whitaker Wright'. They included: 'Getting Round the Globe', 'America as a Health Resort', 'The Strange Adventures of Miss Brown', 'Directors I have Known', 'Detectives who have Known Me', and 'Tales of Finance'.

For all his bravado, Wright's arrest and transfer to prison came as a shock to his system and played havoc with his health. In the space of a few hours, he had switched from being the Lord of the Manor of Witley in a first-class cabin on a luxury ship to a jailbird in a cramped, unlit cell. New York's prisons were notorious for their atrocious conditions, disease and corruption. The exception was Ludlow Street Jail, to which Wright was taken after the hearing. The red-brick complex, with its eighty-seven cells and open courtyard, was intended for civil rather than criminal offenders. Most of the inmates were debtors, and the prison was sometimes called the 'alimony club' since it housed many 'delinquent' husbands who owed money to their former wives. It had a reading room, a billiards room, a grocery store, and cells with well-sprung beds and curtains. It was not unlike a gentlemen's club, and those with cash were able to buy privileges. Unfortunately for Wright, the jail had recently come under sustained fire in the press for mollycoddling its inmates, and the governor gave orders that the prominent new prisoner from England should be denied preferential treatment. To begin with, at any rate, the warders went out of their way to make Wright's life as uncomfortable as possible. If the *Washington Evening Star* was to be believed,

they have put him in one of the smallest and darkest and meanest of cells ... they have forced him to partake of the coarse prison fare, although other well-heeled prisoners have their meals and wines sent in from the best restaurants in New York ... he has to take his corridor exercises with sullen gangs of sailors.

His iron bedstead, it was claimed, had no mattress, he was provided with only one blanket, and he was denied a tin bowl for washing his face. According to another report, he was obliged to spend his last few coins buying 'two tallow candles to see by' so that he could write to family, friends and business associates in England. In yet a further humiliation, he was stared at through the iron bars of the door 'as if he were a beast in a cage'.

Ludlow Street Jail was to be Wright's home for the next four months, and over time he impressed the staff there as a 'game' man. In due course they relaxed their attitude towards him and allowed him a high degree of comfort, turning a blind eye to the cigars and fine wine that were delivered to him through his lawyers. Nonetheless, ultimate hedonist that he was, those first few hours must have seemed like perdition. He began by sending a message to waiting reporters: 'Mr Whitaker Wright presents his compliments to the press and regrets that he has nothing to say this afternoon.'

After a near-sleepless night, he was escorted by foot to the Federal Courthouse in Manhattan to be arraigned before Commissioner Thomas Alexander. The marshal who accompanied him was happy for him to talk to reporters, and Wright was plied with questions as he strolled along the sidewalk. Affecting a confident air, he told them he had nothing to fear. He would waive extradition and return home where 'powerful friends' would exert their influence on his behalf. He was, he said, 'amazed' by his arrest:

It is an outrage and those who are responsible for it will be made to suffer to the full extent of the law. The entire charge against me is technical and in this country no one would ever think of making it. If I had believed it possible that such a charge would be made I would not, of course, have left home. There was a public inquiry more than a year ago, after which it was declared that my hands were clean of any crime, and that nothing but errors of judgment could be advanced against either myself or other directors of the company. My associates, the Marquis of Dufferin, Lord Loch and the other directors, would have nothing to do with a company which was not as free from the taint of suspicion as their own names. They had no reason to be ashamed of their connection with me. They lost a deal of money, as we all did, but that risk must be taken in such business affairs. It is fortunate for directors of American trusts that they are not under the company laws of England. You could not float your industrials in London. The laws would prevent it. There is no difference between what I did in England and what your industrial companies are doing in America.

The more he pontificated, the more fanciful became his assertions. He claimed that after Globe's collapse, he and the Attorney-General had gone through the company books together and that Sir Robert Finlay had said to him: 'Why, old chap, you are not involved in this at all … you have a clean bill of health.' This was the same Finlay who had denounced his actions in the Commons as 'reprehensible'. He went on to maintain that 'the amount of money lost is all bosh', but immediately undermined this pronouncement by conceding that the figure was close to £4 million. When asked why he had come to America in the first place, he had, as ever, a ready answer. He said he had felt free to leave England after 'the Crown officers stated in Parliament that it was not possible to press any charges against me'. He judged that 'an ocean voyage would act as a bracer' and that a journey of several months would restore him 'to the vigour of a couple of years ago'. This would help him to clear up the 'tangled' condition of London and Globe and his other companies. He had intended going to Egypt, 'where I have valuable concessions', and afterwards to British Columbia, California and Western Australia to inspect mining properties. The change of destination to New York, he stated, was entirely down to his health. He would, it went without saying, be happy to return to England, but under his own steam and not as a prisoner. Once his troubles were over, he had 'a notion' that he might return to see the America's Cup races, 'and I don't mind telling you that I think the Cup will be lifted. The latest *Shamrock* will be a wonder.' His comments were read with incredulity in London, not least because he had never in his life met the Attorney-General, and as far as anyone knew he had no mining interests in Egypt.

When he arrived at the courthouse, a large crowd had already assembled. Among them were Sir Percy Sanderson, the British Consulate-General in New York, and the consulate's legal adviser, a Mr Fox, who were there to keep a watching brief for the Official Receiver in London and, if necessary, to insist that Wright stay in jail. The prisoner remained silent as he was formally charged with fraudulently publishing a false company statement, leaving his American lawyer, Maurice Untermyer, to do the talking. The lawyer stated that his client was not a fugitive from justice and would personally prefer to take a steamer back to England immediately to answer the charges. On legal advice, however, he would wait for further action by the British authorities. Applying for bail, Untermyer said it was a 'gross injustice' to lock up the citizen of another country on the strength of a mere cablegram. Commissioner Alexander was unmoved and ruled that Wright must stay behind bars.

Later in the morning, Florence Brown also turned up at the courthouse. The detectives who had arrested Wright on *La Lorraine* the previous day had briefly examined her luggage before leaving her to her own devices. From the ship she had taken a cab to the Albemarle Hotel, overlooking Madison Square, and from there she had moved to the Hotel Kensington on 5th Avenue to avoid reporters. She gave every impression of relishing her notoriety as the 'mysterious young woman' who had accompanied the wanted man across the Atlantic. Carrying a Gladstone bag plastered with foreign labels, she walked briskly down 5th Avenue with reporters giving chase. 'The girl's skill in eluding her pursuers was something remarkable for an ingénue, and she appeared to take great enjoyment in throwing them off the track,' noted the *Rochester Democrat and Herald*.

Florence, it transpired, was on a mission. Like her uncle, she liked to live expensively. In need of funds, she appeared before Commissioner Alexander with a lawyer of her own and requested that the court hand over some of the cash found in Wright's wallet. No more wedded to the truth than her uncle, she claimed that £100 was her own money and that a further £500 had been entrusted to her by her aunt and that she had only lent it to Wright for safekeeping. 'The £500 is mine and cannot be taken from me because of Mr Wright's difficulties,' she argued. Taking a shine to Florence, the commissioner turned over £100 for her immediate needs because he was 'convinced that she had really saved it from her pocket money'. But that was the most he was prepared to give her.

Before the application, Florence had sat reading a newspaper outside the courtroom where she continued to attract considerable interest among the New York press. Tall and pretty, she was dressed in a dark-blue travelling dress and a white blouse. A black-and-white boa and broad-rimmed hat draped with a blue veil completed the ensemble. She looked like a woman who wanted to be noticed. If that was her intention, it worked. One reporter described her as having 'a pleasant face and trim figure'. Another wrote: 'She has a fairly apple blossom complexion, dark hair and large dark blue eyes, with strongly lined eyebrows. Her face is piquantly interesting and pretty, and her manner that of an unaffected gentlewoman.'

It was not only her looks that intrigued the pressmen. They were keen to know if this attractive young woman was really Wright's niece. Could it be, they wondered, that her relationship with the financier was of a more intimate nature? At first, she declined to say anything other than that she had come to America to visit friends in Philadelphia, but she was finally provoked into declaring: 'Yes, Brown is my real name, and I am Mr Wright's niece. Now, really, I don't care to go into family genealogy. It really is annoying to insist upon the actuality of one's identity.'

Asked if she was in possession of large amounts of money or securities belonging to Wright, she shot back:

Decidedly not. The idea that I have any large sums with me is ridiculous. I have nothing more than a few pounds for travelling expenses, and I do not believe Mr Wright had any very large amounts with him either. [The cash found in Wright's Wallet totalled the modern equivalent of £70,000.] Some of the English papers have intimated that we had millions of pounds or some such fabulous sum stored away in our trunks. It is not the custom of English people to travel with large sums.

She remained composed until a reporter claimed – falsely – that back in England Anna had denied that Florence was her husband's niece. 'She can't have said that,' she protested.

Her denials failed to dampen lurid conjecture in the press. 'She is a handsome young lady of some twenty-five summers,' noted the *Adelaide Advertiser* with more than a hint of prurience. 'Perhaps she really *is* Mr

Wright's niece.' Wright himself was so incensed by the insinuations that he felt compelled to issue a statement:

> My wife asked my niece to accompany me as she felt that in my con-
> dition – I had been ill in bed for two weeks – it was not right or
> altogether safe for me to travel alone. It is a cruel shame for anyone to
> say she is not what she purports to be, a highly respectable young lady.

At Tigbourne Court, an indignant Anna told reporters that she hoped Florence would get 'some redress' for the way she had been portrayed in the newspapers: 'The stories putting an unfavourable construction on her journey with my husband are cruel to both of us. Miss Brown accompanied Mr Wright with my full knowledge and consent. I am subject to heart trouble and could not go with him.' Asked if her husband was an American, she replied: 'I do not know. He has always been thoroughly English, much to my disgust. If he had been an American he would have been properly protected.' Professing to 'hate the English', she added:

> I want him back here to face these abominable charges whatever they
> are. If the British authorities had acted properly he would have been
> back here of his own free act before this, but he resents being brought
> here as a prisoner, and will resist it by every means possible.

There was considerable sympathy for Anna among the residents of Witley, even if some were surprised to learn that she was suffering from 'heart trouble' given her healthy appearance. Several sent messages expressing the hope that she would soon be reunited with her husband. Although she was hardly strapped for cash, her finances were

precarious, and shortly after Wright's arrest she was forced to leave
Tigbourne Court and move into a farmhouse – Lower House – on the
Lea Park estate. She told reporters that she was finding it difficult to
pay her bills and had sold some of her jewellery to defray her expenses.
In her husband's absence, she led a reclusive life and, like him, she
claimed to be suffering from insomnia. Despite her troubles, she found
time to pose for a studio photograph which appeared that month in *The
Tatler*. Her elegant evening dress and the fur stole draped across her arm
belied the impression of someone who was feeling the pinch.

In the wider world there were few who shared the hope in Witley that
Wright would soon be free again. John Flower kept up the pressure by
pouring scorn on Wright's claim that the Official Receiver's examination
had found his hands were clean. 'Nothing of the sort was ever said,' he
told reporters in London. He described the way in which Wright kept
dragging in the names of Lords Dufferin and Loch as 'cowardly', adding:
'He is trying to shield himself behind his dupes.' Like Arnold White,
Flower was a conspiracy theorist. He said that unnamed 'exalted personages' had been complicit in the downfall of Wright's empire and predicted
that his trial would be an 'extremely delicate' matter. Wright, he added
darkly, had in his possession 'letters from leading members of the English
royal family showing they were mixed up in his transactions'.

William Burchinell, the Denver speculator who had known Wright
in Leadville, was a rare voice of support. Tracked down by the *Denver
Republican*, he stated his belief in Wright's innocence and declared: 'His
explanations seem clear to me. I believe he lost honestly and that the
trial will come to nothing.' A less welcome appearance from the past
was a firm of Chicago brokers which served Wright with legal papers
in his prison cell in a bid to recover more than $2,000 they claimed he
owed them in respect of grain transactions in the 1880s.

There was more bad news for Wright when Sir Robert Finlay told the Commons that the Crown would not only meet the cost of his extradition, but would consider paying for the trial as well. Wright took this setback badly and declared himself to be unwell. On 19 March, he failed to attend a routine court hearing, complaining that he was too ill to leave his prison bed. In the hope of winning bail for his client, Untermyer told the court that Wright had not slept since his arrest and that fumes from the newly painted walls of his cell had brought on bronchitis. Piling on the agony, he added that Wright was unable to eat, that he had a severe chill and was threatened with pneumonia. His plea for bail was rejected, as was his application to have the case thrown out on the grounds that it was 'frivolous'.

Wright's next move was to offer to return to England of his own accord. He cabled the Official Receiver: 'Not being a fugitive from justice, if you will order extradition proceedings to be stopped, British consul may see me on board steamer for Southampton, on condition that I should not be arrested on arrival, but allowed to proceed to the court voluntarily.' Barnes had no interest in striking bargains. Turning down the offer, he made it plain he wanted Wright brought back as a criminal. In response, Wright sent him an angry letter in which he claimed he had gone on his 'long-contemplated' trip abroad only after he had been assured by his lawyer that Flower's application to have him prosecuted could not succeed. Seething with the righteous indignation he had become expert at projecting, he went on:

> I could not be expected to await the pleasure of Mr John Flower and his allies for ever, so I started on my trip. It is an infamous lie that I travelled under any name but my own, or that I brought with me more money than was necessary for my proposed journey, but it appears

that there is no finality to this persecution. It was quite unnecessary, however, to issue any warrant for my apprehension. I had only to be notified of the fact that further proceedings had been ordered to make my arrangements to come and meet them. I have never turned my back to the enemy, and I shall not do so now. I do think, however, that a hint might have been conveyed to me to expect the eventuality that happened, and I should therefore have been saved the pain and humiliation that I have suffered since my arrival here. This, however, I have no doubt will gratify Messrs Flower & Co, whose malice knows no bounds. Not the least of these wicked and malicious mis-representations is the statement that I have claimed to be protected by distinguished directors and exalted personages, behind whom I seek to screen myself. This is an infamous lie. You and all others concerned, from start to finish, know that I have never on any occasion whatever sought to relieve myself from any responsibility by attempting to put any part of it on others' shoulders.

Still saddled firmly on his high horse, Wright gave a revealing interview in his prison cell to a reporter from the *Washington Evening Star*:

Half of England is hankering to see me working on a sea break-water, in ooze and slime up to my waist. I'll just mention here and now that they'll never see me in that somewhat damp and clammy situation. It was only a little while ago, when shares in one of my mines jumped from a shilling (5p) to £30 [this was presumably an exaggerated reference to Lake View], that my English shareholders regarded me as a gorgeous fellow. Then I was the cleverest chap in the whole British Empire, you know. I was, as you say, 'all right, all right.' I was the greatest public benefactor ever. Then the output of the mine

suddenly slumped and, shortly, ceased altogether. Well, the change in
the attitude toward me would have seemed absurd had it not meant
my actual ruin. They began to call me a blood-sucking vampire, then.
I was the robber of the widow and the orphan, the enemy of little
English homes. I was trying to chuck all middle-class England into
the workhouse. I was a sybaritic deceiver of the poor and lowly. They
didn't stop to reflect that I could have got out from under during
three straight years with a clean profit to myself of from £15 million to £20 million. It made no difference to them that I went down
with the structure I had built up and to which I admitted them on
shilling terms.

Wright's protestations failed to win him any sympathy. Extradition
papers arrived from London on 6 April and proceedings began at once
to have him brought back to England. The hearings dragged on into the
summer and, whether through exhaustion or boredom, he slept through
most of them. A New York court found against him in May, and its
ruling was affirmed by the Supreme Court at the end of June. Refusing
to grant a writ of habeas corpus, Chief Justice Melville Fuller said that
the Companies Act of Great Britain had its equivalent in the penal code
of New York and that the offence was extraditable:

The British statute punishes the making, circulating or publishing
with intent to deceive or defraud, of false statements or accounts of
a body corporate or public company known to be false, by a director,
manager or public officer thereof. The New York statute provides
that if an officer or director of a corporation knowingly concurs in
making or publishing any written report, exhibit or statement of its
affairs or pecuniary condition, containing any material statement

which is false, he is guilty of a misdemeanour. The two statutes are substantially analogous.

Untermyer wanted to fight on, but Wright had had enough. Still convinced that he would never be found guilty in a British court, he threw in the towel and decided to return to England voluntarily. In a cable to the Official Receiver, he again affected the air of a wronged man:

> After four months of vain effort to have my own way, I have finally succeeded in my insistence on returning to meet charges. Eminent counsel here are of the opinion that the offence charged is not extra-ditable, but it would take a year's time to decide that question. As I am innocent I shall hasten home to prove my innocence.

His return to England could not be effected immediately, and he remained locked up in Ludlow Street Jail for several more days. If there was one thing on his conscience, he told a reporter, it was that his absence from home had interrupted his plans for the 'coming out' of his elder daughter, Gladys, and her presentation at court to the King. In a further bid to win him bail, Untermyer produced evidence from Dr Wilhelm Lavigne, the prison physician, that Wright had only months to live if he stayed locked up. According to Lavigne, he was not only suffering from kidney trouble but risked 'succumbing to heart trouble or apoplexy'. Lavigne's report, the wording of which closely resembled Wright's own style of writing, added:

> Mr Wright's determination and courage alone have kept him going. During the recent intense heat he was on the verge of apoplexy. For two days an ice pack was constantly kept about his head and cold baths

were given every two hours. The attacks of vertigo he experienced have been the most serious feature of his condition. Four months of imprisonment here have taken ten years from his life.

A report in the *San Francisco Chronicle* on 4 July suggested that Wright's condition had deteriorated so rapidly that he was on the verge of death.

Wright lies on his cot in a dingy cell suffering from vertigo. Tonight his condition was so serious that the prison doctor had to be called. He said the patent would not recover. Since his transfer to Ludlow Street he has seen no one but the doctors and his keepers. For the last three days he has stayed in bed.

Commissioner Alexander was unmoved by the medical reports and again ordered that Wright must remain behind bars. Back in London, Detective Inspector Willis was determined that this time there should be no hitches. To this end he and his colleague, DI Phillips, sailed from Liverpool to New York on the White Star Liner *Oceanic* to take charge of Wright themselves and bring him back to England. Arriving at Ludlow Street Jail, Willis was surprised to find the prisoner far from 'the verge of death', but relaxing in a 'cosy apartment'. Wright – and Willis could not help admiring him for it – had somehow managed to acquire the use of the head janitor's self-contained flat.

With his love of the theatrical, Wright made the most of the moment. 'Good morning, Willis,' he said. 'Do sit down.' Then he rang a bell, called for a bottle of wine 'off the ice' and filled a glass for the detective. 'It's a pity you got me here today,' he went on impishly. 'Had you been a day or so later, I should have been up country. You would have followed me, of course, but you could have joined me in a little shooting before we started for England.' Apparently no longer suffering from vertigo, kidney trouble or from any of his other reported ailments, Wright pointed out of the window to a courtyard below where he claimed to have effected a dramatic transformation. Willis recalled:

> The courtyard was covered with a lawn as green and as flat as a billiards table cloth. In the centre was a pigeon-loft full of well-bred birds, and Wright asked me what I thought of the vista from his window, remarking that it was he who had brought about the change from a dreary stone-flagged yard to the verdant lawn and pigeonry.

Having shown off his handiwork to Willis, Wright went on a farewell tour of the prison, shaking hands with the wardens and saying that he hoped to return one day and pay them a social visit. It was a bold performance, but for all his conviviality the prisoner looked tired and pale as he boarded the *Oceanic* for the voyage to England. According to the prison doctor, he was in a 'highly nervous state'. There were dark circles around his eyes, and he walked with a stoop. The detectives observed that he had grown an iron-grey beard and had lost some twenty pounds in weight. He seemed depressed, but his spirits revived once the ship was out at sea. A state room had been assigned to him, but he demanded better accommodation, and managed to obtain a suite of three rooms on the promenade deck. He took regular walks along the saloon promenade, mingling with the other passengers and smoking cigars. He ate well and began to put on weight. Still intent on heaping the blame for the Globe disaster on others, he told a *Daily Mail* reporter who had booked a passage on the *Oceanic*:

> The great mistake that I made was in having too child-like confidence in others, in being too trustful, especially in regard to the big

operations which brought down the company. In our exploration and mining operations we were charged to carry on large operations in various parts of the world, and had in many cases to put absolute trust in others. It was impossible for me to be at both ends of the line. I shall never be convicted. My trial is uppermost in my mind. I must clear my name for the sake of my family. In any case, you can take it from me that I shall never serve a day of any possible sentence.

Inspector Willis, who monitored the interview, was struck by Wright's final sentence. He had heard him speak in similar terms to some of the passengers, and was sufficiently concerned to warn his superiors in London that Wright might attempt suicide if convicted and imprisoned. His observation was duly noted and quickly forgotten. For the next few days, Wright remained in a seemingly cheerful mood, but when the ship neared Queenstown on the south coast of Ireland he holed himself up in his suite and refused to see anyone except the detectives. He stayed there until the ship docked at Liverpool early in the morning of 4 August. It was his first sight of England for 160 days.

He appeared to be back to his old self when, wearing a bowler hat and a blue reefer suit, he left the *Oceanic* clutching a leather document case and walked to Riverside Railway Station flanked by the detectives. There he handed in several telegrams before boarding the boat train to London and settling down in a first-class compartment. A reporter managed to grab a few words with him before the train departed.

Q: You seem very light-hearted, Mr Wright.
Wright: Yes, yes. Why shouldn't I be?
Q: But you are coming back to answer very serious charges.

Wright: I don't fear their charges. You can say that others will be fortunate if they feel as happy as I do.

Q: May I take it, Mr Wright, that you have a complete answer to the allegations made against you?

Wright: Certainly, certainly. My hands are as clean as those of a newborn child.

Q: You do seem in good spirits, Mr Wright.

Wright: Why not? My conscience is clear.

Q: And you are sanguine you will be able to clear yourself?

Wright: I wish I was as sure of Heaven as I am that I should clear myself of the unjust allegations made against me.

A large crowd was waiting on the platform at Euston Station to gawp at Wright when he stepped off the train at lunchtime. Pushing through the throng, Willis and Phillips escorted him onto an omnibus and delivered him to the Guildhall police court. There he was formally charged with publishing a false balance sheet with intent to deceive or defraud. Wright had used his time in jail to gather together a formidable legal team, and they were waiting for him at the court to lead him through the initial proceedings. His defence counsel was Richard 'Dickie' Muir, one of the great barristers of the day, with a strong fighting spirit and the ability to inspire fear during cross-examination. He felt honoured to have been entrusted with the case, because he had previously done little or no important work outside the criminal courts. He had, however, achieved a reputation for mastery of detail and thoroughness, and Wright's solicitor believed it would be hard to find a better man. Muir's biographer, Sidney Felstead, wrote of him: 'He took his stand on cold, hard facts and there can be but few men who have succeeded in acquiring such a reputation for inflexible administration of the law … He possessed peculiar qualifications only to be found once in a generation.' In 1910, when the notorious Dr Crippen heard that Muir had been briefed to conduct the prosecution against him, he remarked to his solicitor: 'It is most unfortunate that he is against me. I wish it had been anybody else but him. I fear the worst.' Crippen duly went to the gallows.

The solicitor Wright retained for the case was Sir George Lewis, arguably the most famous lawyer in England, and certainly one of the most adept. 'Lewis would play the game of the law with all the skill he could command, even though he might be fighting for someone whose conduct he deplored,' wrote his biographer, John Juxon. 'But to let his personal opinion of a client colour his judgement would have struck Lewis as mere self-indulgence ... thus he often appeared to be "on the wrong side", championing a perjurer like Mrs Crawford or a swindler like Whitaker Wright.' Oscar Wilde, who found himself up against Lewis in his notorious libel action against the Marquess of Queens-berry, said of him: 'George Lewis? Brilliant. Formidable. Concerned in every great case in England.'

Sitting in the well of the court, Wright showed no emotion as Muir and Lewis began earning their fees. Applying for bail, Muir told the court that he deplored the suggestion 'promulgated by the baser class of newspaper' that his client had confessed his guilt by 'absconding' to New York. Wright, he said, had simply decided to start a new business life in America. Although it was unusual for a fugitive brought back on an extradition warrant to be released before trial, the application was successful, and the magistrate allowed bail in the unprecedented sum of £50,000, half to come from Wright and half from others. The money could not be raised immediately, and Wright had to spend four nights in Brixton Prison while four trusting friends were found to put up £25,000 between them.

Got him! Wright leaves the Oceanic *at Liverpool in the custody of Detective Inspector John Willis.*

One person who was unhappy that Wright had been granted bail was his nemesis, the journalist Arnold White. He had anticipated this would happen and had campaigned against it, even though the case was *sub judice*. Two days before Wright arrived back in Britain, he had written in the *Sunday Sun*:

> On the theory that the law is the same for the rich and for the poor in this country, it is inconceivable that Henry Golding, the labourer who was recently sentenced at Colchester Sessions to six months' hard labour for stealing boots, would obtain bail. Clara Walkley, a barmaid, on Friday was sentenced to three months' hard labour for stealing money from her employer. Why should Whitaker Wright be granted that which would be denied to Clara? Unlike Henry Golding, the labourer who had served in the African War, Whitaker Wright has not risked his life for his country. On the question of bail, therefore, I am obdurate. I have taken all steps that lie in my power to prevent Whitaker Wright being admitted to bail.

Wright at the Guildhall police court, as depicted by Pall Mall Gazette *illustrator Ernest Prater.*

The Lord Chief Justice, Baron Alverstone, took a dim view of the article when White was hauled before him accused of contempt of court. Ruling that the article was 'a direct assault on anybody allowing Whitaker Wright bail', and that it 'virtually assumed the prisoner's guilt', he fined the journalist £100. White refused to pay and was hauled off to jail, coincidentally arriving at Brixton Prison moments after Wright had been released from his cell on bail. His supporters subsequently paid the fine on his behalf and he was allowed to go free.

Wright was at last able to return to his family. As the leaves yellowed at Lea Park, he maintained his usual air of unconcern, vowing that this time he would stay in the country and fight his corner. Not that he had much choice in the matter. Inspector Willis had placed detectives at strategic points around Witley to ensure he did not do another bunk. Those peaceful summer days did not last for long. Committal proceedings began before Mr Alderman Smallman at the Guildhall three weeks later, and were concluded in late November, clearing the way for a full-blown trial in the New Year. Smallman's barbed comment that the case served as 'a solemn warning to persons of high position against lending their names to commercial enterprises of which they had no particular knowledge and in which they become the prey of wicked men' appeared to leave Wright unmoved. As Christmas approached, he remained confident that he would emerge from his trial a free man.

CHAPTER SEVENTEEN

A BALL OR A FUNERAL

Early on, Muir decided that a trial at the Old Bailey would not be in Wright's best interests. He knew Old Bailey juries well. He was worried that they would be confused by the financial complexities of the case and not listen to the arguments. They would find Wright guilty because he had fled the country and because a lot of people had lost a lot of money. A fair trial would be impossible. Wright was all too aware that his escapade with Florence looked bad. He agreed with Muir that it had fostered prejudice in the public mind. 'I was a fool to run away,' he admitted during a meeting in the latter's chambers.

To level out the playing field Muir applied to have the case heard in the Civil Law Courts in the Strand. He believed that a special jury of professional and propertied men guided by a Chancery judge with an intimate knowledge of the Stock Exchange would be better able to grapple with the intricacies of the trial. Consent was several weeks coming, but eventually the Attorney-General granted the application, and the action was set down in the list of Mr Justice Bigham.

The trial judge, Sir John Bigham (left) *continually poked fun at Wright. Prosecuting counsel Rufus Isaacs* (right © GETTY IMAGES) *was 'a loaded blunderbuss' who was turned against Wright with deadly effect.*

Muir considered the case to be the most formidable of his career, and he was relieved to have crossed this initial hurdle. But there was no room for complacency, not least because the prosecution had had an inordinate amount of time to gather evidence. That said, he was convinced of Wright's innocence. He was sure that if he had stayed in England he would have sailed through the trial and would have merely stood before the world as a failed financier. During their many long meetings, he took a considerable liking to his client and was in no doubt that he would stand up well under cross-examination. Even the most skilled of interrogators, he felt sure, would find it difficult to spear this slippery fish. Dedicated to clearing Wright's name, Muir worked on the case in his chambers day and night for weeks on end, never wavering from the view that his client would be acquitted. His biographer wrote:

He believed from the very beginning that Whitaker Wright had been more a victim of his own foolish vanity than of any criminal intent.

His head had been turned by the unending adulation he received in the highest circles of the land and, furthermore, there could be no doubt at all that there were other people who should have been arrested with him.

Muir was not alone in anticipating a 'not guilty' verdict. Even before the trial began, the villagers of Witley began planning a torchlight procession with music by the local Mouse Hill Band to celebrate Wright's acquittal. A triumphal arch was to be erected outside Witley Station on his return from London, and they intended to unhorse his carriage and haul him home themselves in a glorious rebuff to those who had subjected the Lord of the Manor to such a cruel ordeal. At Lower House, a defiant Anna told the *Daily Mail*: 'I am sorry we ever set eyes on England or planted our feet on English soil.' Then, with what the paper described as a 'queenly sweep' of the trailing skirt of her blue silk gown, she added: 'Ah, but he will clear himself. I know he will.'

The trial opened on Monday 11 January 1904 in Court No. 8 of the King's Bench Division of the Royal Courts of Justice. Wright had by now grown more sanguine about his prospects. 'It will either be a ball or a funeral,' he told his legal team that morning. Keen-eyed and heavy of step, he entered the courtroom shortly before 11 a.m. dressed in the flowing frock coat and tall starched collar of a City mogul. His hair had grown greyer over the winter and he had trimmed his beard into a pointed goatee known as an imperial. His resemblance to his erstwhile friend King Edward VII was striking and perhaps intentional. In happier times it was an image that might have impressed investors and awed the public, but it cannot have played well with the jury. With his bull neck, his florid face, his expensively attired corpulent body and his over-confident manner, he was the embodiment of hedonistic tycoonery.

Harry Furniss, a former *Punch* illustrator who spent an hour in the packed public gallery creating an unflattering pen-and-ink drawing of Wright, wrote of him: 'The arrangement of the beard and moustache gives a likeness to another public character – Colonel Cody of "Buffalo Bill" fame. Here is the contrast … Col. Cody is one of the handsomest men I ever met, while Whitaker Wright was one of the ugliest.'

Since it was a civil court, Wright was spared the indignity of the dock and was allowed to sit with his legal advisers below the bench. As an added concession, he was given the use of an ante-room beneath the court where he could consult with his legal team and dine in private. Still the high-living plutocrat, he had instructed a servant from his Whitehall apartment to deliver plates of cold meats to him each lunchtime. The courtroom – small and gloomy, with oak-panelled walls that absorbed much of the light that came through the windows and skylight – was packed. The public gallery was full to overflowing and could only accommodate half of those who sought admittance. At times it was suffocatingly hot. Wright's family stayed away (and, with the exception of his son, would do so for the rest of the trial), but there were plenty of familiar faces. Sitting not far from Wright in the well of the court were the instigators of the prosecution, John Flower and Arnold White. Close by sat Inspector Willis. Lawyers, reporters, stenographers and court officers vied with each other for the remaining space. The tables in front of the legal teams were piled high with documents and books. The ushers had to sit on boxes of exhibits if they wanted to rest their feet. The *Sheffield Daily Telegraph* remarked on the high proportion of female spectators in the gallery. 'The extraordinary number of fashionably dressed ladies present is a conspicuous feature of the Whitaker Wright trial. Mr Justice Bigham's court is crowded all day, the back of the court and the gallery above being gay with feminine toilette.'

And so it began. On that first morning, Wright appeared eager for the proceedings to get under way, but for all his composure, he must have felt a creeping anxiety. The team of lawyers lined up against him was formidable and it did not help that the judge was hostile to him from the start. Although Sir John Bigham was not regarded in legal circles as having the finest of judicial brains, he was quick and clever, and he had a powerful grasp of the principles of commercial law. Eight years on, as Lord Mersey, he would achieve public prominence when he led the Board of Trade inquiry into the sinking of RMS *Titanic*. (Asked why he took the title of 'Mersey', he is supposed to have replied that he would leave the Atlantic for his fellow Liverpudlian, the brilliant F. E. Smith.) In court, he was prone to taking short cuts and had a tendency to be brusque and overbearing. The bias he sometimes exhibited against defendants was never more obvious than in Wright's trial. His obituary in *The Times* a quarter of a century later would note:

> It was easy to see the drift of the Judge's mind ... it was a matter of common observation that Bigham showed hostility to the accused from the outset, and he drew from John Lawson Walton, who was leading for the defence, an unusual protest on the ground that the Judge had raised the laughter of the gallery against his client.

By turns flippant and sarcastic, Bigham continually poked fun at Wright. On one occasion, referring to a piece of paper being held aloft by the prosecution, he remarked: 'Is that a minute of a meeting that was never held?' Of a block of shares sold to Standard, he said contemptuously: '£25,000! That is a mere bagatelle in this case.' And when a witness said Wright had prophesied that the market would 'rise more and more', Bigham put in sarcastically: 'And at the end of the month there was a slump?'

It was when one of his asides drew merriment from the public that Lawson Walton was driven to remonstrate: 'I do protest … it is embarrassing to counsel to have ridicule from the gallery.' The judge stood his ground: 'I think it better to tell both you and Mr Wright what is passing through my mind.' Lawson Walton and Bigham again crossed swords when the judge expressed the opinion that 'no such letter existed'. Lawson Walton replied: 'Your Lordship with all respect is indulging in a vivid imagination.' At other times Bigham was simply short with Wright, as when he told him: 'I wish you would not make statements which are not relevant to the questions, and are simply to confuse us.' Of a large cash sum in Globe's bank account in December 1900, he said tersely: 'It may be what you may call justifiable window dressing, though I do not like it. Or it may be a scheme to throw dust in the eyes of shareholders.' (Bigham is credited in dictionaries of slang with having brought the term 'window dressing' into prominence as a metaphor for the manipulation of figures and accounts to show fictitious or exaggerated value.)

If the scarlet-robed judge was captious, the prosecution team was deadly. The philosopher Thomas Carlyle said a barrister was a loaded blunderbuss: if you hire it you blow out the other man's brains; if *he* hires it he blows out *yours*. As it happened, Sir George Lewis had initially tried to hire the brilliant Rufus Isaacs as the 'blunderbuss' for Wright's defence, but he was too late. The Crown had got there first. Now that same blunderbuss was to be turned against Wright. Isaacs (later the 1st Marquess of Reading) was the son of a fruit merchant and had served as a ship's boy and a jobber on the Stock Exchange before carving out a career in the law. He was experienced in complex financial cases and could not be blinded by science – or by daybooks and ledgers. He had a head for figures, could 'read' a balance sheet and had an outstanding ability to translate esoteric jargon into everyday language. He was a cross-examiner of terrier-like tenacity, with a mind that homed in on the core of an issue with deadly accuracy. He was a kindly man, which made him reluctant to appear in criminal cases, but when he did so he always became a master of detail. It was not his style to bludgeon a defendant who had his back to the wall. Instead, there might be a moment of silence, or perhaps a glance at the jury, before he moved on. His powers of concentration were so great that it was said he could ask a question in cross-examination with the answer he had in view six questions ahead. Margot Asquith, wife of the future Prime Minister H. H. Asquith, described him as one of the four most ambitious men she had ever known. His biographer, Sir Derek Walker-Smith, wrote of him:

> Learned in law, quick and resourceful in argument, penetrative in cross-examination, he had the indispensable adjuncts of forensic success. In addition he was possessed of a memory quite out of the ordinary and a capacity to unravel and elucidate the intricate mysteries of figures, which was unrivalled; in cases like that of Whitaker Wright he was in a class by himself.

Isaacs's son, Gerald, said of him:

> Very quiet, very courteous, rarely raising his voice, he never resorted to browbeating, though he could be severe enough if the need arose. Nor did he ever lose his temper or give the appearance of being ruffled by a witness, however insolent or obdurate. His tactics were never to bludgeon his man, but to lead him gently and politely to destruction … a witness, feeling that this suave and soft-voiced person could not possibly be dangerous, would follow him confidently down the paths

he indicated and would only realise when it was too late the pitfalls that awaited him in the end.

Isaacs's opening speech that Monday morning was consummate. His first task was to familiarise the jury with a host of different companies and their illustrious boards of directors, and to explain how they interlocked with one another. Then he outlined the nub of the case: were Globe's balance sheets and reports for 1899 and 1900 false in material particulars? Were they were false to Wright's knowledge? If so, had they been published for the purpose of deceiving shareholders, defrauding creditors or inducing others to become shareholders? 'If the facts which I propose to put before you are true, it would be scandalous if they did not constitute a criminal offence,' he declared.

On that first day he was on his feet for five hours as he shone a hard-white light through the dense fog of financial transactions that underlay the prosecution's case. Moving smoothly through the complex network of ledgers and amalgamations, he tossed millions of pounds around the court in capital percentages, dividends and loans, with tails in shillings and pence. In all that time he barely once referred to his notes. First to come under scrutiny was Globe's 'cash at bank' figure of £534,455 in the balance sheet for the year ended 30 September 1899. The sum itself was not in dispute. The question was, how had it got there, when twenty-four hours earlier the cash balance had been a mere £89,000? Step by step, Isaacs showed how smoke and mirrors had been used to boost the figure by £445,455 in the course of a single day. Globe, for instance, had sold a large holding of Lake View shares to its sister company, Standard, on 29 September. The shares had exchanged hands at £23 when their market price was only £8. The effect had been to swell Globe's cash balance by £158,424 just in time for the annual report. Afterwards, as the shareholders congratulated themselves on being investors in such a sound concern, Globe had quietly bought back the Lake View holdings. This, said Isaacs cuttingly, was an instance of the 'sound and conservative policy' of which the directors of the Globe were so proud.

Other tricks of the trade had boosted the balance further, but the inflated figure was not in itself the main issue. What really mattered, said Isaacs, were the claims Wright had made about it. He had told the shareholders 'that the cash balance was the best evidence of the prosperity of the company, and that it could have been used to declare a dividend of 25 per cent or even more'. The implication of this statement was clear. Since dividends could only be paid out of profits, he was inferring that the 'cash at bank' sum represented a year of profitable trading. Not, as was actually the case, a day of juggling with the figures.

Isaacs next turned to the 1900 balance sheet. Its postponement from 30 September to 5 December had enabled Globe to convert a loss of £1.6 million into a profit of £432,672. Again, it was all down to sleight of hand. Losses on Lake View Consols, for instance, had been switched into the accommodating books of Standard. The value of other shares held by Globe had been grossly written up. Just one man was responsible for these shenanigans. Wright, said Isaacs, was the 'god in the machine of the three holding companies'. He was 'the ruling spirit from the beginning to the end of the transactions ... the business was always done by the same hand and head ... [H]e himself signed every one of the cheques circulating between the companies.' Isaacs went on:

The London and Globe balance sheet presented to the world at large, to the shareholders and to the creditors a state of things which was absolutely false, and that must have been done with the knowledge of Mr Wright ... there is clear evidence of false balance sheets which could only have been made with intent to defraud … it is inconceivable that any lawyer with the evidence in this case before him should come to any other view than a criminal offence has been committed.

The jury took copious notes while Isaacs was on his feet, and sometimes looked puzzled. Isaacs advised them to 'concentrate your attention on the salient points of the case and not allow yourselves to be diverted into the bye-paths of finance'. By the time he had finished threading his way through the maze of financial dealings, there was a marked change in the atmosphere of the court. Even if they had failed to grasp some of the finer points, the jurors were left with the clear impression that Globe's apparent profits were the result of skulduggery. In particular, the revelation that by the time of Globe's collapse, Wright had offloaded all but 2,503 of his 389,575 Globe shares, using the proceeds to acquire property holdings in and around London, did not play well with them. Wright's team were well aware that Isaacs had scored several direct hits. Sir George Lewis later described his speech as one of the most masterly he had ever heard. Isaacs's biographer wrote:

An advocate less versed in financial affairs could not have found his way with sure enough step through the maze of figures and manipulations; an advocate more temperamental would certainly have given way to irritation. But self-discipline, calmness, and clarity of mind were always foremost in Rufus Isaacs's armoury of qualities.

Wright, too, realised that Isaacs had made a strong impression on the jury, but he remained calm and self-assured as he left the court at the end of that first day. He returned to his apartment at Whitehall Court with a Witley friend, John Eyre, a retired barrister who had stood surety for him. The two had dinner and stayed up until midnight discussing the case. They fell into this routine almost every night until the end of the trial. Wright was far from down-hearted during that first evening. He told Eyre: 'When they hear my side of the story it will be a different matter.'

CHAPTER EIGHTEEN

HOMERIC CONTEST

On the second day of the trial, the court was again packed. Isaacs handed the baton to Horace Avory KC, another formidable barrister with a reputation for being 'cold, utterly unemotional, humourless and relentless'. The strain began to show on Wright's face as Avory, who had been instrumental in securing the conviction of Jabez Balfour, took the prosecution witnesses through their paces. Their individual testimony did not amount to much in isolation, but painted a damaging picture when combined. Wright followed the proceedings intently, taking notes and turning every now and then to whisper to his lawyers. Some of the evidence caused him to shake his head and mutter under his breath. At times he pulled nervously at his beard or fiddled with the rings on his fingers. More than once he was seen to mop his brow with a handkerchief in the stifling atmosphere.

The questioning of the witnesses went on for five days. Edgar Waterlow, whose firm had printed Globe's company reports and balance sheets, said he had noticed alterations on the proofs in Wright's handwriting, including the addition of the words 'balance of profits available for dividends' in the profit and loss account, and the words 'Hear Hear' during reports of speeches. A secretary, John Hyam, described taking minutes at Wright's dictation of a so-called board meeting convened without notice in the Globe lunchroom at which only Wright and one other director had been present. Herbert Peppercorn, solicitor to the late Lord Dufferin, produced notes which showed that Wright had written the bulk of Dufferin's speeches to shareholders. Arthur Russell, the Official Receiver's senior examiner, said Globe's reported assets of £2,332,632 in the 1900 accounts had actually been worth less than half that. Several Globe shareholders maintained that they had been influenced to buy shares because of the 'rosy description' of Globe's prospects painted by Wright and by Lords Dufferin and Loch. Occasionally there were moments of light relief, as when Philip Gangloff, manager of the Le Havre shipping agency, Compagnie Générale Transatlantique, described selling two first-class tickets on *La Lorraine* to Wright and Florence Brown.

Counsel: (pointing at Wright): Can you say whether this gentleman is the gentleman who called with the lady?
Gangloff: I can't remember.
Judge: Perhaps you took more notice of the lady.

As the week wore on, the proceedings became increasingly dry and the public gallery was at times nearly empty. Some of the evidence was so technical that even the judge was forced to admit: 'I do not profess to be able to understand all these exchanges of shares.' Wright himself began to look down-hearted and at times appeared unwell. It was not until the Tuesday of the second week – the seventh day of the trial – that he entered the witness box. This was the moment the press and public had been waiting for, and once again the court was packed. John Lawson Walton, who had been primed by Richard Muir to lead for the defence, rose to examine his client. Wright was pleased to have him on his side. Dignified, lucid and persuasive, the 51-year-old KC was highly respected at both the Bar and in the House of Commons, where he sat as a Liberal MP. His early legal career had been boosted by his close association with the Methodist Church in the West Riding of Yorkshire, which may have been one reason why Wright put his faith in him.

Lawson Walton began by telling the court that his client had been ill over the weekend and suggested that Wright might like to sit while giving evidence. The defendant insisted he was happy to stand. As he leaned forward with his arms on the box and a sheaf of papers at his side, he almost seemed to be enjoying himself, speaking loudly and confidently as if addressing a shareholders' meeting. Two days' rest at Witley had revived him, and he was back to his old self after a nervous end to the previous week. All eyes were on him as he fielded a series of straightforward questions about his career. He provided a brief, sanitised account of his activities in Philadelphia, and boasted of the early successes of his companies in London. Shareholders in the West Australian Exploring and Finance Corporation, he said, had got their money back five times over in cash or shares. The same went for the shareholders of the original London and Globe. All his business transactions, he insisted, had been above board. It was true that he had sent notes to Lord Dufferin for his speeches, but what was odd about that? He believed it to be 'a very common thing in the City for such notes to be prepared for the chairman'.

The questioning turned to Globe's contentious balance sheets. He was in deeper waters here, but he was still swimming strongly, a model of competence and imperturbability. There was nothing wrong with the 1899 balance sheet, he asserted. Stupid misinterpretations had been made by uninformed people. He had merely wanted to bolster Globe at a time of crisis by converting its assets into cash, and had done so with transactions 'not one of which were illegitimate, but happened every fortnight in the City'. As for the 1900 balance sheet, the accountants were responsible for this, not he, and the document had not been submitted to him before it was completed. There was no concealment.

He managed to give the impression throughout that if anything untoward had happened it was someone else's fault. Nothing was ever done without the unanimous agreement of the directors and any errors were down to the accountants. 'I'm not a walking ledger,' he insisted. If there were other mistakes, they were attributable to the mining engineers in Australia who had given him false information. 'There are people who ought to be here instead of me,' he declared.

It was a polished and composed performance, if a little too pat. His air was that of a benevolent autocrat whose good intentions had been misunderstood and who, if only he had been allowed to do so, could have restored his companies to their former state of health. At times he appeared *de haut en bas*, as if striving to explain simple matters to an ignorant audience. 'It is so simple,' he said from time to time. 'You call it simple!' the judge retorted on one occasion. 'Well, it is simple to me,' replied Wright. The occasionally condescending way in which he portrayed himself as a professional in a roomful of amateurs risked antagonising the jury. At times he came close to embodying a toxic cocktail of over-confidence and tone-deaf delivery, but when the examination finished at the end of the day there was a sense in the courtroom that the defendant was on the front foot again. He returned to his apartment that night hopeful that the jury was now firmly on his side. Rufus Isaacs's biographer wrote of the exchange between the defendant and his barrister:

As question and answer passed between them, WW leaning forward almost confidentially and Lawson Walton with his air of quiet, un-hurried certainty, it seemed almost as if the old infallibility had never been challenged; for it appeared not like an examination in court, but like a conversation between two experienced business men in which WW was telling Lawson Walton just what had happened, and what stupid misinterpretations had been made by uninformed persons.

Isaacs, too, was impressed and believed that Wright would be a difficult opponent in cross-examination. He was aware that 'any slips or hesitancy on his part would afford a contemptuous triumph to the infallible WW'. As he rose to question Wright on the Wednesday of the second week, he was supremely well prepared. The cross-examination promised to be excellent sport – two formidable adversaries grappling at the Reichen-bach Falls – and once again the public gallery was packed. In the words of Isaacs's biographer, it was 'a true Homeric contest'. The protagonists provided a bizarre contrast: Isaacs, 'pale, slender, fine drawn with quick movements of head and hand, calm and dispassionate'; Wright, stocky and bull-like, 'with a head disproportionately large even for his massive body', but still imposing and self-confident.

The diminutive KC began with a simple but penetrating set of questions. Why had Wright run away? Why had he done so under an assumed name? Why had he asked his niece to bring £500 from Eng-land? And was it just a coincidence that on the morning he bought tickets for New York he received a telegram from his wife saying that things were going badly?

An indignant Wright denied there had been anything out of the or-dinary about his actions. If he had wanted to flee the country, he would have done so two years earlier. He knew but 'did not care tuppence' about the application before Mr Justice Buckley to have him prosecuted. He had used the name Andreoni because it had been easier to get a berth on a foreign ship using a foreign name. The £500 was for his niece's expenses. And the telegram from Anna? It was 'the telegram of a nervous woman. I never asked for a telegram to be sent. I'll admit anything you say, Mr Isaacs, but I will not have my motives misconstrued.' Sir George Lewis, sitting next to Wright, glanced at the jurors and could see they were not impressed.

Isaacs turned to the payments that had passed to and fro between Wright's companies. 'You received all this money as chairman of one company from yourself as chairman of another?' Wright tried to look unconcerned. He leaned back on the rail behind him. 'I do not like that way of putting it,' he retorted. 'The money was paid by one company to another.' It was a weak answer, and it sparked laughter in the public gallery.

He faced ridicule again when Isaacs pressed him about the added 'hear hears' in the written report of one of Lord Dufferin's speeches. 'He deserved it,' was Wright's justification. 'I didn't put any ["hear hears"] against my own remarks.' Again, there was laughter. Later Wright was driven to say: 'I protest at this giggling in the gallery by people who do not seem to know what we are talking about.'

Isaacs pressed on. He demanded to know why Wright had been at such pains to inject cash into Globe's 1899 balance sheet. Wright replied that the accounts were 'as straight as a die' and insisted that there had been no attempt to misrepresent or mislead. There had been treachery at the mines and the underground railway was eating up cash. The money was needed to keep the company afloat. 'You will never get me to the crack of doom to admit that there is anything the matter with the 1899 balance sheet.' To which Isaacs responded: 'I quite appreciate the impossibility of the task.' More laughter.

The lawyer turned to a payment made by Globe to Brit-Am. It was for £250,000 but had been recorded as £500,000 on the balance sheet. Wright's answer was a fudge:

Wright: I never made up the accounts, or the balance sheet, and I never thought anything about it.

Judge: Never thought about it? Why, it involved £250,000.

Wright: Well, I did not.

Judge: You must have had very weighty matters to think of.

Wright: If you knew, my lord, all I have to do with all these things on my shoulders.

Isaacs: The cash was placed there to impress the shareholders…

Wright: I am not responsible for the inferences the shareholders may draw.

When Isaacs challenged Wright over Globe's failure to record transactions in the minutes, Wright snapped back: 'I was not responsible for the minutes. Would counsel like me to be chairman and secretary and everything?' 'No, I think you were quite enough,' shot back Isaacs to more laughter. Counsel had gained the upper hand and with each new line of interrogation he consolidated his position. Occasionally Horace Avory, sitting next to him, would scribble down messages and pass them to Isaacs who, having scanned them, would put another shattering question. He asked about the unreported loss of £750,000 in Lake View shares. Why had shareholders been kept in the dark?

Isaacs: Did you not want to disclose the true state of affairs?

Wright: Not with regard to every operation of the market.

Isaacs: Did you wish to keep from the meeting the loss of £750,000 on Lake Views?

Wright: No, it was well-known.

Isaacs: There was no reference to that loss at the meeting of 1900?

Wright: It *did* appear in the figures given.

But Wright was wrong. It had *not* appeared in the figures, and during further probing Isaacs forced him to admit as much. Wright had slipped up and his justification for the mistake was lame: 'Things look very different years after they have happened. I'll guarantee to go to the Bank of England and twist and distort anything years afterwards.' As the questions continued, Wright's great bulk seemed to shrink and sag, and his attempts to shift the blame onto others became less convincing. At one point he resorted to saying: 'If the jury had been in the Globe office during the last two months of 1900 there would have been no trouble about this case.' To which Isaacs responded: 'They could soon have made up their minds.' The judge added to Wright's discomfort.

Judge: On 30 September 1899, you as the Globe, sold £72,000 worth of nickel shares in the Standard. Two months afterwards you, as the Standard, bought back the same shares for £80,000. The effect was that you borrowed £72,000 from the Standard for two months.

Wright: I cannot admit it.

Judge: It comes to this, that you paid £8,000 as a bonus for the loan.

Wright: Oh no, my Lord.

As the questioning continued, Wright resorted more and more to answering: 'I don't know.' Several times he described incorrect claims he made at shareholders' meetings as 'slips of the tongue'. Rufus

Isaacs's schoolboy son, Gerald, who was paying his first visit to a law court, recalled:

I have never forgotten the picture of Whitaker Wright as the relent-less cross-examination went on and he found himself forced into admissions or evasions which he must have known to be having an effect on judge and jury. He took on, more strongly every minute, the appearance of an angry and bewildered bull. As question after question went home like darts driven deep into his shoulder, he seemed to back away from the front of the box, as if to put himself out of range of his too nimble enemy … yet, as the hours went by, my father scarcely ever raised his voice. His manner was suave, restrained, almost gentle. The more heated Whitaker Wright grew as the skilful thrusts found their mark, the quieter Rufus Isaacs became.

Isaacs: You made a speech at the shareholders' meeting. You knew there were rumours as to the state of the Globe's affairs.
Wright: No doubt.
Isaacs: You were anxious to put the best face on affairs you could?
Wright: No doubt.
Isaacs: You knew that the important matter to the shareholders was the item of £2,332,000 'value of shares held in sundry companies'?
Wright: The state of the company was the important thing.
Isaacs: The company owed to sundry creditors £570,000?
Wright: Yes.
Isaacs: Your assets were about £2,700,000?
Wright: Yes.
Isaacs: The largest item in the £2,700,000 was the £2,332,000?
Wright: Yes.

Isaacs: It was important to know how much had been written off?

Wright: Yes.

Isaacs: You dealt with that in your speech?

Wright: I answered questions.

Isaacs: You said over a million sterling had been written off for depreciation. That was untrue?

Wright: I do not admit it. You must take the whole report together.

Isaacs: You said: 'over a million sterling'?

Wright: I should have said 'for loss and depreciation'.

Isaacs: Have you any doubt that this statement is absolutely untrue?

Wright: In its connection it is true. But I ought to have said 'loss and depreciation'. It was an extempore utterance.

Isaacs: That is, as it stands, the statement is untrue?

When Wright failed to reply, Isaacs goaded him with the words: 'Would you like to say it was a slip of the tongue?' He went on to point out that the statement had appeared in a report edited by Wright and had not been corrected. Wright was reduced to claiming that 'my time was absorbed. The manager or secretary ought to have looked at it. In this company I had to do everybody's work.' Eventually he sank down onto the chair placed in the box for his use and, in the words of the *Daily Mail*, 'remained a huddled heap of weariness for the rest of the afternoon'. To his friend John Eyre, who was sitting near him, he whispered: 'I fear the worst.' The Australian newspaper *Truth* commented: 'Quietly, suavely, but with the probing tongue of an anteater reaching out to swallow its prey, the diminutive Isaacs questioned and queried, revealing his apparently rock-like antagonist as a man of straw, a faker and swindler.'

The following morning, the judge made a dramatic intervention. He kept the court waiting until 11 a.m. before taking his seat and declaring:

I am daily in receipt of anonymous communications, most of them of an abusive kind, about this case. I should not have taken any notice of them had I not reason to believe that attempts have recently been made of a much more serious matter in other directions to interfere with the course of justice. I desire publicly to warn all persons that such conduct will bring upon offenders the gravest censure and entail the most serious consequences.

He supplied no further details, but the unfortunate impression was left that someone with an interest in seeing Wright acquitted had tried to intimidate the jury. Fairly or unfairly, the finger seemed to point at Wright himself.

Later that day, Isaacs rose to make his closing speech. By now both the public gallery and the floor of the court were packed tight again. Isaacs said he had nothing to withdraw from his opening speech because not a single statement of fact had been disproved. Wright, he declared, was 'a wonderful alchemist who turned base metal into gold by a stroke of his pen'. He had convicted himself out of his own mouth when he admitted in cross-examination that he had published the 1900 balance sheet in order to conceal from shareholders the true state of affairs. By virtue of his position at the head of so many companies, he had been able to 'spin webs of phrases' and manipulate the figures so as to make it appear that Globe not only had its capital intact but had made a large profit. Wright had described his untrue statements at shareholders' meetings as 'slips of the tongue', but remarkably they were always in the interests of the company. It was clear as daylight that the defendant was not honest and had rigged the accounts. Not only that, but while trying to persuade others to increase their holdings in Globe, he was unloading his own. In August and September 1900 alone, he sold 166,000 shares.

Isaacs was on his feet for the rest of the day and throughout Friday. Wright looked increasingly uncomfortable. For much of this time he sketched heads and figures with a quill pen on official court paper. The correspondent for a New York magazine, *The Outlook*, observed that he 'did not give the casual observer the impression of possessing the brain which had conceived and executed such colossal deals'. Busy though he was with his doodles, Wright paid close attention to what was being said. Once or twice he turned and glared at Isaacs, muttering: 'I never said anything of the sort.' Towards the end of the speech, he sat forward with his head in his hands and barely exchanged a word with his legal team. He must have feared the writing was on the wall when members of the public, awed by Isaacs's rhetoric, applauded the KC as he sat down. The judge quickly silenced them.

Wright again spent the weekend at Witley – as did a posse of detectives who stationed themselves near the house to ensure he did not fly the coop. According to friends he was 'cheerful and confident' when he returned to London on Sunday evening. The following morning Lawson Walton began his closing speech. It was a spirited performance. He poured scorn on the suggestion that Globe's shareholders had been misled. John Flower had sent circulars to 10,000 shareholders and just three said they had increased their investments in Globe because of the balance sheets. 'Was there ever a more miserable and abortive result?' asked Lawson Walton. The prosecution had been carried out with 'undisguised vindictiveness' and depended on a small sheaf of transactions – 'pickings from the bones of the Globe that might form a meal for those who wished to found a prosecution such as this'. Wright had been subjected in the box to 'innuendoes of every kind of falsehood and misrepresentation'. The keeping of the books was in the charge of the accountants and they had recorded all the transactions. If Wright had been the class of man suggested, he would have disguised his manoeuvres by tampering with the books, but there was not a scrap of evidence that he had done so. He had acted in what he conceived to be the best interests of the shareholders. If, here and there, a minute was wrong, that was not his fault. In 1900, when Globe 'was struggling in the waves', Wright lost up to £400,000 of his own money in trying to help it. That was the character of the man who, the jury were asked to believe, had tried to deceive the shareholders. Where, asked Lawson Walton, were the other directors while the transactions were going on? Were they really mere waxwork figures under Wright's control? If Lord Dufferin and Lord Loch had been alive, would it have been possible to have made a charge against Wright which did not involve them too? Would the prosecution have dared to have made the same insinuations against them as they had against Wright? No, he contended. The charges would have been swept aside as incredible if preferred against these other men. He concluded with an eloquent appeal:

> Every spot outside this court – the whole outside world – has been ringing with the clamour of denunciation against this man on the part of those who have not stopped to hear my speech, who do not trouble to listen to his defence. He has been brought here by a hue and cry, which has had its reflection in the gallery of this court. I urge you to show the courage of Englishmen, to decide this case not on prejudice.

The next day, the twelfth and last of the trial, Mr Justice Bigham summed up. Ironically, it was Australia Day. He began with ominous words: 'The prosecution was carried on temperately and properly. If Mr Isaacs's view is the right view, it is scarcely possible to use language too strong in describing it.' He dismissed Lawson Walton's arguments that

Wright was no more guilty than were the other directors, and said the conduct of Lords Dufferin and Loch had been consistent with honest mistakes. 'If they [the surviving directors] could throw any favourable comment on Mr Whitaker Wright's conduct, he could have called them. He chose not to.' The judge, who had taken laborious notes throughout the trial, described the manoeuvres that turned Globe's losses into profits as 'almost magical' and said the company was engaged in some sort of 'rig'. Once Wright knew of the company's 'disastrous' position he should have informed the shareholders immediately rather than embark on more 'gambles'.

> Our trading reputation as a nation is of value, and it would be a lamentable thing if frauds when exposed were not punished. The indignation with which I view these transactions might induce me to use language which might perhaps be too strong; but you must remember that the decision in this case rests with you.

He again mentioned that he had been 'pestered with anonymous and ill-considered letters' and told the jurors that if they had received them too they should disregard them. While he spoke, Wright darted quick glances at the jury, but his expression was one of resignation. A court reporter said Wright 'looked like a helpless boxer being pummelled on the ropes. His great body had sagged, his face twitched, while his eyes were ringed with pain.' A barrister who had come in to watch the proceedings, Cecil Mercer, noted that his face was 'the colour of cigar ash'. Isaacs himself told his biographer years later: 'It was as if we saw a man ageing before our eyes.' Sir George Lewis noticed that Wright had mechanically scribbled the initials 'WW' on his blotter several times, along with the word 'intent' in bold capitals, and the Roman numeral VII over and over again. Seven years was the maximum sentence under statute for the crime of which he was accused. He had also drawn what looked like prison gates. He was clearly expecting the worst. In the words of Anna's notorious telegram, 'everything looked bad'.

CHAPTER NINETEEN

HORROR IN ROOM 546

The jurors filed out of the courtroom at 2 p.m. to consider their verdict. Wright ran his eye over each in turn, trying to read their minds. Despite the judge's hostile summing-up, his spirits had revived and against all the odds he appeared confident of a successful outcome. As he lunched on cold beef in the ante-room he had been allocated below the court, he assured Sir George Lewis that the jury would find him not guilty, or at least be so bemused by the evidence that they would be unable to agree on a verdict. He seemed to be pinning his hopes on the jurors being in the same befuddled state as their counterparts in *Alice in Wonderland*, who 'wrote down all three dates on their slates, and then added them up and reduced the answers to shillings and pence'.

It was not an unreasonable expectation. Even Bigham had commented that the case was 'intricate and wearisome' and that 'parts of it passed the wit of man to understand'. At one stage in the proceedings he had asked the jury: 'Do you understand these transactions?' and was met with shakes of the head. Journalist Max Pemberton, who covered the trial for the *Daily Mail*, later called it 'a most intricate and indeed monotonous proceeding, impossible to explain or make entertaining for the average newspaper reader in one column, or even thirty. I doubt whether a score of men in the crowded court found the case in the least degree intelligible.'

Moment of truth: Wright stands to receive his sentence from Sir John Bigham.

Wright knew it did not bode well when word was sent down to him that the jury had returned after forty-five minutes of deliberation. Clearly they had not felt the need to discuss the case in any great detail. Outwardly calm, he walked back to the courtroom and took his place below the bench. Interlacing his fingers on the table in front of him, he again peered through his spectacles at the jurors' faces. He must have known for certain what was coming when they studiously avoided his gaze.

The judge took his seat and a hush fell over the packed courtroom as the foreman announced the jury's unanimous verdict. Wright was guilty. Somewhere in the public gallery a woman cried out, but Wright himself remained impassive save for a slight contraction of his forehead. Lawson Walton rose immediately to his feet and asked Bigham to grant a stay of execution with a view to an appeal. He stressed that whatever

Wright may have done, he had not been motivated by personal gain. The judge ignored him, and Wright was told to stand. Deathly pale, shoulders squared, the convicted man stared straight ahead as Bigham pronounced the sentence that Wright had anticipated while doodling on his blotter during the summing-up.

> In my opinion the jury could have arrived at no other opinion than that which they expressed in their verdict. I confess that I see nothing that in any way excuses the crime of which you have been found guilty, and I cannot conceive a worse case than yours under those sections of the Act of Parliament which define your offence. In those circumstances I do not think I have any option except to visit you with the severest punishment which the Act permits, and that is that you go to penal servitude for seven years.

Bigham was not alone on the bench as he delivered the sentence. He had been joined by a fellow judge, Mr Justice Darling, whose list had finished for the day and who had an interest in the case because he had been present at the contempt of court proceedings the previous year against the journalist Arnold White. Sitting unrobed on Bigham's right, Darling had an unnerving experience as the drama unfolded. Years later, he told his biographer, Derek Walker-Smith:

> I looked at Whitaker Wright as sentence was passed upon him, and saw his hand go in the direction of his pocket. I was horrified. 'Good heavens!' I thought, 'he has got a gun, and is going to have a shot at Bigham.' These people are always too strung-up to aim straight, and he is bound to miss Bigham and hit me. What a way to end my judicial career – shot, and not even in my own court.

Darling was not the only person to notice Wright's sudden hand movement. Several newspaper reporters spotted it too. Much to Darling's relief, no gun materialised (although it would turn out that his initial thought had not been as fanciful as it seemed), and with a degree of thankfulness he rose to his feet with Bigham and prepared to leave the bench. Below them, Wright was still staring straight ahead. 'My Lord,' he declared, 'all I can say is that I am as innocent of any intention to deceive as anyone in this room. That's all.' Some of those present thought they detected a slight tremor in his enunciation of the last two words, as if he was on the verge of breaking down, but his *cri de cœur* fell on deaf ears. Bigham, having thanked the jurors, was already on his way out, with Darling trailing slightly nervously behind him.

In the courtroom there was mayhem as reporters rushed to file their stories. Though most had expected a guilty verdict, the severity of the sentence came as a surprise. Few had expected Wright to be given more than three years. Among those watching the drama was Wright's son, who had listened to the summing-up from the public gallery and now had the job of telling his mother what had happened.

Wright himself remained calm amid the pandemonium. As Sir George Lewis recalled later, he was 'absolutely cool and firm'. Having protested his innocence to the bench, he appeared to want to make a further pronouncement for the benefit of the press, but before he could do so two court officials – the assistant superintendent, Arthur Smith, and the tipstaff, John Dixon – called him forward and escorted him out of the courtroom through a side door. They took him down some stairs and along a corridor into the private ante-room – Room 546 – that had been placed at his disposal throughout the trial. From here he would be removed by the police to Brixton Prison to begin his sentence. Or so it was intended. As the prisoner and his minders walked along the dimly lit passageway, Wright asked Smith what he made of the verdict and sentence. Smith, who afterwards described Wright as 'the coolest man I ever met', replied that he thought it seemed 'a bit stiff'. Wright told him nonchalantly: 'We shall soon upset it in the Court of Appeal.' He then told Smith he would like to see his son, but the latter could evidently not be found and the message never got through.

Waiting for Wright in the ante-room were his friend John Eyre and Globe's former chief accountant, George Worters. Wright walked in and said to Eyre: 'Well, this is British justice. What have I done? I am amazed. I have done nothing to deserve this. I think it is disgraceful.' A minute or two later, Sir George Lewis also came in. Wright indicated to the court officials that he wanted to be left alone with his three companions, and they obligingly left the room, locking it from the outside and standing on guard in the corridor.

Had the trial been held at the Old Bailey rather than at the Royal Courts of Justice, the rest of the afternoon might have turned out less dramatically than it did. At the Old Bailey, or in any other criminal court, the police would have taken immediate charge of the prisoner and, if they had not done so beforehand, they would have subjected him to a thorough search. Nor would they have taken their eyes off him for a moment, let alone have allowed him to spend time in private with his friends. In the Royal Courts, things were not done like that. It was no one's duty to search Wright, and the procedures were altogether more informal. 'Well, gentlemen,' said Wright when the two court officials had shut the door behind them. 'You have all been very good. I am most grateful for all you have done for me.' Eyre, overcome with emotion, walked to the window to calm himself, causing Wright to say light-heartedly: 'I really think that I am the most composed of all of you.'

Eyre suggested that a message should be telephoned to Anna in

Witley. He was apparently unaware that Wright's son was already seeing to this. Wright told him: 'No, there is plenty of time for doing that. Now do sit down.' A coal fire was burning in the grate and Wright crossed the room to stand in front of it. Removing his gold watch and chain from his pocket, he handed them to Eyre, saying: 'I shan't have any use for these in that place. I give them to you to keep for me.' Eyre replied: 'I shall keep them for you until we meet again, and then I shall give them back to you.'

Wright, still perfectly composed, asked for a cigar. Lewis gave him one and poured him a glass of whisky. Wright smoked and drank a little while Lewis talked to him about an application for a new trial and discussed the disposal of some of his personal possessions. Nothing in Wright's demeanour suggested anything other than a resolve to have the conviction overturned. *The Times* reported later: 'The prisoner appeared to be determined to convey to his companions the impression that he was in no way broken in spirit. He spoke hopefully of the possibility of a new trial and the probability of a reduction of the sentence.'

Moving restlessly around the room, Wright said at last: 'Everything that can be done has been done.' Then he went to the door and signalled to the two court officials that he wished to go to the adjoining wash-room. Nodding their assent, they watched him enter the washroom but did not go inside with him. He emerged a minute or two later and went back into Room 546, where he asked Worters for another cigar. The accountant took one from Wright's silver holder and handed it to him along with a lighted match. As Wright lit the cigar, a change came over his demeanour and his hand began to tremble. Dropping the match to the floor, he lurched towards the window and gasped: 'Stamp out that light.' Then he collapsed backwards into a chair.

For a moment, Wright's companions thought that he had been overcome with emotion and was making a supreme effort to control himself, but it soon became obvious that something was desperately wrong. While Worters extinguished the still-flaming match with his foot, Lewis ran to the chair and took his client's hand. Wright appeared to be struggling to speak, but no intelligible words came out. Lewis observed that he was breathing heavily and assumed he was having a heart attack. He was also aware of a distinct smell on Wright's lips, redolent of bitter almonds. He went to the door and asked the court officials to send for a doctor. Then, with the help of Worters and Eyre, he laid the stricken man on the floor against the chair, loosened his clothes and opened the windows to let in air. By the time a Dr Atkey arrived from King's College Hospital some fifteen minutes later, Wright was writhing semi-conscious on the ground. 'He has only a few minutes to live,' declared Atkey after a brief examination, and a moment or two later the writhing ceased. At 3.55 p.m., the doctor pronounced him dead. Barely an hour had passed since the jury had returned its verdict.

One of the first to hear the news was Rufus Isaacs. He was in consultation in his chambers with a solicitor and an actress when his clerk came in to tell him what had happened. He was so upset that he was unable to continue the meeting. Like most people at this stage, he assumed that Wright's death was due to natural causes and that his relentless cross-examination had helped to precipitate it. It was only with partial relief that he learned later that he was not directly responsible for the turn of events. According to a barrister friend, Edward Abinger, the episode 'troubled him for a long time'.

Wright's body remained on the floor of Room 546 for the next four hours while discussions took place in the Home Office about what should be done with it. As a convicted felon, Wright's person had become the property of the Crown, and there were those in officialdom who argued that he should be buried in a prison graveyard. The matter went to the Home Secretary himself, who ruled that the body should be handed over to the family once an inquest had been held.

In the meantime, the officials who had gathered in Room 546 had made a bizarre discovery. A cursory search of Wright's clothing had revealed nothing out of the ordinary – keys, gold cufflinks, a silver matchbox, 7s 6d (37.5p) in loose change and a purse containing five gold sovereigns. It was only when Police Constable Veale of the coroner's office conducted a second search that he found a cocked, fully loaded six-chambered revolver in the right-hand hip pocket. The American-made weapon appeared to be quite new, and speculation immediately grew that Wright's death might not have been the result of a heart attack.

At 8 p.m., the body was placed in a simple black coffin and carried out through a side entrance of the Royal Courts. From there it was taken to the City of Westminster Mortuary in Horseferry Road, more usually the repository of bodies dragged from the Thames. By now newsboys had appeared at almost every street corner bearing placards with the startling words 'Whitaker Wright Dead!' Court illustrator Harry Furniss noted: 'Hard-grained businessmen paused. Many openly expressed their regret; many too, exclaimed: "Poor devil" or "plucky chap".'

The following day a pathologist, Dr Ludwig Freyberger, confirmed what many had begun to suspect. In a last – and certain – throw of the dice, Wright had swallowed potassium cyanide, ironically the same toxic chemical used in the extraction of the gold and other precious metals that had made him his fortune. The news of his conviction and suicide caused a worldwide sensation, making front-page news across Britain, the United States, Canada and Australia. The *New York Times* observed:

The career of this man, who was known on three continents for his stupendous financial operations, closed in a startling tragedy. Even in his life, which, with his rise from poverty to enormous wealth, was full of dramatic incidents, there was nothing that could compare with the manner of his death. All London tonight is thrilled with the news of it. No such human tragedy has been enacted in England for many a year.

The inquest was held in the red-brick coroner's court in Horseferry Road two days after Wright's death. With its stained-glass windows, dark pews and pulpit-like coroner's desk, the packed courtroom was evocative of the kind of wayside chapel in which Wright's father and Wright himself had once preached. Many of those who had participated in the trial attended the hearing. Among them were Sir George Lewis, John Eyre, Richard Muir and John Worters. An author and criminologist, John Churton Collins, was allowed to view the body in the mortuary during the proceedings, and some years later he provided a graphic and unflattering account in his memoirs of what he saw:

The general impression was a large broad face most strikingly coarse and plebeian. The mouth, which was partially open, as well as the lips, was large and most grossly sensual: the lips looked swollen and were a ruby crimson in remarkable contrast to the yellow face; the chin was mean, with a short, scrubby, grey tuft for a beard. The skull was shaved, no hair visible, and white. The forehead most mean, remarkably receding, except along the frontal bone, where it was strikingly developed, tense and corrugated, as if anxious thought had ploughed so deep that the repose of death could not smooth it out, as though the whole force and power of the man was concentrated there, this frontal development extending about an inch, and then the forehead receded into absolute meanness – and wretched collapse. In the frontal development, and in that area alone, was there anything to redeem the features from mere animalism from those of the average low type of petty tradesman or huckster ... altogether it was a repulsive spectacle, death giving it no sort of dignity or charm.

Wright's twenty-year-old son was the first witness to give evidence. Dressed in black, he gave his name as Whitaker Wright before leaving the stand and going into the mortuary to identify the body formally. One newspaper described him as a 'tall, smart-looking young man, with jet-black hair, dark moustache, keen eyes, and a chin of the square, determined type'. He looked momentarily stunned when he returned to the courtroom, but he quickly recovered himself and made a determined effort to keep his emotions in check. 'The young man's restraint was almost heroic,' said one report. He confirmed that he had seen his father at Witley the previous weekend, adding that his state of mind had seemed normal and that he had never heard him so much as intimate that he contemplated suicide. All eyes were on him as the coroner thanked him and spared him any further questioning. The court was so packed that he had to stand for the rest of the hearing. Sir George Lewis was one of a string of subsequent witnesses who testified that they had never foreseen that Wright would take his own life. He told the court: 'He spoke after the trial as a man prepared to grin and bear it rather than as a man who contemplated suicide.'

Other witnesses backed this view – all except Detective Inspector Willis, who recalled Wright's pledge on the *Oceanic* the previous August that he would never serve a day of any prison sentence. One way or another, there was no escaping the fact that Wright had deliberately killed himself. Dr Freyberger's post-mortem had revealed that the lower side of the dead man's tongue was corroded. This indicated that he had kept a cyanide pill in the back of his mouth for some time before he swallowed it. Exactly when he placed it there was never resolved. Some witnesses said he had been clutching a handkerchief towards the end of the trial and that he held it to his mouth for a brief interval after sentence had been pronounced. (This could have been the hand movement observed by Mr Justice Darling.) Others thought he might have put the pill in his mouth as he was being led by the bailiffs down the dark passage that led to Room 546. According to one fanciful theory, he had hidden the capsule in his beard. Yet others believed that he had inhaled the poison through his second cigar (in truth he probably lit the cigar to maintain his composure, knowing he was about to die).

The consensus, however, was that he had placed the pill in his mouth while he was alone in the washroom. Since cyanide is liable to render a person unconscious within thirty seconds, this seemed the most likely scenario. Whatever the case, he had measured the dose with his usual extravagance and his good mind for detail, for it was enough to kill several men. 'Every organ in the body emitted the unmistakeable smell of prussic acid,' Freyberger told the hearing. (The autopsy also showed that the body was 'exceptionally well nourished', but revealed that the heart was about twice the normal size and very flaccid.) Instructing the jury to return a verdict of suicide, the coroner, John Troutbeck, said: 'It was the action of a cool and determined man.'*

The presence of the gun in Wright's hip pocket would always remain a matter for speculation. Most believed it was a back-up in case the poison failed. Others maintained that Wright had intended to shoot himself in the courtroom – in full view of scores of people – if the jury found him guilty, but either lost his nerve or missed his chance when the bailiffs hustled him

---

* Wright's death sparked a spate of copycat suicides. On the day of his funeral, printer Emil Beck of Notting Hill, London, having read in a newspaper about the trial's dramatic end, told his son-in-law: 'I am sure it was an easy death.' Hours later he was found dead in his shop with a bottle of potassium cyanide at his side. George Craven, aged sixty-one, an Islington jeweller, remarked to a friend that Wright had had 'a beautiful death' and shortly afterwards swallowed a lethal dose of poison. Colour-Sergeant Benjamin Cooke of the 3rd Grenadier Guards, on reading of Wright's death, reached for his pistol and shot himself. At an inquest in Enfield, a chemist, Mr Lewis, complained about the dangers of publicising Wright's death after a cart driver killed himself with potassium cyanide, which he had claimed he wanted for killing rats.

away to the ante-room. The writer Arnold White had a typically fanciful theory. He was convinced that he and John Flower, as ringleaders of the move to prosecute Wright, were the intended victims, and that Wright had planned to shoot them both before turning the gun on himself. He claimed that on the last morning of the trial he had seen Wright place his hand on his hip pocket several times as if to assure himself that the weapon was there. 'Each time I slid to the edge of the chair on which I was sitting, prepared to duck under the table,' White said later. 'He knew the end had come, and had he at any time been able to draw a bead on me without anyone else being in the line of vision he would have shot me.'

'The young man's restraint was almost heroic.' Wright's son
gives evidence at the inquest in Westminster.

The suggestion that Wright meant to take down innocent men with him seems far-fetched, but the fact that both White and Mr Justice Darling believed he had been reaching for a gun in court is intriguing. It may well be that the showman in Wright found the idea of a grand exit in front of scores of people appealing. Whatever his exact intentions, it was, in the words of *The Times*, 'a miserable end, and one which pleads powerfully for a pitiful judgement on the culprit'. The *Illustrated London News* put it more simply: 'This sybarite, inured to luxury, could not or would not face the hardships of the prison-house.'

CHAPTER TWENTY

BROKEN-HEARTED WIDOW

News of Wright's conviction and sentence – but not yet of his death – was telephoned to Anna by her son shortly after the end of the trial. Her reaction was one of anger. She went to the front door of Lower House and spoke briefly to the journalists who had gathered in the lane outside. 'It is a gross injustice,' she told them. Later that evening, John Eyre arrived from London with the news that her husband was dead. If she had any prior knowledge that he had planned to kill himself, she hid it well. 'Thank God he has escaped prison,' she proclaimed to the waiting pressmen, before going back inside the house and reportedly falling into a faint.

The news flashed around Witley 'with amazing rapidity'. In the words of the *Surrey Advertiser*, 'it spread a gloom over the entire neighbourhood. It was at once felt that the district had sustained a great blow, that the poor had lost a generous and liberal friend, and that the neighbourhood would be infinitely the poorer.' The Mouse Hill Band was stood down, and the triumphal arch remained locked in its shed. Journalists who scoured the village for reactions to the day's events could find no one with a bad word to say about the late Lord of the Manor. One resident declared: 'He was a thousand times more likely to be defrauded than to defraud … they hounded him down.' A local tradesman added: 'He employed a lot of labour and made life better for everyone in the neighbourhood. He was a very good man for the working classes, and no doubt would have continued to be so had he lived.' Another said simply: 'He never robbed the poor.' The *Morning Post* reported that 'the kindness and generosity of the dead man are held in high appreciation in the village', while the *Surrey Advertiser* eulogised:

In justice to the deceased, it is only right to say that he did not, like Jabez Balfour, with whom he has been compared, bring widespread ruin and misery to thousands of poor people, whose confidence was gained by mean and despicable hypocrisy. Whatever his dealings in the City of London, in his Surrey home at Witley Mr Wright had made himself exceedingly popular among the poorer section of the community, for whose welfare he always showed great solicitude.

The eulogies and the outpourings of sympathy spread far beyond Witley. The next morning, floral tributes, letters and telegrams began arriving at Lower House from all over the country. One letter in particular touched Anna. Signed by thirty-one former Globe employees, it said: 'Your beloved husband was always held in the highest esteem by all of us, and his memory will ever be cherished with the greatest respect.' A wreath from the London motor car dealer, Moffatt Ford, carried a message with which not many Globe shareholders and creditors would have agreed: 'To a great and exceedingly brave man, who certainly did not realise that he was doing wrong, but chose to suffer death rather than dishonour, who courted death with a superb courage passing the wit of man to understand.'

It is unlikely that Wright's immediate family had any more sympathy with this sentiment than Globe's shareholders. Although Anna remained unswervingly loyal to her husband's memory, there was no escaping the fact that his suicide had been a cool, calculated and entirely selfish act. He must have known there was a good chance that he would never see his wife or children again when he had left Witley the previous Sunday and started down the road that led to his last unfinished cigar. Yet he gave them no warning of his intentions and, as far as is known, left no farewell note. Nor, apparently, did he give any consideration to the traumatic effect his suicide would be likely to have on them (his younger daughter was only fifteen). The manner of his death was all the odder given his seeming confidence after the trial that the conviction would be overturned, or at least that the sentence would be substantially reduced. Some of his friends took the view that he had always played for high stakes and that life itself was just another counter to be gambled away. The prospect of spending years in jail may not have been the only reason he took his life. Knowing that he would probably never see his beloved Rosalie again was perhaps another factor. In the wake of his death, the *Victoria Daily Times* called him 'one of the most selfish specimens of the human species' ever to have lived.

In the City of London, the talk for the rest of the week was of little else but Wright's death. So gripped was the public imagination that Madame Tussauds made immediate plans to create a waxwork model of him to go on display in their Baker Street museum, replacing one of the arsenic murderer, Florence Maybrick, who had been released after fourteen years in jail the day before Wright died. Across Britain, and in many other countries, Wright became the subject of tub-thumping church sermons. In Dundee, the Revd Walter Walsh noted that Wright's last words had been: 'Stamp out the light.' He went on: 'These words were a fitting commentary on a life spent in deception, in selfishness, in vulgar ostentation and wealth-piling, a life that could only be lived by continuously stamping out the light of love, of conscience, of brotherly kindness and feeling.'

Dr E. R. Dille, pastor of the First Methodist Church in Oakland, California, delivered the kind of stinging reproof that Wright's own father might have written half a century earlier:

> Nemesis is on the track of every wrong-doer. Whitaker Wright was counted one of the fortunate men of his day. Men hung around him, straining their ears to get a tip on the market as bees hang around honeyed flowers. He bought paintings and art treasures; his city mansion was a palace; his country villa was ducal in its magnificence. But his life was a series of lies. No man can look at Whitaker Wright and still determine to be rich quick at all hazards. Wealth is honourable provided it is honourably obtained – providing that men in enriching themselves also confer benefit upon society. But all wealth gained by lying and deceit is like Dead Sea apples stuffed with ashes and soot. And such wealth is as much a curse as was Judas's thirty pieces of silver for which he sold his master.

As they denounced Wright from their pulpits, neither of these reverend gentlemen could have had any inkling that the subject of their harangues had once been a minister of the church himself. In the meantime, Wright's family and friends had turned their minds to the thorny issue of the funeral. They decided on a simple ceremony at Witley parish church the following Saturday, but matters were complicated because ecclesiastical law at that time dictated that suicide was sinful and that those who died by their own hand were to be denied the complete rites of Christian burial. In less enlightened times, Wright's body might have been ignominiously buried at a crossroads, and well into the twentieth century suicide remained a criminal act. Given this, the Revd John Seymour, who had recently replaced John Eddis as the vicar of Witley, made discreet inquiries to find out what form of service would be acceptable to the church hierarchy.

If the funeral presented problems, at least the family were spared any difficulties over the release of the body. The coroner's court handed it over immediately after the inquest, and Wright's son took responsibility for bringing it back to Witley. The oak coffin was taken to Waterloo Station, where a small crowd of curious spectators respectfully removed their hats while it was placed in the brake van of the evening train. Before the train departed, Wright's son placed two wreaths on the coffin and knelt before it in silent prayer. When the coffin arrived at Witley Station an hour later, a carriage drawn by two black horses was waiting to transport it to Lea Park. The police were taking no chances, and a sergeant from the Surrey constabulary sat on the box seat in case of trouble. The great mansion was opened up for the first time in two years to receive the coffin, and for the next forty-eight hours it lay amid a profusion of wreaths, flowers and palms on trestle tables in the candlelit marbled hall (a veritable '*chapelle ardente*', as the *Surrey Advertiser* called it). From then on, until the day of the funeral, it was watched over day and night by Lea Park's household servants. Outside, men with dogs guarded the entrances to the estate to keep out snoopers.

Anna, always a private person, decided from the outset to stay away from the funeral, partly because she was in a state of shock, but also because she disliked the idea of being subjected to the gaze of hundreds of strangers. Her husband's philandering may have been an unstated factor in her decision. To make her decision easier for her, the vicar obligingly bicycled to Lea Park the night before to conduct a brief private service attended by the family, a few close friends and a handful of servants. Messages of sympathy continued to arrive at the house by the sack-load. By Friday evening, the family had received more than 1,000 telegrams and letters.

On the morning of the funeral – 30 January – the doors of Lea Park were thrown open to villagers who wanted to pay their respects. A harsh east wind and driving rain gave the park a desolate look. The driveways and paths, untended since the collapse of Wright's companies, were unkempt and overgrown, and dead leaves lay on the porches of the empty outbuildings. The gardens, terraces and greenhouses all bore signs of neglect and decay. The mansion itself looked bleak and uninviting. Abandoned scaffolding blemished its unfinished south wing. The great dolphin's head, still spewing water into the Big Lake, was one of the few visible reminders of past glories.

Hundreds of people, driven as much by curiosity as out of a wish to pay their respects, trooped into the gloomy entrance hall to gaze in silence at the flower-bedecked coffin. If they hoped to catch a glimpse of the grieving widow, they were out of luck, for Anna had taken to her bed. Although she was not seriously ill, some of the more excitable newspapers reported that she was 'at death's door'.

A little after midday, a team of workmen hoisted the coffin onto a horse-drawn glass hearse, which set off at walking pace through the park. Four black mourning coaches followed in its wake. The first was occupied by Wright's son and daughters, and the second and third by family friends and business associates. In a gesture which Wright would have commended, the family made over the fourth coach to Lea Park's housemaids. On arriving at the edge of the estate, the cortege picked up speed and proceeded at a trot down the narrow, wooded lanes to Witley. The Surrey countryside was at its most depressing. The rain had not lifted, and the pinewood surroundings were enveloped in a grey, watery mist. The coaches slowed down again as they reached the outskirts of the village twenty minutes later. Here they were joined by estate employees who followed on foot in double file. The sodden streets were strangely quiet. Villagers stood in silence outside their houses, heads bowed, hats doffed beneath their umbrellas. The shutters of shops were closed and the blinds of cottages were drawn as a mark of respect. As the procession approached All Saints Church, a tarpaulin sheet that had been placed over the brick-lined grave to prevent it flooding was discreetly removed from sight.

The coffin was received at the church gates by the vicar and by his predecessor, John Eddis. Behind them, some 500 people stood in the rain-swept churchyard, including members of the London Stock Exchange, ex-Globe employees, representatives of the charities Wright had backed, and the royal physician, James Reid. (Reid, as it turned out, would shortly become yet another victim of the deceased's machinations. Several years earlier, Wright had persuaded him to become a trustee of Anna's estate. A month after Wright's death, Sir George Lewis sent Reid a demand for £9,000 for negligence in the conduct of Anna's affairs. Anxious to avoid any hint of scandal because of his royal connections, the physician paid up £5,000 in an out-of-court settlement. The nature of his 'negligence' is unknown because he burned most of the papers relating to the case. Family members helped him clear the debt but for the rest of his life he was never free from financial worry. Many others who had come into contact with Wright knew how he felt.)

Witley had never seen a funeral like it. No fewer than sixteen police officers, including a superintendent, mingled with the crowd, but no one was out to cause trouble and there was little for them to do. Scores of wreaths lay by the graveside. Many, such as the one from Witley Working Men's Slate Club, testified to Wright's popularity locally. Among the family wreaths was one from Wright's 'loving children', another from JJ 'mourning the loss of the best of brothers', and a third 'from his sorrowing nieces, Florence and Gertrude Brown'. Anna's wreath, which was composed of white blooms including lilies of the valley, bore the inscription: 'From his broken-hearted widow'.

In a commercial venture which Wright would surely have applauded, a boy who earned his living selling newspapers in Throgmorton Street outside the Stock Exchange had travelled to Witley with a large basket of violets and lilies to sell to mourners. A stockbroker, Murray Griffith, impressed by his initiative, paid for the lot and told him to distribute them among the crowd. Memorial cards were handed out bearing the words:

> Past his suffering, past his pain,
> Cease to weep, for tears are vain,
> Calm the tumult of thy breast,
> He who suffered is at rest.

Anyone who had been expecting a full-blown funeral was disappointed. The vicar had discovered that only a severely curtailed service recently devised by the Bishop of Winchester for deaths by suicide would be acceptable. It was just seven minutes long, with the committal prayer omitted, and was held not in the church but outside in the churchyard beneath umbrellas. Seymour led the mourners in Psalm 143: 'The enemy pursues me, he crushes me to the ground; he makes me dwell in the darkness like those long dead.' At the end of the service, a group of Lea Park servants lowered the coffin into the grave, and girls from the village threw flowers on top of it. Their grief was genuine enough. Whatever the Lord of the Manor had got up to in the City, he had always done well by Witley. The headstone was an unexpectedly modest affair. It carried a line from The Song of Solomon: 'Until the day breaks, and the shadows flee away'. Above this were the words: 'To the memory of James Whitaker Wright, born at Prestbury, Cheshire Feb 9th 1846, died January 26th 1904.'

Like Wright's company accounts and prospectuses, even this brief inscription was careless with the truth. He had been born not in Prestbury, but 40 miles away in Stafford.

CHAPTER TWENTY-ONE

FINAL RECKONING

Wright's metamorphosis from villain to victim did not last for long. Initially there was a near-hysterical outcry against the harshness of the system that had crushed him, and on both sides of the Atlantic there was criticism of Bigham's handling of the case. The *New York Times* accused the judge of having acted as 'prosecuting counsel'. Other newspapers said his summing-up displayed the 'utmost bias' and thought the sentence 'extreme'. Barrister and author Cecil Mercer, writing under the pen name of Dornford Yates, said Bigham was normally a good judge and that his 'remarkable bias' in the Wright case was inexplicable. The anger was such that Bigham received threatening letters in the wake of the trial and had to be given police protection. On the day of the funeral, London's *Saturday Review* commented: 'We wish we could say that Mr Justice Bigham presided over a trial with that dignity and impartiality which are the noblest traditions of the British Bench. But we cannot … the judge made no secret of his opinion of the prisoner's guilt.'

The outrage at what was perceived to be a miscarriage of justice was especially evident in Witley. Sir Edward Marshall Hall, a barrister who lived on the edge of the Lea Park estate, deemed the trial so unfair that he tried to persuade Anna to start proceedings to have her husband's name cleared. She rejected his advice on the grounds that it would not bring him back; that it would cost a lot of money which she no longer had; and that all her friends knew that he was innocent anyway. Marshall Hall was not alone in his anger. Edwin Lutyens, who designed the Lea Park boathouse and bathing pavilion, held Wright in higher esteem than most politicians. 'Whitaker Wright was a soul of honour compared to the blarney of ministers and others out on the cadge for votes,' he wrote to his wife. Local playwright Alfred Sutro described Wright as 'a paladin of rectitude compared with some of the robber chieftains who came after him'. The villagers raised no objections when the family erected a granite memorial in Witley churchyard in 1905, not unlike the one Wright had put up in Philadelphia, bearing an inscription with which they could all concur:

> Whitaker Wright.
> Lord of the Manor of Witley.
> He loved the poor.

It was not only in Witley that Wright was given the benefit of the doubt. 'The poor fellow was as straight as a string,' opined a former United States senator, George Turner, who had negotiated with Wright over the sale of the notorious Le Roi gold mine. Wright's counsel, Richard Muir, described his client as a man who had been 'hounded to death simply for having failed', and who would have been acquitted but for his 'single mistake' of having fled to America rather than staying to face the music. Even many of those who did not regard Wright as innocent somehow saw him as less guilty or guilty of lesser crimes than the likes of Jabez Balfour, Ernest Terah Hooley and Horatio Bottomley. It was perhaps telling that, unlike these others, Wright was awarded a 1,650-word entry in the *Dictionary of National Biography*. The Irish politician T. P. O'Connor, recalling Wright's death twenty years later, said: 'I feel even today that he was quite as much sinned against as sinning.' The *Saturday Review*, while not absolving Wright of all guilt, said that others had committed far worse crimes than he had, and that his story was symptomatic of a greedy world:

> Courage and ingenuity, even in crime, command a kind of respect. We cannot echo the cruel glee expressed so freely over this man's end. The world is not altogether free from responsibility for the commercial frauds which have been so frequent of late. There are many men flourishing today in Mayfair who are only luckier gamblers than the poor wretch whose grave we will chatter over for another twenty-four hours.

Whether they judged him guilty or not, many believed that Wright had shown commendable restraint in refraining from making revelations about 'people in high places'. According to this school of thought, he had spared establishment figures, including the King himself, from embarrassment and humiliation by not naming them in court. The American press, in particular, trumpeted this notion, calling Wright a 'martyr' and a 'scapegoat'. Although there was not a jot of evidence to suggest that Wright had 'dirt' on any member of the royal family, or on anyone else for that matter, an Oregon newspaper commented that 'he who was not a gentleman died like a gentleman that gentlemen might go free'. Most of the British press rejected the 'martyrdom' thesis, but not the *Westminster Gazette*, which claimed that 'distinguished people are involved and some of them have had happy escapes'. The *Financial News* (one of the papers that had been in Wright's pay) went further: 'Wright might have made disclosures which would have seriously discomfited some people, but as he was loyal, as well as courageous, he carried his secrets to the grave. To protect others from divulging what he chose to conceal, he destroyed many papers, thus completing his sacrifice.'

Praise for Wright did not end there. Others admired him for the fortitude he had shown during the trial and for his dignity in death. Something about his melodramatic suicide appealed to the British and American sporting instinct. 'A game finish to a hard fight', was how some saw it. Others called his death 'heroic'. The poet and novelist Edward Verrall Lucas wrote of seeing newspaper placards as he walked through London announcing first Wright's conviction and then his sentence. 'At Trafalgar Square it overtook me,' he recalled. 'DEATH OF WHITAKER WRIGHT. He had done it then! Brave fellow. I honoured him for the deed and, after many years, still do so.' The *Washington Times* observed that 'the consummate coolness with which Wright comported himself during the last scene, while knowing that his mortal existence was limited to a few minutes, was astounding ... [I]t cannot, we believe, be paralleled in the whole dark history of self-destruction.' Even Wright's determined foe, Arnold White, was impressed:

Though for three years I have striven to bring about this trial, I feel so deeply the reticence that is imposed by death that I prefer to say nothing with the exception that Mr Whitaker Wright showed himself throughout his examination a brave man, and that he went through the fearful ordeal of the sentence with the greatest courage and dignity.

In some quarters, there was even praise for Wright's business legacy. The *Rossland Evening World* felt he deserved gratitude for having given the town 'a new lease of life'. It added:

> [I]t certainly would not be the position of a Rossland newspaper to speak anything but good of the man who has filled so large a place in our annals … Rossland certainly has no kick coming at Whitaker Wright whatever may have been his misdeeds … he deserved a better fate.

As the weeks passed, the plaudits petered out. For all those who believed that Wright had redeeming qualities, many more had nothing good to say about him. Unsurprisingly, the negative view of Wright prevailed. Even his defenders could not deny that in his quest for riches he had ruined lives, damaged the reputation of the mining industry in the London market for the foreseeable future, and scarred the mining regions in Australia and Canada with which he was associated. The *Australian Mining Standard* noted that 'for a time Kalgoorlie was a stench in the nostrils of the London investor'. Mines in British Columbia became synonymous in the public mind with swindles, and mining stocks took years to recover. The *Financial Times* commented that 'while we must deplore the sad sequel, it is impossible to avoid the admission that a pestilent influence has been removed from the City'. In Pennsylvania, where Wright had started his business career, the *Philadelphia Inquirer* declared that Wright had 'set traps to catch the unwary and to rob the confiding … [T]he fact that a conviction was reached cannot be regarded as a matter of anything else than satisfaction.' *Blackwood's* magazine, long Wright's bitter enemy, summed up the general feeling:

Everything was swagger and no room was left for business. Swagger directors, swagger offices, swagger bankers, a swagger house at the West End, a swagger palace down at Surrey, a swagger yacht at Cowes, swagger entertainments – all matched each other. The whole thing was a gorgeous vulgarity – a magnificent burlesque of business.

In time, his story came to be seen universally as one of deception, fraud, greed and cunning, combined with an effrontery and shamelessness that surpassed even that of later notorious swindlers like Ponzi, Maxwell and Madoff. Yet it is perhaps a little too easy to write him off as an out-and-out crook. Certainly, he played hard and fast with the truth throughout his career, but no more so than a thousand other company promoters who made and lost fortunes in the comparatively unfettered market conditions of the day. Many astute observers of the time, including Globe's lawyer, Richard Haldane, believed him to be an essentially honest man who made a lot of money for a lot of people, and who only crossed the line into criminality towards the end of his career, and then unwittingly and out of desperation. While the large sums he gave to charity might be dismissed as cynical attempts to curry favour with the establishment and to bolster his reputation in the City, his less-publicised efforts to better the lives of working-class people in and around Witley indicate a genuine desire to help those not so fortunate as himself. If he was far from good, he was surely not all bad either.

It is less easy to defend him against charges of gross incompetence. Shrewd as he was, he must have known that his business methods were unsustainable in the long run. Probably he saw the writing on the wall as early as 1897, at least three years before the ultimate collapse of his empire. Yet he was too buoyed up by his own triumphs, too ready to believe in his own infallibility, and too distracted by the fruits of his success – his houses, his boats, his mistress – to take the necessary action to avert disaster. Pouring cash into the underground railway, when no return could be expected for many years, was a colossal mistake, as was his foolhardy spending splurge on Lake View shares. Against this background, his misrepresentation of Globe's true position in the 1899 and 1900 balance sheets may perhaps be viewed as an example of ineptitude and panic rather than as a descent into wholesale criminality.

Nor is it possible to defend him against the accusation that he was a man without a vestige of conscience. He brought loss, misery and hardship to the lives of countless people, from the small-time creditors of his printing business in Halifax to the investors in his forty-one companies in London, from Edward Drinker Cope in Philadelphia to Lord Dufferin in Ireland, from the wife he left a widow to the children he left fatherless. Yet there is no record of him having ever apologised, either in public or in private, to those whose lives he disrupted and wrecked. On the contrary, he dismissed anyone who dared to complain about their losses as a 'squealer', having first been at pains to point out that none of it was his fault anyway. Contrition was not in his make-up. The word 'sorry' was not in his vocabulary.

Despite his undoing, Wright died rich by the standards of the day. He left all his £148,200 estate to Anna, who lived on in Witley for another twenty-seven years, ending her days in relative comfort in Winkford Lodge, just outside the park wall. (Inevitably there has been speculation over the years – never substantiated – that he salted away a much larger sum than that recorded by his executors.) Tragedy continued to stalk Anna. Her younger daughter, Edith, married Captain Edward Crispin in October 1912, and the couple went to live in Port Sudan, where Crispin was a medical officer. Four months later, Edith died in childbirth at the age of twenty-four. Anna's son also predeceased her.

Four years after his father's death, John Whitaker Wright was commissioned as a lieutenant in the Queen's (Royal West Surrey) Regiment. He married Wietty Smijth-Windham of Hampshire in 1912 and took the opportunity to change his name by deed poll to John Windham Wright, ostensibly to please his father-in-law, who had no sons, but probably because he also wanted to shed his name's toxic associations. He served with his regiment throughout the First World War, reaching the rank of Lieutenant-Colonel, but died of pneumonia in Germany three months after the end of hostilities at the age of thirty-five. His death meant that by the time of her fifty-eighth birthday, Anna had survived her husband and five of her six children. Only her daughter Gladys (who married Edward Crispin's brother, Gilbert) outlived her.

Anna died in 1931 and was buried alongside her husband in Witley churchyard. She left £28,853 in her will, to be divided among her surviving daughter and her grandchildren. If she had harboured doubts about her husband's actions, she kept them to herself. An Australian politician and writer, Randolph Bedford, who had known the couple and kept in touch with Anna after Wright's death, wrote that 'she believed in him to the end – believed in him as much in the poverty that came with the ruin as in the days of greatness'.

After Wright's death, the Lea Park estate sat empty for almost two years. Various consortia drew up plans to create a sanatorium there, then a racecourse, then a hotel and golf course, but no one was prepared to pay the £500,000 asking price and the schemes were abandoned. Eventually the estate was forced to parcel out the property in auction. The local community banded together in 1906 to purchase the Devil's Punchbowl and Hindhead Common, donating them to the National Trust. The house and park were bought by William Pirrie (later Viscount Pirrie), the chairman of the Belfast shipbuilding firm Harland

and Wolff, which built the *Titanic*. (There has been speculation over the years that the grand staircase on the *Titanic* was modelled in part on the one at Lea Park.) Pirrie lived there until his death in 1924, when the house was bought by Baron Leigh of Altrincham, an industrialist and newspaper owner whose publishing stable included Wright's old enemy, the *Pall Mall Gazette*. During Leigh's tenure, the name of the estate was changed to Witley Park. In 1951, the property was bought by food magnate Ronald Huggett, who pulled down the palm court and stripped the house of its treasures. The following year the house was destroyed when a fire broke out in the ballroom. A more modest house was built on the site, and the stables were converted into a conference centre with a meeting room named after Wright. In 2011, Witley Park became the property of businessman Gary Steele.

Wright himself has remained an object of fascination down the years, no more so than in the literary world, where he has made scores of appearances in novels and plays. 'You must not say you pay your bills, because to do so would hurt the feelings of Whitaker Wright,' instructs one of the protagonists in L. P. Hartley's *The Boat* (1949). Even before his death, Wright was the inspiration for multimillionaire rubber magnate Joel Stormont Thorpe – 'huge of body, keen of brain' – who was the central character in American novelist Harold Frederic's *The Market Place* (1899). H. G. Wells was fascinated by Wright, using him as the basis for financier Edward Ponderevo in *Tono-Bungay* (1909) and drawing on aspects of his life for *The Research Magnificent* (1915) and *The World of William Clissold* (1926). In Theodore Dreiser's *The Stoic* (1947), Wright made an appearance as Abington Scarr, owner of an underground railway. More recently he was cast as a villain in F. R. Maher's fantasy thriller, *The Last Changeling* (2013) and in Craig Stephen Copland's *The Stock Market Murders* (2016). In Salema Nazzal's *The Folly*

Under the Lake (2015), he appeared as multimillionaire Walter Sinnet. At least two plays, *A Balance of Trust* (1995) and *Love and Business* (2016), have featured Wright. As did a 2006 episode of the TV series *Hustle*, in which 'James Whitaker Wright III' sought revenge on the bank he claimed ruined his grandfather.

Here and there, more tangible mementoes of Wright's life are still in evidence. At Leadville, Colorado, the rickety Wright Shaft head-frame still stands atop the old Denver City mine on Fryer Hill. The Lea Park nymphs sculpted by Orazio Andreoni today grace the riverside garden of York House, Twickenham, while the female figures representing the four seasons can be seen at the Winter Gardens in Weston-super-Mare. The Bakerloo railway, which Wright kick-started into life, proved to be the pioneer line of the modern system of underground travel, and is today one of London's busiest tube lines with more than 110 million passenger journeys a year. Wright's counsel, Richard Muir, frequently travelled on the line, and often remarked on the irony of fate that a man whose life had ended so ignominiously should have been responsible for the ultimate success of such an enormous venture.

The sunken hideout at Witley also remains, exuding the decay of a fading grandeur beneath the waters of what is today called Thursley Lake. Now a Grade II listed building, it is often described as Britain's greatest folly. Its white paintwork is decorated with rust trails, the windows are veiled with green after decades of submersion, and the mosaic floor and plush furnishings are long gone. Yet it remains a spellbinding place, strong and watertight, a testament to the architects and engineers who designed it more than 120 years ago … and to the folly of Whitaker Wright.

BIBLIOGRAPHY

Abinger, Edward, *Forty Years at the Bar* (London: Hutchinson, 1930)

Ainslie, Douglas, *Adventures Social and Literary* (New York: E. P. Dutton, 1922)

Beckerlegge, Oliver A., *United Methodist Ministers and their Circuits* (London: Epworth Press, 1968)

Bedford, Randolph, *Naught to Thirty-Three* (Sydney: Currawong Publishing, 1944)

Belfort, Roland, *A Tale of City Crisis: The Nineteenth Century and After,* Vol. 56 (London: Constable, 1929)

Black, Charles, *The Marquess of Dufferin and Ava* (London: Hutchinson, 1903)

Blainey, Geoffrey, *The Rush That Never Ended* (Parkville: Melbourne University Press, 1963)

Blumenfeld, Ralph, *R. D. B.'s Diaries* (London: Heinemann, 1930)

Brayley, Edward W., *A Topographical History of Surrey* (London: G. Willis, 1850)

Camplin, Jamie, *The Rise of the Plutocrats: Wealth and Power in Victorian England* (London: Constable, 1978)

Cherif Bassiouni, Mahmoud, *International Extradition: United States Law and Practice* (Oxford: Oxford University Press, 2014)

Churton Collins, Laurence, *Life and Memoirs of John Churton Collins* (London: J. Lane, 1912)

Clifford, Henry B., *Rocks in the Road to Fortune; or, The Unsound Side of Mining* (New York: Gotham Press, 1908)

Covick, Owen and Vickers, Beverley, *The Trials of Whitaker Wright* (Melbourne: History of Economic Thought Society of Australia, Sixteenth Conference, Melbourne, 2003)

Davidson, Jane, *The Bone Sharp: The Life of Edward Drinker Cope* (Philadelphia: Academy of Natural Sciences, 1997)

Dempsey, Stanley and Fell, James, *Mining the Summit: Colorado's Ten Mile District, 1860–1960* (Norman: Oklahoma Press, 1986)

Dill, R. G., *History of Lake County, Colorado* (Chicago: O. L. Baskin, 1881)

Dudley Edwards, Ruth, *The Pursuit of Reason: The Economist 1843–1993* (Boston: Harvard Business Press, 1993)

Duguid, Charles, *How to Read the Money Article* (London: Effingham Wilson, 1901)

—, *The Story of the Stock Exchange: Its History and Position* (London: Grant Richards, 1901)

Dumett, Raymond E. (ed.), *Mining Tycoons in the Age of Empire, 1870–1945* (Farnham: Ashgate, 2009)

Emlen Hall, G., *Four Leagues of Pecos: A Legal History of the Pecos Grant, 1800–1933* (Albuquerque: University of New Mexico Press, 1984)

Eveleth, Robert, *Lake Valley's Famed Bridal Chamber* (New Mexico: New Mexico Geological Society Guidebook, 1986)

Farmer, John and Henley, William, *Dictionary of Slang and Colloquial English* (London: Routledge, 1912)

Faust, Drew Gilpin, *The Republic of Suffering: Death and the American Civil War* (New York: Knopf, 2008)

Felstead, Sidney, *Sir Richard Muir: A Memoir of a Public Prosecutor* (London: The Bodley Head, 1927)

Furniss, Harry, *Harry Furniss at Home* (London: T. Fisher Unwin, 1904)

—, *Some Victorian Men* (London: The Bodley Head, 1924)

Gailey, Andrew, *The Lost Imperialist: Lord Dufferin, Memory and Myth-making in an Age of Celebrity* (London: John Murray, 2015)

Gilbert, Michael, *'Fraudsters': Six Against the Law* (London: Constable, 1986)

Gribble, Francis, *Seen in Passing* (London: Ernest Benn, 1929)

Haldane, Richard, *Richard Burdon Haldane: An Autobiography* (London: Hodder & Stoughton, 1929)

Haldane, Robert, *With Intent to Deceive: Frauds Famous and Infamous* (Edinburgh: William Blackwood, 1970)

Hays Hammond, John, *The Autobiography of John Hays Hammond* (New York: Farrar & Rinehart, 1935)

Headley, Gwyn and Meulenkamp, Wim, *National Trust Book of Follies* (London: Vintage, 1986)

Hoover, Herbert, *The Memoirs of Herbert Hoover: Years of Adventure, 1874–1920* (New York: Macmillan, 1951)

Horne, Mike, *The Bakerloo Line: A Short History* (London: Douglas Rose, 1990)

Jackson, Stanley, *Mr Justice Avory* (London: Victor Gollancz, 1935)

—, *Rufus Isaacs: First Marquess of Reading* (London: Cassell, 1936)

Johnson, Johnnie, *Surrey Villains* (Newbury: Countryside Books, 2004)

Jones, Barbara, *Follies and Grottoes* (London: Constable, 1953)

Judd, Denis, *Lord Reading* (London: Weidenfeld & Nicolson, 1982)

Juxon, John, *Lewis and Lewis: The Life and Times of a Victorian Solicitor* (London: Collins, 1983)

Kynaston, David, *The City of London, Vol. 2: Golden Years, 1890–1914* (London: Random House, 2015)

Lang, Gordon, *Mr Justice Avory* (London: Herbert Jenkins, 1935)

Lingenfelter, Richard, *Death Valley and the Amargosa: A Land of Illusion* (Oakland: University of California, 1986)

Livingstone, Belle, *Belle Out of Order* (London: Heinemann, 1960)

Lucas, Edward: *The Barber's Clock: A Conversation Piece* (London: Methuen, 1931)

Lustgarten, Edgar, *The Illustrated Story of Crime* (London: Weidenfeld & Nicolson, 1976)

Lyall, Alfred, *The Life of the Marquis of Dufferin and Ava* (London: John Murray, 1905)

Malmgreen, Gail, *Silk Town: Industry and Culture in Macclesfield, 1750–1835* (Hull: Hull University Press, 1985)

Milford, Homer, *History of the Lake Valley Mining District, New Mexico* (Santa Fe: Abandoned Mine Lands Archaeological Report, 2000)

Mouat, Jeremy, *Looking for Mr Wright: A Tale of Mining Finance from the Late Nineteenth Century* (Boise: *Mining History Journal*, Vol. 10, 2003)

—, *Roaring Days: Rossland's Mines and the History of British Columbia* (Vancouver: UBC Press, 1995)

Nicholls, Ernest, *Crime Within the Square Mile: The History of Crime in the City of London* (London: John Long, 1935)

Nicolson, Harold, *Helen's Tower* (London: Constable, 1937)

O'Donnell, Bernard, *The Trials of Mr Justice Avory* (London: Rich & Cowan, 1935)

Olson, R., *A Golden Life* (Los Angeles: California Club, 1999)

Pemberton, Max, *Lord Northcliffe: A Memoir* (London: Hodder & Stoughton, 1922)

Pennsylvania Historical Commission, *Philadelphia: A Guide to the Nation's Birthplace* (Harrisburg: Telegraph Press, 1937)

Percy, Clayre and Ridley, Jane (eds), *The Letters of Edwin Lutyens to his Wife, Lady Emily* (London: Collins, 1985)

Plazak, Dan, *A Hole in the Ground with a Liar at the Top: Fraud and Deceit in the Golden Age of American Mining* (Salt Lake City: University of Utah Press, 2006)

Radclyffe, Raymond, *Wealth and Wild Cats: Travels and Researches in the Gold-Fields of Western Australia and New Zealand* (London: Downey & Co., 1898)

Reading, Marquess of, *Rufus Isaacs, First Marquess of Reading* (London: Hutchinson, 1945)

Reid, Michaela, *Ask Sir James: The Life of Sir James Reid, personal physician to Queen Victoria* (London: Hodder & Stoughton, 1987)

Rendel, Lord, *The Personal Papers of Lord Rendel* (London: Ernest Benn, 1920)

Robb, George, *White-Collar Crime in Modern England: Financial Fraud and Business Morality, 1845–1929* (Cambridge: Cambridge University Press, 1992)

Rossland Board of Trade, *Rossland in 1898* (Toronto: Grip Printing & Publishing, 1898)

Stephen, Leslie and Lee, Sidney (eds), *Dictionary of National Biography, Supplement* (London: Smith, Elder, 1912)

Strattman Linda, *Fraudsters and Charlatans: A Peek at Some of History's Greatest Rogues* (Stroud: The History Press, 2006)

Sutro, Alfred: *Celebrities and Simple Souls* (London: Duckworth, 1933)

Taine, Hippolyte, *Notes sur L'Angleterre* (Paris: Hachette, 1874)

Twain, Mark, *Roughing It* (Hartford: American Publishing Company, 1872)

Vallance, Aylmer, *Very Private Enterprise: An anatomy of fraud and high finance* (London: Thames & Hudson, 1955)

Walker-Smith, Derek, *Lord Reading and His Cases* (New York: Macmillan, 1934)

—, *The Life of Lord Darling* (London: Cassell, 1938)

Waller, Philip, *Writers, Readers, and Reputations: Literary Life in Britain 1870–1918* (Oxford: Oxford University Press, 2006)

Ward, Edwin, *Recollections of a Savage* (London: Herbert Jenkins, 1923)

Webb, George, *Science in the American Southwest: A Topical History* (Tucson: University of Arizona Press, 2002)

White, William, *Walt Whitman and the Sierra Grande Mining Company* (Albuquerque: *New Mexico Historical Review*, July 1969)

Wright, James, *Our Father* (Ripon: J. J. Wright, 1863)

Yates, Dornford, *As Berry and I Were Saying* (London: Ward Lock, 1952)

—, *B-Berry and I Look Back* (London: Ward Lock, 1958)

INDEX

Abaris Mining Corporation 63–65, 68

Abinger, Edward 283

Abrahams, Messrs Michael 224

Adolphus of Teck, Prince 161

Adolphus of Teck, Princess 161

Akers-Douglas, Aretas 222–223

Albemarle, Lord 71

Albert, Prince 87

Alexander of Serbia, King 112

Alexander, Thomas 230, 232, 233, 241

Alverstone, Baron 203, 247

American Museum of Natural History 49

Andreoni, Orazio 103, 218, 308

Aquila, Gilbert de 94

Argyll, Duke of 88

Ashburton, Lord 112, 113

Asquith, Margot 255

Atkey, Dr 283

Avery, Horace 261

Baker, Bartrick 146–150

Baker Street and Waterloo Underground Railway 108, 170, 178–180, 308
and construction 133–135
and planned disposal 191, 194

Balfour, Arthur 127–128, 210, 212–213, 215

Balfour, Jabez 157, 193, 196, 261, 290, 301

Baring, Susan 113

Barlow, Magistrate 228

Barnato, Barney 124, 127, 156

Barnes, George 195, 196, 197, 199, 200, 237

Bartlett, Herbert Henry 108

Battle of Gettysburg 21

Battle of Pine Knob 21

Beck, Emil 287 (n)

Bedford, Randolph 306

Belfort, Roland 29, 61, 71, 85, 113, 127, 128, 163, 164
and Rosalie 159–160, 175

Bell, Alexander Graham 13

Bevis, Charlie 163

Bigham, Sir John 249, 252, 262, 267, 268, 272, 273, 274, 277
   and hostility to Wright 253, 254, 299
   and jury intimidation 270–271
   and sentencing of Wright 278–280
Birieson, Mary Anne 7
Bishop, Joseph 118, 216, 217
Bismarck, Otto von 87
Black, Charles 87, 90, 202
Blumenfeld, R. D. 174
Bottomley, Horatio 94. 96, 124, 158, 301
Bratnober, Henry 165
British American Corporation 138–142, 144–146, 169, 170, 198, 267
   and collapse 193, 197, 203
   and reconstruction plan 196
Brixton Prison x, 245, 247, 280
Brock's Fireworks 14
Brodrick, St John 119
Brousson, L. M. 150
Brown, Florence (niece) 217–219, 225, 227, 228, 232–235, 249
   and Philip Gangloff 262
   and Wright's funeral 296
Brown, Gertrude (niece) 217, 296
Brown, James 217
Buckley, Sir Henry 210–211, 217, 219–220, 222, 266
Burchinell, William 33, 236
Burns, Fanny 90

Callahan, Henry Clay 164
Calvert, Albert 67
Card, Henry 118
Carlyle, Thomas 254
Carnegie, Andrew 174
Carson, Sir Edward 206, 212, 213
Carson, Revd R. J. 21
Cassatt, A. J. 53
Chippewa Consolidated Mining Company 33
Chloride Mining and Reduction Company 62

Choate, Joseph 174
Churchill, Jennie 155
Churchill, Lord Randolph 71
Churchill, Winston 155
Clarke, Enid 108
Clay, James 3
Clifford, Henry B. 49
Cobbett, William 95
Cody, William ('Buffalo Bill') 252
Collins, John Churton 285–286
Conan Doyle, Sir Arthur 95, 190
Connaught, Duke of 128, 209
Conran, H. L. 177, 182
Cooke, Benjamin 287 (n)
Cope, Annie 48
Cope, Edward Drinker 26, 36, 37, 71, 113, 305
   and Lake Valley 40, 41, 48–49
   and Leadville 31–32
Copland, Craig Stephen 307
Coward, Mr 150
Cradock-Hartropp, Edmund 81
Craven, George 287 (n)
Crawford, Virginia 245
Crippen, Dr Hawley 224, 245
Crisp, Sir Frank 104 (n)
Crispin, Edward 305
Crispin, Gilbert 306

Daly, George 40, 41, 42
Darling, Mr Justice 279–280, 287, 288
Darwin, Charles 7
De La Warr, Earl 71
Denver City Consolidated Mining Company 30, 32, 35
Dickens, Charles 8, 170
Dill, R. G. 32
Dille, Dr E. R. 292
Disraeli, Benjamin 156
Dixon, John 280
Donoughmore, Lord 81
Drake, Edwin 11, 15
Dreiser, Theodore 307

Dryon, Arthur 216
Dudley, Countess of 161
Dudley, Earl of 161
Dufferin and Ava, Marchioness of 93, 161
Dufferin and Ava, Marquess of 113, 116, 131, 160, 195–196, 266, 305
   and British American Corporation 138, 140, 141
   and Canada 10–11
   and collapse of London and Globe 185, 188–191
   and death of son 171
   and illness and death 201–202
   and John Flower 236
   and Lea Park 95
   and London and Globe 87–92, 167, 168, 170, 172–173, 177–181, 231, 262, 263, 273, 274
   and *Pall Mall Gazette* 148
   and Standard Exploration 166
   and *Sybarite* 112
Duguid, Charles 149, 183
Dumas, Alexander 83

Eckstein, Friedrich 197
Eddis, Revd John 116, 153, 293, 295
Edelsten, F. W. 62
Edison, Thomas 14, 15
Edward I, King 9
Edward VII, King 161, 209, 211, 226, 240, 251, 301
   as Prince of Wales x, 86, 110, 111, 113, 128, 158, 162–163, 174
Edward VIII, King 161
Eliot, George 95
Elizabeth I, Queen 87, 95
Eton College 60, 117, 161, 197
Evans, Revd William Davies 27
Eyre, John 258–259, 270
   and Wright's death 281–283, 285, 289

Farrer, Gaspard 144

Felstead, Sidney 162, 244
Fielden, Revd Randle 177
Filby, Mr 150
Finlay, Sir Robert 205, 210, 212, 213, 231, 237
Flower, John 220, 237, 238, 272, 288
   and Attorney-General 205, 207–208
   and Mr Justice Buckley 210, 217, 219
   and Official Receiver 236
   and Wright's trial 252
Ford, James 176
Ford, Moffatt 157, 290
Fox, Mr 232
Fraser, Sir Malcolm 67
Frederic, Harold 117, 307
Freyberger, Dr Ludwig 284, 286–287
Fuller, Melville 239
Furniss, Harry 252, 284

Gangloff, Philip 262
Garnett, Sir Richard 190
George III, King 161
George Jackson and Sons 97
Gilbert and Sullivan 72
Gladstone, William 155
Golding, Henry 246
Goodbourne, Mr 97
Gordon, General Charles 154
Gough, William 223
Gough-Calthorpe, Somerset 73, 74–75, 79, 113
   and Lord Dufferin and Ava 88, 173
   and Official Receiver 198–199
   and Standard Exploration 130, 195
   and *White Heather* 109, 111
Gould, George Jay 197
Grace, W. G. 127
Graham, Charles 57
Grant Duff, Sir Mountstuart 92
Greeley, Horace 16
Greene, Francis 224
Griffith, Murray 296
Gunnison Mining Company 56–57

Haldane, Richard 128, 304
Halifax Bankruptcy Court 8
Hall, Lydia 4
Hamilton-Temple-Blackwood, Archie
    (son of Lord Dufferin and Ava) 171
Hamilton-Temple-Blackwood, Freddie
    (son of Lord Dufferin and Ava) 181
Hannan, Patrick 125
Hardy, Thomas 184
Harmsworth, Alfred 149, 174
Harrison, George 104 (n)
Hartley, L. P. 307
Hays Hammond, John 80
Heinemann, William 131
Henry VI, King 95
Henry of Prussia, Prince 174
Henry, Sir Edward 222–223
Henty, G. A. 125
Hoffman, Charles 55–56
Hooley, Ernest Terah 71, 93, 124, 134, 149,
    301
Hoover, Herbert 206
Huey, William 51
Huggett, Ronald 307
Hyam, John 262

Isaacs, Gerald 255, 269
Isaacs, Rufus 83, 250, 254–258, 264,
    265–272, 274, 283
Iveagh, Lady 161
Iveagh, Lord 161

James Veitch & Sons 97
Jekyll, Gertrude 97
Joel, Woolf 124, 157
Johnson, Benjamin 57
Jones, Harry 158
Jones, Kennedy 174
Juxon, John 245

Kaufman, Charles 68, 70, 82–83, 126, 175
Kennedy, Myles 197
Knowles, Yalden 117

Labouchere, Frank 154
Lambert, George 211
Lavigne, Dr Wilhelm 240
Lawson Walton, John 253, 254, 263, 265,
    272–273, 278
Lea Park 93–108, 111–121, 153, 190, 197, 247,
    297, 300, 308
    and disposal of 221, 306–307
    and Mottram Hall 161–162
    and Relief of Mafeking 173
    and Wright's funeral 293–295
Lee, Robert E. 71
Leeson, Detective 225
Leigh of Altrincham, Baron 307
Leopold II, King 112
Lethbridge, George 155
Lewis, Sir George ix, 245, 266, 274, 277
    and Sir James Reid 295
    and Wright's death 280–283, 285, 286
Leyman, Emanuel 57
Lick Observatory 64, 98
Lipton, Sir Thomas 174, 209
Livingstone, Belle 158–159
Loch, Lady 109, 161
Loch, Lord 79–80, 88, 167, 231, 262, 273,
    274
    and Baker Street and Waterloo
        Railway 135, 179
    and Charles Mackintosh 138
    and John Flower 236
    and Pall Mall Gazette 148
    and resignation 172
    and Standard Exploration 166
    and White Heather 109
London & Globe Finance Corporation
    155, 166–170, 222, 231, 232, 254, 256–258,
    261–264, 266–274
    and Baker Street and Waterloo
        Railway 107
    and British American Corporation
        138, 144
    and collapse 175–184
    and formation 78, 84

and John Flower 205–206, 208, 210
and Lord Dufferin's appointment 87,
    89–91
and Official Receiver 197–202
and *Pall Mall Gazette* 146, 147
and reconstruction plans 187–193, 196
Lorne, Marquess of 85
Lothian, Marquess of 118
Louise, Princess 85
Lovell, 'Chicken Bill' 28
Low Moor Cricket Club 8
Lubbock, Sir John 112
Lucas, Edward Verrall 302
Ludlow Street Jail 229–230, 240–242
Ludwig of Bavaria, King 99
Lufkin, George 39
Lutyens, Edwin 97, 104, 300
Lyall, Sir Alfred 202

McClusky, George 227–228
MacDonald, Bernard 142
McHattie, John 118
Mackintosh, Charles 137–142
Macleay, Sinclair 176, 194, 198
MacNeill, Swift 222
MacRea, Douglas 150
Madame Tussauds 291
Madoff, Bernie 304
Maher, F. R. 307
Malcolm, Henry 176, 200
Marconi, Guglielmo 123
Marks, Harry 150
Marshall, George 94
Marshall Hall, Sir Edward 300
Maxwell, Robert 304
Maybaum, Mr 57
Maybrick, Florence 291
Mercer, Cecil 274, 299
Meynell, Alice 159
Millard, John 180
Montague Hare, John 117
Moody, Detective 225, 227, 228
Morgan, Thomas 5

Mount Moriah Cemetery 23
Muir, Sir Richard 162, 244, 249–250, 263,
    300
    and Baker Street and Waterloo
        Railway 308
    and Wright's death 285
Munro Ferguson, Ronald 89, 184, 185

Nazzal, Salema 307
Newcastle, Duchess of 161
Newcastle, Duke of 161
Newnes, George 6
Nicholson, Benjamin 168
Nickel Corporation 114, 172, 210
Nicoll, Sir William 183
Nicolson, Harold 87–88, 95, 104, 181, 185,
    189, 201
Nightingale, Florence 73
North Horn Silver Mining Company
    36
North, John 94, 96

O'Connell, Mary 22
O'Connor, T. P. 111, 117, 129, 301
O'Hagan, Henry Osborne 129

Pattisson, Jacob Luard 188
Pedro II, Dom 13
Pelham-Clinton, Lady 109
Pelham-Clinton, Lord Edward 73, 79
    and Edmund Cradock-Hartopp 81
    and Lord Dufferin and Ava 88
    and Standard Exploration 130, 195
    and White Heather 109, 111
Pemberton, Max 277–278
Penn Conduit Company 52
Peppercorn, Herbert 262
Perry & Company 108, 134
Peyton, Isaac 83, 140, 146
Philadelphia Woollen Manufacturing
    Company 12
Philler, George 54
Phillips, Henry 223, 241, 244

Pirrie, William 306–307
Plimsoll, Miss 88
Ponzi, Charles 304
Porfirio, Diaz 62
Portland, Duke of 120
Potter, Beatrix 59
Potter, Rupert 59
Powers, R. C. 208

Queensbury, Marquess of 245

Radclyffe, Raymond 66, 131–132, 150
Raglan, Lord 73
Reid, Sir James 113, 295
Rendel, Lord 202
R. G. Dun & Company 50
Richard II, King 95
Roberts, George D. 30–31, 32, 40, 41, 42,
    45, 47, 49, 53, 68
Roberts, Lord 190
Robinson, Lady 109
Robinson, L. S. 55–56
Robinson, S. S. 42
Robinson, Sir William 79, 85, 109, 179
Rockefeller, John D. 174
Rolleston, Launcelot 188
Rose, C. E. 150
Rosebery, Lord 185
Rucker, Martin 111–112
Russell, Arthur 262
Russell, Francis 116
Russell, Lord John 116

Sanderson, Sir Percy 232
Saunders, Alfred 177
Saville, J. H. 224
Sawyer, Henry 46
Scheurich, Fraulein 117
Schwab, Charles M. 53
Seal, Mr 192
Security, Land, Mining and
    Improvement Company 52
Seymour, Revd John 293

Shedd, William 29
Sheridan, General Phil 43
Sheridan, Richard Brinsley 202
Shipsides, Miss 7
Shireland Hall School 5–6
Sierra Grande Silver Mining Company
    41–49
Silliman, Benjamin 43–44, 46, 48
Simmons, Percy 208
Sitting Bull 87
Smallman, Alderman 247
Smijth-Windham, Wietty 306
Smith, Adam 185
Smith, Arthur 280, 281
Smith, F. E. 253
Smith, James 9
Speaight Limited 161
Spencer, Lord 92
Spensley, Howard 73, 81
Stafford, Anson 42
Stafford Jail 4
Standard Exploration 129–130, 138, 166,
    169, 170, 195, 203, 257
Steele, Gary 307
Stokes, Ellis 57
Straight, Sir Douglas 146, 147
Stubbs, Sarah 2
Sudeley, Baron 128, 183
Summerville, Maggie 22
Sutro, Alfred 116, 300

Tabor, Horace 28
Taine, Hippolyte 156
Tarbet, A. H. 144
Tennyson, Lord 95
Thellusson, Percy 163
Thorp, John 99
Trembath, William 39
Troutbeck, John 287
Turner, George 300
Twain, Mark 18, 33, 149

Untermyer, Maurice 232, 237, 240

Veale, Police Constable 284
Veitch & Son 101, 103
Verne, Jules x
Victoria Chemical Works 9
Victoria, Queen 73, 85, 87, 113, 123, 161, 174, 193
Voules, Horace 150

Walker-Smith, Derek 83, 99, 255, 279
Walkley, Clara 246
Walsh, Revd Walter 292
Walters, Rex 108
Warwick, Countess of (Daisy Greville) 86, 159, 184
Warwick, Earl of 81, 86
Waterlow, Edgar 261
Watkins, Mr 107
Watson, George Lennox 162
Watson, Paxton Hood 96, 97
Webb, Philip Carteret 95
Webb, Richard 95
Weightman, Isaac 20–21
Weightman, Sarah 21
Wellington, Duke of 87, 118
Wells, H. G. 307
West Australian Exploring and Finance Corporation 68–73, 263
Whistler, James McNeill 131
White, Arnold 50, 62, 209, 220, 222, 228
    and Arthur Balfour 210, 212, 213
    and contempt of court 246–247
    and George Lambert 211
    and John Flower 208, 236
    and Wright's death 302
    and Wright's trial 252, 279, 288
Whitman, Walt 45–46, 47–48
Wilde, Oscar 27–28, 67, 245
Wilhelm II, Kaiser x, 109, 111, 163, 173, 174
Willis, John 223, 224, 225, 241–244, 247, 252, 286
Winchilsea, Earl of 71
Worters, George 175, 176, 199, 281–283, 285
Wrede, Princess Leopoldine von 111

Wright, Anna (wife) 14, 160–161, 215, 220, 221–223, 236, 251, 281
    and California 64
    and deaths of children 22–23, 305–306
    and donations to charity 154–155
    and Eldridge House 53, 54
    and Eton College 161, 197
    and Florence Brown 217, 234–235
    and Sir James Reid 113, 295
    and Lea Park 107, 117
    and marriage to Wright 20–21
    and Mount Vernon 94
    and telegrams to Wright 217, 266, 275
    and Wright's death 289–291, 293–294, 296
Wright, Edith (daughter) 54, 117, 305
Wright, Ernest (son) 22
Wright, Frederick (brother) 5
Wright, Gladys (daughter) 54, 117, 240, 306
Wright, Revd James (father) 1–10, 120–121, 285, 292
Wright, J. B. 7
Wright, Jay (son) 22–23
Wright, John Joseph (brother) 5, 7–10, 13–15, 65, 110
Wright, John Whitaker (son) 280, 281, 286, 288–289, 293
    and birth of 54
    and death 305–306
    and Eton College 117, 161
Wright, Mabel (daughter) 22–23
Wright, Mary (grandmother) 3
Wright, Matilda (mother) 2–4, 10, 23
Wright, Matilda (sister) 5, 217
Wright, Robert (brother) 5
Wright, Walter (nephew) 21
Wright, Whitaker 16–19, 37–38, 59–91, 109–110, 124–135, 187–203, 205–248, 299–308
    and Canada 9–11
    and childhood 1–6
    and collapse of London and Globe 169–186

Wright, Whitaker *cont.*
    and Countess of Warwick (Daisy
        Greville) 86–87, 184
    and death of 281–292
    and escape to New York 215–226
    and funeral 292–297
    and Lake Valley mines 39–50, 82
    and Lake View mine 81, 83, 126, 131,
        138, 164, 167, 199, 203
    and Lake View Consols 82, 146,
        165–166, 170, 172, 173, 175–176,
        181–182, 201, 238, 267, 305
    and Leadville 26–36, 58, 82, 308
    and Lea Park 93–108, 111–121, 153,
        161–162, 173, 190, 197, 221, 247
    and Le Roi gold mine 137–145, 151, 154,
        155, 167, 196, 300
    and Methodist Church 6–7
    and *Pall Mall Gazette* 146–151
    and Philadelphia 11–15, 20–23, 25, 40,
        50–58, 263, 303, 305
    and Rosalie 159–160, 162, 163, 175, 180,
        215, 216, 291
    and trial ix-xi , 249–280
    and 'Wright Brothers' 7–8

Yerkes, Charles Tyson 158